Fly Fishing Is Spoken Here

Fly Fishing Is Spoken Here

⛧

EDITED AND WITH AN INTRODUCTION
AND AFTERWORD BY

Stephen Sloan

Paintings and Illustrations by

James Prosek

THE LYONS PRESS
GUILFORD, CONNECTICUT
AN IMPRINT OF THE GLOBE PEQUOT PRESS

The Lyons Press is an imprint of The Globe Pequot Press

10 9 8 7 6 5 4 3 2 1

Printed in the United States of America

ISBN 1-58574-772-6

Library of Congress Cataloging-in-Publication Data is available on file.

For all the trout
that have risen to a fly

Contents

INTRODUCTION 3

JAMES PROSEK *on Izaak Walton* 11

ERNEST SCHWIEBERT *on Trout Fishing* 23

THE WHIRLING DISEASE FOUNDATION *on Whirling Disease* . . 37

BILL LOGAN *on Fly Tying* 53

ART NIERENBERG *on Fishing without Limits* 65

FEN MONTAIGNE *on Fishing in Russia* 77

JOSEPH HEYWOOD *on THE SNOWFLY* 93

ROBERT LINSENMAN *on Streamer Fishing* 113

JOSEPH HUMPHREYS *on Nymph Fishing* 127

VALERIE HAIG-BROWN *on Her Late Father, Roderick Haig-Brown* 139

JAMES CRONNIE *on Loch Lomond* 155

JACK SAMSON *on the San Juan River* 169

JAMES MCBROOM *on THE RIVER BOOK* 183

JOAN STOLIAR *on Trout in the Classroom* 197

RAMÓN ARANGUREN *on Trouting in Argentina* 211

HOAGY CARMICHAEL, JR., *on Being Everett Garrison's Boswell* . . 223

JOAN SALVATO WULFF, *the First Lady of Fly Fishing* 237

LEFTY KREH *on Casting Etiquette, and much more* 251

AFTERWORD 271

Fly Fishing Is Spoken Here

INTRODUCTION

This book is a collection of radio interviews from "The Fishing Zone," a weekly radio show I host with accomplished personalities from the fly-fishing world. I hope they bring to your life as much knowledge and delight as they have brought to mine. Each of the following interviews brings back fond memories for me of the particular time and place where it occurred, whether I happened to be on my telephone at home; in a phone booth in Madrid; on location beside a Scottish loch or streamside in the Patagonian Andes; or on a cellular phone at Beaver Lake, Arkansas; Fisherman's Paradise on Spring Creek near State College, Pennsylvania, or the Texas Hole on the San Juan River in New Mexico. As one would expect, each interview revealed for me the detailed understanding and depth of knowledge that the participant brought to bear on his or her topic. I learned something each Sunday morning.

Yet I now realize, in reading these interviews, that they represent something more—that they in some modest and often subtle way help reveal the universality and diversity of fly fishing. If this collection does nothing else, it at least dispels some preconceptions people have about fly fishing: that in some way it is mystical, beyond the grasp of ordinary folk, effete, or a pastime somewhere between idle diversion and monomania. How better to explain the breadth of sentiment about fly fishing than to show it in the diversity and richness of the voices of those who practice it?

Readers should come away from this book with a truer understanding of the sport of fly fishing and of the particular contribution of each of the participants. But, also, I feel I owe it to my audience to provide some understanding of my angling perspective. For although each of the eighteen participants is encouraged to discuss his or her relationship to fly fishing, I am not. While it's true that readers will still learn a great deal about me from my half of the interviews, I think they should know more.

I struggled a little bit with this and ultimately decided to provide a complete and thorough transcript of my own words on fly fishing, captured at a particular time and in a particular place. The following is the text of an after-dinner speech I delivered at 9:00 P.M. on October 14, 2000, as part of the Fly-Fishing Hall of Fame induction ceremony at the Catskill Fly Fishing Center and Museum in Livingston Manor, New York.

As many of you know, I broadcast a fishing radio show called "The Fishing Zone" every Sunday morning at 6:00 A.M. eastern time to more than two hundred stations serving one thousand cities throughout the United States. This coming Sunday will be my 470th consecutive live broadcast. The show is based on fishery, conservation, and ecological issues. Authors who write about these subjects are guests. Many in the audience tonight have appeared on the show.

The show started about eight years ago. I had begun calling into a weekly fishing radio show run by others to provide three minutes of political commentary. After about a year, the producers asked me to take over the show and assume financial responsibility for it. I did.

I told them I would underwrite the program, income minus expenses, but they had to keep soliciting advertisements and stay on the air. I would continue to call in my weekly political commentary. We also agreed that nonprofit fishery and conservation groups like the Catskill Fly Fishing Center and Museum, IGFA [The International Game Fish Association], the South Street Seaport, the American Museum of Fly

Fishing, and others with whom I had a trustee presence or relationship would receive free advertising; any businesses or commercial endeavors would pay the going advertising rate. The producers agreed to this arrangement.

The next week, I was listening from my car to the freshly renamed "Fishing Zone" radio show with my cell phone ready to make my weekly call. I soon heard the following:

"Don't forget Sam's Bait and Tackle in Lindenhurst, Joe's Boat Canvas in Syosset, and Al's Deli in Plainview."

The next day, I called the office and asked who these advertisers were and whether they were paying for their airtime. I was told by Joe, the show's host, "They're friends of mine." I told him in no uncertain words, "We buy the time; they pay us."

"Okay boss," was his terse reply.

The next week, I tuned in again and heard a repeat performance of the previous week. The following week, I went down to the station with my wife, Nancy, and waited for Joe to show up. He waltzed in with about three minutes to spare before airtime. I told him I was going into the broadcasting booth with him, and if those non-paying advertisements came up again, I would cut him off.

He turned to me and snarled, "If you think you can do this f------ show, then go ahead and do it. I'm out of here." He walked out the door and was gone.

I turned to my wife and said, "Nance, we're going to do the radio show, and I want you to come in the booth with me."

She looked at me incredulously and said, "You always put me in these impossible situations!" Panicking further, she continued, "No notice! No warning! What are we going to talk about?"

"I am going to ask you one question, just one," I said, trying to do some quick damage control.

"Well, what is it?" she asked in exasperation.

"I am going to ask you what you don't like about fishing. That will kill an hour, and next week I can get organized."

That was "The Fishing Zone" as of 469 weeks ago.

The show has given me tremendous insight into the fishing, environmental, and philosophical souls of many anglers, writers, and scientists. For example, I now realize that when we talk about wild trout and wild salmon, we are talking about a concept that is fundamental to the entire environmental conservation movement. By convincing the public and politicians of the notion that wild fisheries matter, we are implicitly selling the whole ecological package. Wild anything is synonymous with clean water, pristine forests, no logging or clear cutting, and clean habitat. The latter extends to farmers whose livestock use our waterways as bovine latrines. The metaphor extends to what I call "the asphalting of America." Developers create parking lots where rainwater runoff flows unchecked and unabsorbed into our rivers and streams.

If we sing the wild trout anthem, we must be eternally vigilant against anything that can affect Cemetery Pool on the Beaverkill, the Ledge Pool at Henryville, Spring Creek at State College, or Charlie Fox and Vince Marinaro's beloved LeTort. Preserving wild trout and salmon means zero tolerance for the diminution of any fishery habitat.

This led me to think about why anglers should support a hall of fame. The answer came to me in a line from a T.S. Eliot poem:

"Time present and time past are both present in future time"

A hall of fame dedicated to fishing greats is a necessity for the following four reasons: first, to commemorate our piscatorial comings and goings; second, to record for the general public events in real fishing time; third, to record events in real political time; and, fourth, to record events in scientific time

First, let me comment on our piscatorial comings and goings. This hall of fame, and indeed any fishing hall of fame, contributes to the sum knowledge of our sport by recording the fishing experiences of its inductees. They have answered the angler's prayerful question posed by Roderick Haig-Brown:

What fly shall I use? The answer lies not in knowing his or her way among the 50,000 varieties, nor in searching the infinity, but in developing for himself or herself some logically based system of selection that allows oneself to bring order out of the pure corner of chaos and go about his business with some measure of confidence. Good minds have always found a quality of enjoyment and satisfaction because fishing is the richest and most complex of all sports, but it is not found in full measure without preparation.

6

Part of that "preparation" that Roderick Haig-Brown has written about is the history here and now in the Catskill Fly Fishing Center and Museum that we honor tonight.

Secondly, the general and fishing public will be able, hundreds of years from today, to read and review the trout-fishing legacy created by our inductees during their lifetimes—a capability that only adds to the already rich history of the sport. It is no wonder that THE COMPLEAT ANGLER by Izaak Walton is the third most published book in the world, exceeded only by the Bible and Shakespeare's plays. We fly anglers are in august company tonight. We are carrying on a proud tradition that Walton initiated more than three centuries ago.

Our third goal is to record events in political time. To my colleagues in arms who have fought the environmental battles, your contributions and recognition are here in the [Catskill Fly Fishing Center and] Museum and now in the hall of fame. Your membership in the museum's hall of fame ensures that no one can revise our history for political purposes, or attempt to eradicate our advocacy efforts to keep our streams and waters clean and full of wild trout. Here in the Catskills and, indeed, throughout the United States, it can never be said that no one cared about some dead fish society in the Catskill Mountains. Just look around you tonight.

Lurking behind each potential ecological disaster are the words of "Deep Throat" of Watergate fame: "follow the money." The answer to those special interests seeking to take our clean gravel, clear-cut our timber, divert our sustainable water flows, or otherwise pollute our clean water is in this hall, in this room tonight, and in the hearts of each of us who come to fish these beautiful waters. In the political arena, we must learn to cast our ballots as deftly as we cast our flies. This hall of fame is the cathedral where trout anglers can stand together, united in the belief and faith that protecting their streams and rivers serves a higher purpose.

Fourth and finally, this hall of fame serves a scientific purpose. It is a fact that the sum of humankind's knowledge [during the decade from 1990 to 2000] has doubled. Will we trout fishermen be prepared for the next ecological crises? The next whirling disease? The next freshwater pfesteria? The next freshwater poisonous dinoflagellate? Or some other resistant trout-decimating virus? The next trout-killing pesticide, compliments of the chemical industry and its money-hungry lobbying arm? If you do not think it can happen, read TOXIC DECEPTION, by Dan Fagin and Marianne Lavelle. We are now at risk that runoff will storm our streams and possibly kill every stone fly, mayfly, or caddis fly in a watershed. Science helps us understand these threats so that we can counter them.

This hall of fame protects us; it gives safe harbor to trout and trout fishermen everywhere. It is the citadel of learning, of means for preservation of our history and understanding of our sport. It is the touchstone we can point to over and over again. We need more science to help us understand the trout's universe and what role we anglers play in it, both as fishers and concerned citizens. Will science develop methods to seed streams where insect hatches have been destroyed? Can we restore the glory that was the caddis and the grandeur that was the green drake?

Again, I must turn to Roderick Haig-Brown:

> *When an angler, no matter how novice, learns the feeling that sooner or later in the month will come a day when the river looks right to a certain pool, when the weather seems too fresh and inviting to stay home... If the hunch proves itself, one has learned something; if it doesn't, one has still stolen another day from all the days that slip by with rods in our cases and reels silent.*

Are we ready to welcome the new millions of eager trout anglers? Where will the next generations go to establish their trout-fishing roots? Here! Here! Here! *Yes, in coming here, they will join the many lifetimes of observations, writings, and experiences that constitute our collective memory. They and you should visit and learn. Trout language explains the world to us literally or metaphorically.*

Trout is spoken here.

Trout is whispered in reverence here.

Trout is exalted here.

Trout is a language we are helping to be spoken forever.

I want to thank so many for their help and encouragement in putting this work together. I am indebted to my wife, Nannette, who loves to see me fish and has supported me unconditionally in my endeavors in the conservation and fishing communities; to my daughter, Suzanne, my partner in marine affairs, for all her encouragement, and to Robert Sloan, my son, who used his business acumen to gain access for me into the world of Japanese fishery matters and encouraged me to put this book together. Special thanks to Steve McCabe from Wordwright Editorial Services, Inc., a fellow Washington and Lee graduate and patient copy editor. To all the nearly 500 guests who have appeared on "The Fishing Zone" radio show, I wish to thank you for getting up on a Sunday at 6:00 A.M., or earlier as we go west, to provide us with live interviews. Finally, I owe special thanks to the Talk America Radio Network, which expanded distribution of "The Fishing Zone" from three stations to its present coverage of more than two hundred.

This book is about trout fishing; a second book, describing the state of our ocean fisheries, is in progress.

As always, tight lines, and a very good drift.

Stephen Sloan
New York City, 2001

JAMES PROSEK

on Izaak Walton

AN INTERVIEW WITH JAMES PROSEK ON IZAAK WALTON;
CHRISTIANITY AND FISHING; MILTON, DONNE, CROMWELL,
AND ELIOT; AND SOMETHING CALLED 'TECHNOCRACY.'

*James Prosek is a graduate of Yale University with a degree in English
literature. He is the author, most recently, of EARLY LOVE AND BROOK TROUT
(2000, The Lyons Press, New York). Prosek began to fish when he was nine years old.
Fishing provided solace, and eventually became a kind of religious experience for him
and led him on the trip that culminated in his writing THE COMPLETE ANGLER: A
CONNECTICUT YANKEE FOLLOWS IN THE FOOTSTEPS OF WALTON (1999,
HarperCollins, New York). Written about Izaak Walton, Prosek's book is 322 pages
of life philosophy and concludes, much as Walton's original COMPLEAT ANGLER did,
that everything the author ever does, whether it is fishing or not, is fishing. As Izaak
Walton wrote in 1653: "THE COMPLEAT ANGLER is not about fishing, but about life.
Or rather, it is about fishing—but fishing is life."*

*When Prosek sat down to talk with Steve Sloan of "The Fishing Zone" radio show,
he revealed much of what went into THE COMPLEAT ANGLER, as well as some of the*

11

larger issues behind it. For instance, in this interview, Prosek talks about his experiences as a scholar of both Walton's writings and that author's favorite streams. Prosek also compares the religious and political climate of Walton's time with the effects of something he calls "technocracy" in our time.

MR. SLOAN: James Prosek has just written a new book that is a real treat; it's called THE COMPLETE ANGLER: A CONNECTICUT YANKEE FOLLOWS IN THE FOOTSTEPS OF WALTON. It's a spellbinding book, written in a high literary style. I thought I would flatter you a little this morning.

MR. PROSEK: I'll take it *(laughing)*.

MR. SLOAN: Not only is the book well written, it is ingenious, it is different, it addresses a subject that we all know, and yet it has a different approach. Additionally, it is illustrated with your watercolors, which are quite extraordinary. I collect angling art, and I would be proud to have one of those hanging on my wall.

MR. PROSEK: Oh, wow, I appreciate that.

MR. SLOAN: Well, tell us how this project started. You were at Yale University, I think, when you decided to trace Izaak Walton's footsteps, so to speak.

MR. PROSEK: Yes. With my great interest in fishing influencing everything I do, I decided to write my senior thesis as an English literature major on Izaak Walton and his book, THE COMPLEAT ANGLER. It just sort of seemed like a logical next step, and so I applied for various travelling fellowships between my junior and senior years. For instance, my first proposal was to go fishing in the waters of the Tigris and Euphrates rivers. I'd always been interested in going fishing there, but they didn't really like that idea very much.

MR. SLOAN: Well, the cradle of civilization might have been the cradle of fishing.

MR. PROSEK: Right. But it's also the cradle of combat, because the Kurds are fighting the Turkish Army there.

MR. SLOAN: True.

MR. PROSEK: So, my next proposal was to go fishing in the footsteps of Izaak Walton, which seemed to make a lot more sense. And then I ended up doing my senior thesis on Walton and his COMPLEAT ANGLER, but, really, the book isn't so much about what I wrote about for my thesis; it's more about my travels through England and the people I met in Walton's wake.

MR. SLOAN: One astounding fact that jumps right out at the beginning, and was part of your proposal, was that THE COMPLEAT ANGLER is the most popular sporting book ever.

MR. PROSEK: Yes. Amazing, isn't it? It's actually the third most frequently printed book in the English language...

MR. SLOAN: Right.

MR. PROSEK: ...after the Bible and the works of Shakespeare.

MR. SLOAN: That's an incredible statistic that frankly I did not know until I read this book.

MR. PROSEK: It is kind of remarkable.

MR. SLOAN: It *is* remarkable. Tell me, this is a book not only about fishing but somewhat about historical detective work, too, because you—and I don't know if it's ever been proposed before by anyone else—think that the words "compleat angler" were basically a pun, a disguised code for the times in which Walton lived, with Cromwell in his glory and raging through England and putting down Anglicans at every turn.

MR. PROSEK: Walton's book title, THE COMPLEAT ANGLER, was, as far as I'm concerned, code for "The Complete Anglican." You see, Walton was a staunch Royalist and a supporter of King Charles I when the Anglicans were being bashed by the Puritans. This was during the English Civil War in the 1660s, and Walton published THE COMPLEAT ANGLER shortly after the king had gotten his head cut off. Walton's religious beliefs were certainly being reevaluated; I mean, his whole world was being turned upside down, in a sense. I think he knew he was poking some fun at the Puritans in this book.

You know, it's not really a book of religious allegory or a polemic; it's a book on fishing. But let's just say that some of his thoughts on the times generously leak into his writing, I think. But, it's also a book about how to live life simply and contentedly like a good Christian, like a good Anglican. Walton quotes the Bible frequently and early on gives the argument that all fishermen, like the apostles of Jesus from Galilee, are good and follow peace.

MR. SLOAN: So, he got this idea of the dialogue form from the Bible, right?

MR. PROSEK: Well, not exactly. Walton borrowed the dialogue in THE COMPLEAT ANGLER from a text of 1577 called THE ART OF ANGLING, in which the same characters appear.

MR. SLOAN: I see. Walton's book is really a dialogue among three people, I believe. You hear the name Cotton associated with Walton many times. What was the relationship of Walton to Cotton?

MR. PROSEK: Walton considered Charles Cotton as somewhat of an adopted son. I'm not sure how they first met. Cotton was a fairly well regarded poet at the time, and we know him because he wrote an addendum to the fifth edition of THE COMPLEAT ANGLER in 1676, at Walton's request, on fly fishing. And it still holds up as one of the greatest modern treatises on fishing with an artificial fly. It even gives directions on how to tie flies.

Cotton extends Walton's dialogue. Walton's dialogue is mostly between the *piscator*, the fisherman, and the *venator*, the hunter, but then Cotton extends the dialogue after Walton's book when he had discourses on fly fishing with the *piscator* and the *viator*, the traveler. Cotton has them go fishing along the River Dove and talk about different subjects. They talk a little bit about Walton, but where we're really indebted to Cotton is for his giving us, as I said, probably the first great treatise on fly fishing.

MR. SLOAN: What rich times he lived in. That book was written in, what, 1648, 1650?

MR. PROSEK: Actually, it was most likely written in the few years before its publication date, 1653.

MR. SLOAN: And Walton was also a friend of John Donne, the metaphysical poet.

MR. PROSEK: That's right.

MR. SLOAN: There was a quotation from Donne's "Meditation XVII," from his DEVOTIONS UPON EMERGENT OCCASIONS, that I've never forgotten because I once had to answer a question about it for a college admissions test many years ago. The question read, "Please comment: 'No man is an island, entire of itself; every man is a piece of the continent, a part of the main.'" I've used that quote many times since to describe the state of our ocean fisheries and how each country is interconnected in fishery matters. Over-fishing by one country affects the entire world.

James, is the Walton book your second or your third book? I read JOE AND ME.

MR. PROSEK: It's my third book.

MR. SLOAN: What are your other books?

MR. PROSEK: The first book I did was TROUT: AN ILLUSTRATED HISTORY. I painted them all and wrote little histories about each one. And JOE AND ME was my second.

MR. SLOAN: I'd like to get back to Izaak Walton and 1650 for a moment.

MR. PROSEK: Sure. Well, we know that Walton was a friend of John Donne, and he also might have known John Milton, I'd like to believe, at the same time. Milton's PARADISE LOST was published, I think, in 1667...

MR. SLOAN: Right.

MR. PROSEK: ...and THE COMPLEAT ANGLER had come out in 1653. It's interesting that they were published in the same churchyard, that they had the same publisher. So, it's possible that he and Milton could have come across each other. As I said, he very likely knew John Donne pretty well and maybe even fished with him. When John Donne died, Walton wrote Donne's biography as a preface to the publication of Donne's sermons and poems. None of Donne's work was published while he was still alive. So Walton's first published work was his biography of John Donne. He then wrote a biography of another friend of his who was a prominent Anglican clergyman, Henry Wotten.

After Sir Henry Wotten died, the English Civil War interrupted everything, and Walton couldn't write about these prominent Anglican clergymen because anything written about Anglicanism was discouraged—the author was fined. The Anglican clergymen were being pushed out of their places of work and Anglicans were being persecuted.

MR. SLOAN: Yes, they were being persecuted.

MR. PROSEK: So that's why you see Walton sort of sticking it to the Puritans in THE COMPLEAT ANGLER, which is, at least in part, that code we talked about earlier for "The Complete Anglican."

MR. SLOAN: James, isn't Walton's book the wellspring of so much angling literature down through the years? I mean, here's a quote: "Good company makes the way seem short." And you yourself wrote JOE AND ME, which is the story of a game warden who caught you poaching at an early age and then befriended you. You had been hopping fences and fishing...

MR. PROSEK: Yeah *(laughing).*

MR. SLOAN: ...in the Bridgeport Hydraulic property in Easton, Connecticut. But, how many people like to fish alone? Not many. You like company; you like to take a friend with you.

MR. PROSEK: Absolutely.

MR. SLOAN: You talk to him in the car, talk to him on the stream, have lunch, whatever. I mean, that's part of the sport of fishing.

MR. PROSEK: Even though the act of fishing, when you're actually in the stream, or wherever you happen to be, is kind of solitary. It's nice to know that someone's there, that you can walk over and talk to him when you want to, or that you can rendezvous for lunch.

MR. SLOAN: There's one quote you have from Walton's book that I'd like you to speak to. The words Walton lived by were basic to Christ's teachings in the New Testament of "love, joy, peace, modesty, patience, and diligence." Those last two words—patience and diligence—remind me of a play T.S. Eliot wrote, THE COCKTAIL PARTY.

MR. PROSEK: Oh, really?

MR. SLOAN: Yes. Because in it, there's a quote. Eliot's play is really a verse play about psychiatry, basically—T.S. Eliot's answer to psychiatry. And Eliot writes, "Seek your salvation with patience and diligence." That reference to patience and diligence jumped right off the page at me. And here we are looking at the roots of those words in Walton in 1653, well before Freud and well before Eliot.

MR. PROSEK: Amazing, isn't it?

MR. SLOAN: So much came right from Walton—including your own fishing philosophy. Tell us about the places that he fished. How different was it and is it from what we know here in America?

MR. PROSEK: Well, Walton mostly fished chalk streams.

MR. SLOAN: Right.

MR. PROSEK: At least, what they call or we call chalk streams, which are a lot like certain limestone streams in central Pennsylvania fed by big springs, usually with very clear, clean water. And a lot of the streams Walton fished are very much like they are today, but in part that's because they've been owned by the same families for centuries—owned by members of the aristocracy, dukes, barons, earls, and lords. The water's mostly private, so the streams are in very, very good condition.

MR. SLOAN: You said these were very clear, cold, spring-fed streams.

MR. PROSEK: Yes. Walton was born in Stafford in the Peak district, where there are many beautiful spring-fed streams, among them the Dove and the Wye. He lived his middle years in London and fished the Lea, a tributary of the Thames, which is where THE COMPLEAT ANGLER is staged. The last thirty years of his life he spent in Hampshire, in the south. That's when he fished rivers, mostly, like the Test and the Itchen, which are world-famous trout streams, beautiful spring-fed streams that come from limestone outcroppings and are very fertile because they have a lot of dissolved limestone that promotes insect life and plant life and makes for big, fat, healthy trout.

MR. SLOAN: When you fished them, and you describe in detail your fishing, did you get a sense of history? You were trouting not only in the footsteps of Walton but the fish you were after—the wild ones, anyway—were certainly descendants of those that Walton had pursued over three hundred years ago.

MR. PROSEK: Yes. It's possible that some of the fish were actually descendants of ones that Walton had caught. Those were the thoughts that were going through my head, and, sure, I was looking around for Walton's ghost. But I had a good time and had good company. I met a lot of anglers who followed in some sense Walton; they were a kind of good, simple, content people—true servants and true disciples of Walton who enjoyed nature and fishing.

MR. SLOAN: Well, let's take that word "simple" for a minute, James. You make a comment in the book—and I have always felt this way myself—that angling is joy, but the minutiae involved with it is really overdone today. I mean, you know there are people who make a cult out of fly fishing for trout and salmon. They really overdo the sport. I really believe one should go out and enjoy oneself and use the tools that one has. For instance, I see fellows trying to fish with dry flies in high, discolored waters in March or April, proclaiming that that is the pure and only correct way of fishing. They know that they're not going to catch anything, but they actually disdain anyone who uses a Woolly Bugger or a nymph. I don't agree with this kind of elitism.

MR. PROSEK: Well, they're living proof of what I think is called *technocracy*.

MR. SLOAN: Technocracy, right?

MR. PROSEK: Right. It's just the term that's meant to describe the tendency of some folks to get too technical in any pursuit. Technocracy takes people away from the simplicity and beauty of fishing, and they lose sight of the original reason behind why you want to do it. I like to fish with as few flies as possible, but, at the same time, certain situations call for very specific kinds of flies. I'm less prone to impose rules on myself, like fishing only with a dry fly upstream, than other people are. I'm not a purist. I fish with bait.

MR. SLOAN: I heard of a fellow who is now fishing without a hook. He just counts the number of rises and strikes he can get from the same fish. He's satisfied never to hook, land, or release a trout.

MR. PROSEK: That's interesting. The biggest part of the fishing experience really is getting the fish to take the fly.

MR. SLOAN: Sure. Getting back to your book, what's the wellspring for it? From the time of Walton's book, we have produced some rich angling literature. What books have come closest to what Walton was espousing? You've mentioned Vince Marinaro's MODERN DRY-FLY CODE as one.

MR. PROSEK: Since Walton, there have been thousands of fishing books. As you know, it's probably the densest literature *(laughing)* of any pastime or sport—of anything, for that matter, except maybe gardening. Fishing has a longer history than most sports. I mean, it started out of necessity: people had to eat.

MR. SLOAN: Right.

MR. PROSEK: And then somehow it became a recreation, mostly with Walton, and people started to then regard it as kind of a metaphor for life. So, we have accumulated a lot of penned romantic literature about fishing. Vincent Marinaro is one author whose books I enjoy a lot. There are a lot of great fishing books, and Walton seems to have spawned many of them.

MR. SLOAN: James, Walton took this sport, in his own words, as sort of a religion. We know that he was an Anglican. My personal belief is that there's a pantheism involved when I am fishing, either in a stream or the ocean. God may be in a church or temple, but he also may be found on a trout stream, and certainly I feel God is out in the ocean when I'm fishing there.

MR. PROSEK: There's no doubt that a lot of people do feel a kind of spiritual source when they get away and escape their daily jobs. Walton was doing the same thing. He was escaping: THE COMPLEAT ANGLER proceeds with two characters, a fisherman and a hunter, walking out of the center of London to fish the River Lea, which is a tributary of the Thames. Metaphorically, though, when they walk out of London, they're not only escaping their daily jobs to go fishing but they're leaving behind some of the turbulence of the times. The Cromwellian suppression that was taking place in London and all the strife inherent in a civil war that was raging through the country during Walton's lifetime all get left behind by his two characters. But, to get back to your initial point, I really *do* think Walton regarded fishing as somewhat of a religion. Well, on Sunday mornings he probably went to church, but shortly after that he got his fishing rod and headed down to the stream.

MR. SLOAN: James, why don't you describe what kind of tackle Walton would have used on these streams?

MR. PROSEK: He describes using a wooden rod, probably an eighteen-footer, that may have been made of greenheart, and then a length of line, about the same length as the rod, made of braided horsehair, which tapered down to sometimes just one single hair. When Cotton talks about fishing with a very fine line, I think that's what he meant.

MR. SLOAN: So there you have the beginning of what we would know today as tapered leaders.

MR. PROSEK: Yes. But they didn't really cast the fly. They just sort of reached out and dapped it on the surface. They liked a little breeze that would help them blow the fly across the stream, if the breeze was blowing in the right direction. It was kind of simple, but I'm sure it was very effective.

MR. SLOAN: What were the flies like in those days? I mean, were they dressed as we know them today?

MR. PROSEK: I don't know whether any flies have survived from back then, but we can divine what they might have looked like from their descriptions. You know, they probably looked like some of our contemporary wet flies.

MR. SLOAN: Right.

MR. PROSEK: You see, they didn't have the various stiff-hackle dry flies that people like Theodore Gordon and Edward R. Hewitt made famous here in the United States and people like Frederick M. Halford started using in England. I'd think they were just some feathers and thread tied on a hook. I'm sure there were also beautiful little flies, well made. Remember, they didn't have fly-tying vises back then; they just made the flies while holding them between their fingers.

MR. SLOAN: You describe in your book the Rheingold Fly, named after a horse that you were fond of as a young man.

MR. PROSEK: Yes. I tied some little ant flies from single hairs from the golden-colored horse's mane. I was friends with this horse, which lived down the street from me when I was a kid. Anyway, I had an opportunity to use these Rheingold flies on some difficult trout in England. I caught a nice trout on one of them, which was sort of a nice continuum. You see, I was catching a fish on my best friend's hair, which was the same material Walton used for his line and maybe some of his flies. It just sort of extended the whole experience for me.

MR. SLOAN: What about access to streams in England? You stated that some of the streams were owned by the same families for centuries. Was it difficult getting on the water Walton himself fished? Is the public excluded from these holdings?

MR. PROSEK: Well, in some sense it's good that they've been private for centuries because they're still in very good condition. As far as access is concerned, some streams, like the River Dove, have public footpaths along the rights of way, so you can access them. At the very least, you can walk along a lot of them.

As far as getting permission to fish, on any one of Walton's rivers, you can buy some really good day tickets for maybe twenty pounds. So for thirty dollars a day, you can fish a really good stretch of water. Otherwise, you have to figure out how to meet some people, unless you're going to pay a hundred pounds a day to fish a beat on the River Test. I did something as simple as calling the Izaak Walton Museum in Great Bridgeford near Stafford, where Walton was born, asking if anybody could take me fishing on the River Dove. They said, "Yes, as a matter of fact, there's this guy named Tony Bridgett who takes people fishing who are interested in Izaak Walton."

But in other cases I made some friends through Yale alumni over in England. Friends of friends of theirs owned fishing rights to some of the better rivers. These people introduced me to some other people. I just built up a network of people who fished and became friends with some members of the Fly Fishers' Club, in London. It was fun and interesting.

MR. SLOAN: James, another thing that was interesting to me was some of the discussion in your book about otters. I know how destructive they can be, eating trout like popcorn. I've seen a couple of otters out at Henryville, Pennsylvania, that looked to me like they weighed thirty or forty pounds.

MR. PROSEK: Really?

MR. SLOAN: They get in the stream, and they're lightning fast. They can clean out the fish population. But the funny thing that struck me was that Walton had the same problem with otters three hundred years ago.

MR. PROSEK: Yes. In fact, that's how he meets or makes acquaintance with the hunter in the opening chapter of THE COMPLEAT ANGLER. Remember, the hunter is walking out of London with the fisherman. The hunter is going to hunt otters, and they get along because, as you said, the fisherman knows that otters kill the fish so he therefore likes the otter hunter.

MR. SLOAN: Sure. And what was Walton's comment about grayling in the book? Did he consider grayling a trash fish in one of the streams you fished?

MR. PROSEK: No, Walton did not consider grayling a trash fish, but in some streams now they do. In the Itchen as well as the Test, the river-keepers were telling me to keep and kill the grayling, as well as the rainbow trout in some cases, because apparently there were never any grayling native to the River Itchen, and they just wanted the native brown trout in there. But the brown trout they have in there now are from all over different parts of England and even Europe. They're not necessarily the original native strain of brown trout.

MR. SLOAN: Do we make too much of a fish's native strain? As long as the trout arc happy and in a suitable environment and feeding well, shouldn't we be satisfied?

MR. PROSEK: In some streams, maybe. But where you know that the original fish are already gone, it doesn't really matter. If you have a stream that has native, indigenous fish in it, you don't want to be putting in a non-native fish. There are places, like in Turkey, for instance, where there are many beautiful native brown trout streams that have not been contaminated at all because they haven't introduced non-native trout to them.

MR. SLOAN: How far east in Turkey do you have to go before you've got some trout fishing?

MR. PROSEK: I traveled with a friend of mine from southern Austria throughout Turkey, and we caught trout in the northwest and in the southwest right near the Mediterranean coast. So, you don't have to go far from Istanbul. We also caught trout in the headwaters of the Euphrates in eastern Turkey, and we fished in the headwaters of the Tigris near the Iraqi border, where the Kurds are fighting the Turkish Army. In short, there are trout all over the place.

MR. SLOAN: And they're doing well?

MR. PROSEK: As well as can be expected. They're doing well despite places where people fish for them with nets and, even worse, explosives.

MR. SLOAN: James, before we wrap up here, I think we ought to mention your Web site, www.troutsite.com. What's on your site?

MR. PROSEK: The site's got information about the book and reprints of some articles I've written. You'll also find information on fishing in different places around the country.

MR. SLOAN: James, it's been good talking to you. I want to thank you again for taking us back in history to Izaak Walton with your new book, THE COMPLETE ANGLER: A CONNECTICUT YANKEE FOLLOWS IN THE FOOTSTEPS OF WALTON, published by HarperCollins. You'll go trout fishing again soon, I'm sure. Meanwhile, good luck with the book and your other travels.

MR. PROSEK: Good talking to you.

ERNEST SCHWIEBERT
on Trout Fishing

AN INTERVIEW WITH ERNEST SCHWIEBERT ON NATURE
VERSUS NURTURE IN THE INTELLIGENCE OF TROUT, THE
GREAT MYTH OF THE CATSKILLS, AND HIS EXPERIENCE AND
TIMES AT HENRYVILLE, PENNSYLVANIA.

*I*f you fish for trout, Ernie Schwiebert hardly needs an introduction. He is one of the best-known authors and authorities on trout in the world. His books TROUT and MATCHING THE HATCH are modern classics. Schwiebert's ability to convey his nearly encyclopedic knowledge of fly fishing and understanding of the ways of trout and salmon and their various habitats in clear and engaging prose has established him as one of the leading writers on the sport of fly fishing. Schwiebert's "other" life is that of an award-winning architect and urban planner, a field in which he holds a doctorate from Princeton University. Both his vocation and his avocation have resulted in travel to every part of the globe and, with it, the opportunity to explore the world's great trout and salmon rivers. Schwiebert lives and works in Princeton, New Jersey.

The following discussion between Schwiebert and Sloan finds two old friends getting reacquainted. Schwiebert answers questions on topics such as trout intelligence and how it is influenced by everything from angling pressure to a fish's origins in a *hatchery or the wild; to time spent in Henryville, Pennsylvania; to some specific details on his preferred gear for fishing Brodhead Creek. Readers will find Schwiebert's answers—as well as some revealing non-answers—in the following interview.*

MR. SLOAN: I'm pleased to have as my guest today one of the greatest trout fishermen to have ever picked up a rod, and that's not an overstatement. Ernie Schwiebert, author of MATCHING THE HATCH, SALMON OF THE WORLD, REMEMBRANCES OF RIVERS PAST, NYMPHS, TROUT, DEATH OF A RIVER-KEEPER, and A RIVER FOR CHRISTMAS, has just written a new book called THE HENRYVILLE FLYFISHERS. Ernie and I and a few other dedicated trout fishermen founded the Henryville Conservation Club out in Henryville, Pennsylvania, near Stroudsburg, some thirty years ago.

William Trego, Ernie's publisher at Meadow Run Press, will join us today by telephone to talk trout and about that extraordinary place that is Henryville, Pennsylvania.

MR. SCHWIEBERT: Thank you for your kind words, Steve. It's a pleasure to be here.

MR. SLOAN: Ernie, before reading your new book, I didn't realize on what hallowed water I had been fishing. But before I get into all that you have done for and with fishing in your lifetime, and since this is the dead of winter, I have a quick question: what is the effect of cold weather on trout streams like those at Henryville—the Analomink, Paradise Creek, or the Brodhead—out there in Pennsylvania?

MR. SCHWIEBERT: What happens during the winter is that life in the stream is a little bit dormant. The stream certainly isn't bad, and it's definitely not empty. A lot of people think that summer is the time when fish have plenty to eat and winter is when they don't. But that's not really true. There is probably more food available to trout in March—between January and March, actually—than at any other time in the year. But that food is underwater because all the fly hatches that will take place in late winter and early spring and early summer reach maturity during the dead of winter. In January, the streams and rivers are full of nymphal diet forms down among the stones and cobbles and everything else on the bottom.

The metabolic activity of fish is directly tied to the temperature of the water. Because the water temperature has dropped during winter, it makes the fish very sluggish. They don't eat as much, and they digest what they do eat more slowly. As a result, their systems are slowed down, even though there's plenty to eat. But all the clocks are still ticking out there: the eggs that the brown trout laid in the fall will be hatching soon, and the little brook trout eggs in the feeder tributaries are ticking in the gravel. And the same is true of the insect life: all those little diurnal clocks are ticking away as degree-days accumulate. What we will be seeing as a hatch of flies in the spring is already starting to happen in egg and larval form in the middle of winter. It's just that we're not aware of it.

MR. SLOAN: We may not be aware of it without your wonderful description, but our angling clock is ticking, even in the dead of winter. Somewhere about forty days before the opening day of trout season, we get energized. We start visiting the tackle shops and tying flies like mad.

MR. SCHWIEBERT: *(laughing)* That's right. We begin to think that those first false spring days we get sometimes in late January or February are the real thing, and we pine for trout waters.

MR. SLOAN: Ernie, you and I have known each other since 1960, when we were fortunate enough to become members of a club that later bought the Henryville property. Nobody I have ever fished with or seen fish is better with a fly rod than you, Ernie. Just watching you read a trout stream while you fish is an extraordinary experience.

MR. SCHWIEBERT: Well, thank you, Steve.

MR. SLOAN: No, I mean it, Ernie; your reputation is well earned. But you've also been a prolific writer, and some of your books spring to mind immediately: MATCHING THE HATCH, SALMON OF THE WORLD, REMEMBRANCES OF RIVERS PAST, and NYMPHS, which is a classic along with MATCHING THE HATCH. Your book TROUT is probably *the* definitive work on trout fishing, and that is saying a lot, considering who your predecessors were.

MR. SCHWIEBERT: Well, there has probably been more writing about trout in the history of angling than any other topic, probably several thousand books altogether, since Izaak Walton got it all started with THE COMPLEAT ANGLER in the 1650s. It is really quite an amazing body of literature.

MR. SLOAN: You're right, Ernie. I've been thinking about it, too. The reason that I think people like trout fishing, especially business people and even nonbusiness people, is that trout fishing is just problem solving all day long in a very pleasant way.

MR. SCHWIEBERT: That's a very good way of putting it, Steve.

I have a lot of doctor friends, some of whom I have taught to fish, and they say it's very much like medical diagnosis, in that one observes phenomena in nature and tries to determine what is going on. Then you reach several hypotheses as to what the problem might be or how one might break the code and solve the problem.

For example, when you're watching a group of fish rising in front of you in springtime, you're asking yourself, "What are they feeding on? Exactly what are they doing?" One looks at them in very much the same way that a doctor observes a patient. In fishing, one observes things in nature, comes up with several possibilities and solutions out of one's experience, and then begins testing them. My doctor friends say they can't think about the office, the problems of their patients, an upcoming surgery, or anything like that while they are fishing. They become so engrossed in this kind of fishing because it is a form of chess playing, a pure form of observation and diagnosis and solution. Like the practice of good medicine, this form of fishing is not passive and doesn't involve just sitting back and waiting for something to happen.

MR. SLOAN: Ernie, we have been at this sport, you and I, for thirty to forty years now. Are we starting to need more and more finesse? Are the fish getting smarter? Do we need better and better flies, smaller flies—to use a phrase, "matching the hatch"—to make trout rise? To me it seems like we are headed that way.

MR. SCHWIEBERT: I think there are three factors that are involved here. The first is hatchery fish, the second is fishing pressure, and the third is one that we have seen since Colonial times: we have had only speckled char, the so-called eastern brook trout, in our fishery since those times. Let's face it, the brookie is a very beautiful fish but not a terribly smart one. When brown trout from Europe were introduced to our streams in the 1880s, we saw a bit of a revolution in the sense that this was a fish that had survived fishing pressure for twenty to twenty-five centuries. By contrast, our native fish had seen nothing but tribal pressures and pursuit by rather small local colonial populations for quite a long time.

There is a substantive difference between the two species. Our ancestors did not like brown trout very much; they claimed it was not as pretty as the brook trout. Well, you could also make the argument, I guess, that a pheasant is prettier than a grouse. But the brown trout also was not as tasty, they argued. Well, that point is also arguable both ways. But there was no argument that the brown trout was harder to catch. All the gaudy brook trout flies of the nineteenth century were not working very well on brown trout.

Mary Orvis Marbury, the daughter of Charles Frederick Orvis, who founded the Orvis Company back in the middle of the nineteenth century, wrote a famous book on fly patterns. She was a fly dresser and tied all of the Orvis family's flies in the nineteenth century, including flies that were shown at the World's Columbian Exposition in Chicago, the Crystal Palace in London, and all sorts of famous places. Anyway, in her book of fly patterns, she made the observation that a lot of the flies depicted were quite fancy and gaudy. She predicted that the arrival of the brown trout would mean fly tyers would need to upgrade and refine their act a little bit. She was right.

Of course, on the other side of the equation, we've got hatcheries pumping out very gullible fish that know nothing of their natural foods and nothing of their natural enemies, including us. We humans are a friend to them from the time they are an inch long until the time we put them out in the fish truck, at which point we do not feed them anymore, begin fishing for them, and suddenly become their enemies. These hatchery fish are not really trout. They look like trout, but they are not really trout. They do not behave in the way that a trout does as we have come to respect and expect and love, quite frankly.

MR. SLOAN: How long does it take for them to develop that behavior? Do they lose their imprint forever, or do they suddenly get acclimated after a period of time and then become wild fish?

MR. SCHWIEBERT: It is very clear that private stocking, at least to the extent that the stocked fish are not actually killed the first time they make a mistake, does allow the fish to acclimate a bit. But I would never, *ever*, try to make the argument that they become fully wild fish, because I think they do not. One of the reasons they don't is that nature is very, very harsh in the way she handles things. Less than 1 percent of the fry that have hatched, and a very small percentage of the eggs laid at random in our rivers in the wild, will actually emerge. Of the ones that do hatch successfully, less than 1 percent survive. *Wow!* Talk about Darwinian selection: the best and the brightest are the only fish left.

MR. SLOAN: Now, getting back to the point you were making, I have always thought that when people talk about wild fish versus hatchery fish, the wild fish proponents try to make clear that we are buying all of the environment and the ecosystem as part of the package. You can't have one without the other. If one accepts the proposition that wild fish populations should be supported, one is also supporting the notion that natural selection and all its benefits come along with it.

MR. SCHWIEBERT: Yes, that's right. I think fishing pressure is a big piece of it. We seem to think that everything out there is still pristine and wild, and we are somehow separate from it. We all know about the obvious effects we have had on the environment. But we have had a discreet effect on nature in a great many less obvious instances, as well. Teaching the remaining pheasants to run, because the ones that flew are dead, is a classic example of what I'm talking about.

I think the same thing is true of fish, and exposure to population density is what explains the difference between the behavior of brown trout and our brook trout. If one goes into the remote latitudes of arctic Europe, where there are few people, places like northern Russia and arctic Finland, Sweden, and Norway, you will find the brown trout there to be just as stupid as a wild Labrador brook trout. That was a revelation to me. The 1880s brown trout that were planted in United States streams, by way of Cold Spring Harbor Hatchery on Long Island, the Caledonia Hatchery up in northwestern New York, and then from the Northville Hatchery in Michigan, were genetic stocks that we got from England, Scotland, and Germany.

Now, I'm not sure about the brown trout from Scotland, because there were a lot of people who had lived around Loch Leven for a long, long time. And certainly the English fish from Hampshire, which is an hour away from London, and the German brown trout from the Black Forest had seen fishing pressure for millennia. There was quite a difference in the way these brown trout behaved under fishing pressure—a true difference between hatchery trout and wild trout. I think you're right about the semantic confusion that comes up when anglers, serious trout fishermen, talk about wild fish: clearly, they're not talking about the wild fish of Labrador or the wild fish of, say, arctic Russia and Lapland.

In short, when we say wild fish now, Steve, I think what we are talking about are fish that have been stream-bred on their own. Therefore, they are aware of their natural foods and their natural enemies from the time that they are less than an inch long. They have also seen fishing pressure and people. So we *have* affected the genetics, in the sense that the ones that disappeared first were the gullible and the foolish. We have affected trout behavior, as well. This has been the effect across twenty, thirty, forty, fifty, or perhaps hundreds of generations, I would guess.

MR. SLOAN: Bill Trego, when Ernie came to you with his last book project [THE HENRYVILLE FLYFISHERS], did he say, "I want to do this book on Henryville, Pennsylvania"? How did this project get started?

MR. TREGO: I have known Ernie for probably ten years or so, and I can't really recall who approached whom. Actually, it was the officers of the Henryville Conservation Club who were really behind the effort; it was their intention to publish a book about the history of the club, and they had Ernie working on it. Somewhere along the line, I was asked to become involved and act as publisher. I was thrilled to be able to do so, and I'm thrilled to have published the book. I think it's a magnificent book and reflects Ernie's effort one hundred percent. The seed of the book was the wish of many members of the club over the past twenty-five or thirty years to commemorate the Brodhead and the history of the region.

MR. SLOAN: Ernie, I didn't realize that we were treading on such hallowed ground and fishing such significant waters at Henryville. I will never walk or fish there again without a new perspective, I can tell you that.

MR. SCHWIEBERT: Well, it is true. Somebody once said there is not any real tree farming because we have not yet, particularly in the case of the Pacific Northwest, seen a generation of eight-hundred- to one-thousand-year-old Douglas firs since we invented tree farming. The same is true in history: we are not yet aware of what has happened all around us. It's a pity in a way, because I think it enriches our lives to know what has gone before.

MR. SLOAN: It certainly does. Tell us about Captain Brodhead, who lived in the Henryville area. The Brodhead stream comes in behind our waters at Henryville. What was the area like 200 years ago?

MR. SCHWIEBERT: The Brodhead clan goes clear back to some of the first English settlers who intruded on the Dutch. One has to remember that the Delaware Water Gap region in those days was frontier. The Brodhead clan lived there in the 1700s, before the French and Indian Wars. It was all absolutely wild country. Most of northern and western New Jersey was wild country. There was an original Brodhead, a member of the British Grenadiers, who finally decided that rather than being called New Amsterdam, Manhattan ought to be called New York. William Penn and his sons were the ones who received their original Royal Grant and then finally a treaty grant called the "Walking Purchase." By the way, the Walking Purchase was an infamous fraud perpetrated by Penn on the native peoples of the area. Penn and his sons acquired big tracts north of Philadelphia that reached up into the Pocono region. The Brodhead clan headed by Daniel Brodhead bought a rather large plantation.

MR. SLOAN: Including our property at Henryville?

MR. SCHWIEBERT: No; I don't think it reached that far upriver. It was about fifteen hundred acres, and according to history it varied a little bit—but so did surveying and other land titles in those days. It was quite a plantation, right at the Water Gap on the mouth of Brodhead Creek. In those days, it had an Indian name, which still survives in the name of a small town, Analomink. People just began to call it "the creek on Brodhead's place," or Brodhead's plantation, or Brodhead's Manor. Then it slowly became Brodhead Creek.

But this family was fascinating. Daniel Brodhead became a brigadier general under Washington, and before that he saved our bacon in the French and Indian Wars. He was in command of Fort Pitt at one point, and he saved our forces at Newtown, New York. He marched right through the wilderness from Pittsburgh up to Wyomissing on the Susquehanna and fought a great battle against American colonial loyalists and the British and their Indian friends up near Newtown, New York, just outside Elmira.

MR. SLOAN: Sounds like there's another book coming.

MR. SCHWIEBERT: *(laughing)* You bet. It has been a fascinating story. That whole region is rich in history, considering who visited Henryville and fished there.

MR. SLOAN: Check out some of these names: Thaddeus Norris.

MR. SCHWIEBERT: Thaddeus Norris was a famous tackle-maker from Philadelphia.

MR. SLOAN: And how about Phillippe, the rodmaker?

MR. SCHWIEBERT: Yes, Samuel Phillippe. He was a gunsmith, a gunmaker, and a violin maker; he even made metal musical instruments. He was also an excellent rod builder. He was based in Easton, Pennsylvania. We tend to forget that before railroads and roads, Easton was a major city because of its location at the confluence of the Delaware and Lehigh rivers.

MR. SLOAN: Give us a little critique on Henry Andrews Ingraham.

MR. SCHWIEBERT: Henry Andrews Ingraham visited Henryville as a very young man, right after the Civil War. He fished there and participated in the early years of the Anglers' Club of New York, which was founded just after the turn of the century. Oddly enough, the club was founded with a nucleus of people who had met fishing at Henryville, Pennsylvania, on the Brodhead, because it was such a famous destination. Henryville became famous both because of the fishing and because of the fact that the Delaware, Lackawanna & Western Railroad reached Henryville with regular rail service in 1852. Up until that point, it was quite an ordeal to travel there. Sometimes it took as much as twenty hours to get there by stagecoach from Philadelphia. Think of that: there was very little time to make a weekend trip of it.

MR. SLOAN: Here are two more names: Robert Barnwell Roosevelt and Gifford Pinchot

MR. SCHWIEBERT: Robert Barnwell Roosevelt was the uncle of Theodore Roosevelt. The two families lived side by side, down around Gramercy Park in Manhattan. Everybody knew the Roosevelt clan. Theodore Roosevelt's father died while Teddy was still at Harvard. So his uncle Robert, who was a naturalist, a fly fisherman, and a hunter of note, and wrote extensively about the outdoors, became a surrogate father to him. Teddy's family lived in a big brownstone next door to his uncle, and there is a rather famous note that Roosevelt wrote when he won his first presidential election. Remember, he was vice president when McKinley was shot in Buffalo. On the night of the electoral inauguration, he wrote a brief note to Robert Barnwell Roosevelt, thanking him for being there for him and being his surrogate father. He regretted that his real father could not enjoy the moment but thanked his uncle for all his help.

Gifford Pinchot was a colleague of Theodore Roosevelt. He was the father of the United States Forest Service and a founder of Roosevelt's Bull Moose Party, and he later became governor of Pennsylvania.

MR. SLOAN: Well, here are two presidents who fished there: Grover Cleveland and Benjamin Harrison.

MR. SCHWIEBERT: That's correct. They fished there during the 1880s. Harrison's appearance is a bit of a mystery; he simply pops into the old ledgers of Henryville House and then disappears again. The curious thing is that he and Cleveland were political rivals. I don't know whether his visit was a peacemaking trip or exactly what it was. No one probably ever will know, because it was a meeting that has sort of escaped the history books. Cleveland lived in Princeton, New Jersey, in those days. Later in life, he became chairman of the board of trustees of Princeton University. He fished quite a lot, and that's how he got to Henryville with Henry Van Dyke, who was also from Princeton. Pinchot comes into the picture quite a bit later, with Theodore Roosevelt. Pinchot, of course, did some great conservation work with Roosevelt, such as the creation of Yellowstone National Park—which basically started public access to the government's land.

MR. SLOAN: The book also contains a passage about General Phil Sheridan and George Armstrong Custer, who both fished Henryville, Pennsylvania.

Bill Trego, before we get into Custer and Sheridan and a couple of other notables, Henryville was fished by some famous artists, such as Julian Alden Weir and Willard Metcalfe. I have owned some works by both of these painters.

MR. TREGO: You're very fortunate. While they're not very well known, they are both very great American painters.

What appealed to me about THE HENRYVILLE FLYFISHERS is that it is a very broad and large story—just as Ernie has been elucidating for us—but within that large story are many smaller stories. It is a fascinating book. Most of the comments that I have received about the book from our readers and our customers are about the latter half of the book, which describes the events of the club through the past twenty-five or thirty years.

What the reader ends up with is a very intimate insider's view of what it means to be a member of a private trout club, what problems arise, and how they are resolved. People die, new members come in, land becomes available and has to be purchased, or the issue is debated as to whether or not it should be purchased, and there is usually no money in the treasury. All these things come up in the life of other private clubs. Most people out there, myself included, are not members of private fishing clubs and never will be.

Ernie provides a very intimate view of what it *really* takes to conserve the waters, to attend all the local planning meetings and file lawsuits on occasion, just to protect the waters. I should say that the Henryville waters are the most pristine northeastern trout waters I have ever seen. They are just a joy to fish. Walking into some of the more remote areas of the club is like entering a time warp. You get the sense that it could be the late 1600s. The book offers both a history of the region and a history of the activities of the club.

MR. SLOAN: Yes, and a lesson in civics, in a way. A group of people got together under a common bond and decided that they really liked a unique area of the world and, through some rather difficult but fortuitous negotiations, wound up not only owning it but taking care of it. And that is part of the ongoing problem.

MR. SCHWIEBERT: You're right: it *is* more than a fishing club; it's almost a responsibility of stewardship when, through accidents of family history and their own fate, a group of people band together to protect and conserve something. We decided to do it privately because of what had happened to the family that had owned it for six or seven generations and then fell on hard times because they were land rich and cash poor. Our purchase was not forced but, rather, fortuitous for both parties. Once you are aware of the Henryville history, you realize that it is a lot more than our own fishing that we are protecting here. Henryville is a bit of a shrine among the trout-fishing faithful, and it precedes the Catskills in the history of American fly fishing. This fact, of course *(laughing)*, upsets a few apple carts.

MR. SLOAN: Yes. That was one of the most interesting stories that you bring out in the book. For a long, long time, most others and I had always felt that the Beaverkill and the Catskill region was the cradle of American fly fishing.

MR. TREGO: It is a popular myth but not entirely true.

MR. SCHWIEBERT: Steve, when you realize that the Delaware, Lackawanna & Western railroad reached Henryville with regular daily service in 1852, and the Ontario & Western did not reach Roscoe, New York, where the Willowemoc and the Beaverkill meet, until 1872, one is forced on technical grounds to rest one's case as to which river was fished earlier.

MR. SLOAN: Ernie, you may not have heard this before, but there are three great names in American fly fishing—LaBranche, Hewitt, and Gordon—and now I want to add a fourth: Schwiebert.

MR. SCHWIEBERT: That's some pretty heavy company.

MR. SLOAN: I can't think of any better foursome than that if you want to talk, read, or are interested about trout fishing. Besides this book, Ernie's written a number of others, especially TROUT, but you have made a lifetime study of our sport.

Now, I've got to ask you just one more question. What rod do you use at Henryville?

MR. SCHWIEBERT: *(laughing)* You know, I do not use just one, unfortunately. Fly fishing is pretty close to being an addiction, and I don't think of myself as a type of a collector, but I would suspect that everyone in my family would disagree.

MR. TREGO: He keeps all his worms out of sight and locked up.

MR. SLOAN: Speaking of worms, I just came back from the San Juan River in New Mexico last October, and I did fish the San Juan Worm. I asked myself: is it really a fly?

MR. SCHWIEBERT: Well, I'd be less worried about that than you are, Steve. You know, you are not imitating earthworms with a lure like the San Juan Worm, because there are such things as aquatic worms that live in water. These worms look like ordinary angleworms, but they aren't the same. These aquatic worms are what a San Juan Worm imitates, and they are quite prolific in warm-water streams—more so than in trout streams. Because we have built dams on big western rivers like the San Juan and the Big Horn, or the Green River at Flaming Gorge, these rivers are now tailwater fisheries that were warm-water fisheries in frontier times. These aquatic worms are present in larger numbers in these tailwater fisheries than they are in regular trout streams. In using the San Juan Worm fly, you are imitating what the fish eat and what they see there. The worms get particularly displaced and available in high water.

MR. SLOAN: Wait a minute. The question still remains: what rod do you use at Henryville?

MR. SCHWIEBERT: *(laughing)* Well, let me make one more point about the San Juan Worm. I do not fish it—although not because I object to it esthetically and not because you are imitating something the fish eat, because they do eat it and it is an imitation. I do not fish it because the San Juan Worm, as tied by most people today, uses too large a hook. I do not like to kill fish anymore. I do not object to it, but I myself just do not like to do it anymore. When a hook of the size needed to tie the San Juan Worm is used, the damage inflicted by the hook itself makes it very difficult to release the fish successfully.

MR. SLOAN: Even barbless?

MR. SCHWIEBERT: Even barbless. It has a pretty big point and pretty big bend.

MR. SLOAN: Is that why you fish small flies, too?

MR. SCHWIEBERT: No, I fish small flies because I am imitating what the fish eat. Most of the things that the fish eat in a trout stream in the East, for example, are probably less than half an inch long.

MR. SLOAN: Ernie, we will leave the question as to which rod you use at Henryville until another time. Until then, tight lines and a good drift.

MR. SCHWIEBERT: Thanks, Steve.

During editing of this transcript, Mr. Schwiebert removed the aura of mystery surrounding his choice of tackle at Henryville by providing the following explanation:

> *"I fish an eight-foot, four-weight Thomas & Thomas Paradigm at Henryville because I enjoy fishing cane, but I don't like to put it aboard airplanes. I can drive to fish the Brodhead. The rod was specially built for me by Tom Dorsey and takes a four-weight double-taper line. It will handle both ninety feet of line and 7X tippets."*
>
> *—The Editors*

❧❧

The Whirling Disease Foundation
on Whirling Disease

An interview with the Whirling Disease Foundation on the current status of the disease, its pathology and transmission, and the prospects for its containment and management.

*T*he Whirling Disease Foundation faces a seemingly insurmountable task.
The foundation is fighting to manage one of the most devastating threats that rainbow trout and other salmonid populations have ever encountered. Whirling disease is caused by a water-borne metazoan parasite, Myxobolus cerebralis, *that penetrates the head and spinal cartilage of fingerling trout, where it multiplies rapidly and puts pressure on their organ of equilibrium. This pressure prevents normal development of the spine and causes the trout to swim erratically, often in a characteristic whirling or tail-chasing pattern, preventing the trout from feeding and avoiding predators.*

Whirling disease has taken the most significant toll on wild rainbow trout populations since it was first introduced to North American waters from the Eurasian continent in the late 1950s. And while other salmonids—most prominently brown trout—can become infected but not display any symptoms of the disease, all salmonids can carry the disease and transmit it to other fish. Regardless of species, when each infected fish dies, it can release millions of M. cerebralis *spores into the water.*

The spores, in turn, are extremely hardy: they can withstand freezing and desiccation and can survive in a stream for twenty to thirty years. Eventually, the spore must be ingested by its alternate host, the common aquatic worm known as Tubifex tubifex, *where the spore takes on the form that once again can infect trout fry. It is this ease of transmission and vitality of the spore that make whirling disease every bit as devastating to the trout population as AIDS is to the human population. The parasite is sure to continue to spread to waters now clean because it is so easily and unknowingly transported by animals, birds, and humans.*

When Dave Kumlien and Tom Anacker of the Whirling Disease Foundation spoke with Sloan from the Whirling Disease Foundation offices in Bozeman, Montana, they discussed a number of critical issues surrounding the disease.

MR. SLOAN: Chances are good that if you fish for trout and you have not yet heard of whirling disease, you soon will. That's because whirling disease is one of the most significant threats to trout ever encountered and, sadly, one that is proving impossible to eradicate. A trout infected with the disease will start chasing its tail, cannot feed itself, dies, and then infects its stream when spores are released from its carcass.

You would be surprised at how many states are affected by whirling disease. Twenty-two in all, and this number is expected to grow: Alabama, California, Colorado, Connecticut, Idaho, Maryland, Massachusetts, Michigan, Montana, Nevada, New Hampshire, New Jersey, New Mexico, New York, Ohio, Oregon, Pennsylvania, Utah, Virginia, Washington, West Virginia, and Wyoming.

We'll be talking today by telephone with two leaders in the battle against whirling disease, Tom Anacker and Dave Kumlien, the president and the development director, respectively, of the Whirling Disease Foundation, in Bozeman, Montana. We'll be looking to learn more about this disease from Tom and Dave and what we, as fishermen, can do to stem its advance. For example, where do trout contract this kind of parasite?

Dave, I just read off that list of more than twenty states where whirling disease is found. It sounds pretty serious when one thinks of the kind of trout waters found in most of those states.

MR. KUMLIEN: Yes, it is a serious problem. When Tom gets on he can give you a clearer picture because he knows more about the science than I do. But I think you're right in your estimate of up to twenty-two states. It is a serious problem, and, unfortunately, just not a lot is known about whirling disease. It is being studied now, obviously, but it was not something that was being closely studied back when it was first encountered, especially in wild trout populations. So it caught a lot of people by surprise when it started to show up in the wild trout areas and spread so rapidly.

MR. SLOAN: Dave, you are tasked with raising and collecting the money that will keep the research effort alive until a cure is found. Please tell people where you are located and the correct name of the organization.

MR. KUMLIEN: The full name of our group is the Whirling Disease Foundation. We work out of a small office in Bozeman, Montana, that houses our president, Tom Anacker; an executive administrator, Sue Higgins; a secretary, and me. Our address is P.O. Box 327, Bozeman, Montana, 59771-0327. The foundation's phone number is 406/585-0860, and we have a Web site, as well, at www.whirling-disease.org.

MR. SLOAN: Tom Anacker has just joined us. Tom, Dave and I were just talking about how rapidly and extensively whirling disease has spread in North America. What's the most recent estimate of the number of states that have infected fisheries, twenty-two?

MR. ANACKER: That's right, Steve. Twenty-two states, primarily in New England and the West, have infected trout populations, and the disease is spreading toward the Mid-Atlantic states.

MR. SLOAN: Tom, describe for us what this trout-decimating disease really is. Is it a worm, a parasite? Where do you think it comes from?

MR. ANACKER: Well, the disease itself is caused by a parasite that alternates between two different hosts as part of its lifecycle. And those two hosts are fish—specifically, trout and other salmonids—and a common aquatic worm called the tubifex worm.

Whirling disease has a relatively complex life cycle that was really not completely understood until the mid-1980s. That's a large part of the problem: our knowledge is relatively young as far as scientific history goes. The disease was spreading quickly, while our understanding of it was not. But we do know that the origins of whirling disease are on the European Continent with hatchery-raised brown trout. Ironically, these European brown trout have built an immunity to the disease over the years even though they can still carry the parasite and transmit it to other salmonids.

Whirling disease spreads through a typical host-parasite relationship that has evolved over the millennia so that both European brown trout and the parasite spore, called *Myxobolus cerebralis,* prosper in the presence of each other. However, this symbiotic relationship has wreaked havoc when European brown trout came to North America and the parasite hit species that had no experience with it—specifically, the wild North American rainbow trout.

MR. SLOAN: So rainbows are the trout that are most at risk? Why is that?

MR. ANACKER: That's right: rainbows have been hit the hardest. This is because of the way the disease spreads. The host is the fish itself—the rainbow trout or other salmonid. The lifecycle of the parasite that actually causes whirling disease requires the tubifex worm as part of the cycle.

To describe this lifecycle briefly, we can start with the mature form of the parasite, which is a spore embedded along the spinal and cranial elements of an infected fish. When the fish dies or is eaten, the whirling disease spore is released into the water column. At that point, the tubifex worm, through its normal feeding patterns, will pick the spore up and actually ingest it. The spore is very small, about the size of a red blood cell, but is covered by a very tough, environmentally resistant covering.

Next, the ingested spore undergoes a metamorphosis in the gut of the worm and transforms into a stage called the *triactinomyxon,* or TAM for short, that can infect fish. The TAM is released out of the worm and floats into the water column. Under a microscope, the TAM looks like a grappling hook, with three hook-like tentacles. This is the stage that affects the fish. The TAM will float passively in the water column and, when it comes into contact with the skin of a fish, attach to the trout and at that point inject the pre-spore material.

MR. SLOAN: That's incredible. It's hard to believe that a process so complex could allow the disease to spread so quickly.

MR. ANACKER: You're right; it really is a tremendously complex parasite/host relationship.

Getting back to the infection stage of the cycle, each TAM has sixty-four so-called "shotgun shells" that actually inject *sporoplast* material into the skin of the fish. Once injected, this *sporoplast* material enters the fish, seeks out the nervous system, and travels up the nerves—primarily to the area around the brain casing and along the spinal column. In very young fish, there is a lot of cartilage in those areas. This parasite travels up the nervous system to these cartilaginous regions and just starts eating—consuming, digesting, destroying —the cartilage and begins reproducing and growing toward the adult form of the spore.

MR. SLOAN: That sounds like Pac Man—Pac Man on its spine.

MR. ANACKER: That's a very good descriptive analogy of essentially what it looks like.

Whirling disease is insidiously odd. Here we are—all of us who have been trout fishing in a stream or river—crossing a pool or sitting on a rock or looking down from on top of a bridge, watching the water pouring over the trout, while all the while, something invisible and deadly is just waiting for an opportunity to get on the skin of the fish and kill it and infect many others.

The larger fish are more resistant to it than the smaller ones because at three, four, or five months' age, their cartilage is naturally turning into bone. As the cartilage hardens into bone and there is more ossification, the parasite causes less impact. The real devastating effect of whirling disease occurs to the very young fish. These fish are just emergent—two, three, or four months of age—and that is the most dangerous time for them in terms of susceptibility to the disease. While older fish can have the infection, they do not necessarily have to show any symptoms of the disease

MR. SLOAN: So it's almost like humans being HIV positive but not showing any of the symptoms of full-blown AIDS. Fish can be infected with whirling disease and transmit the spores but not be impacted by it.

MR. ANACKER: Exactly. You could have older rainbow trout in a stream but no recruitment—no new fry reaching maturity—because all the juveniles are going to get attacked by whirling disease and die. Here's an analogy for the effect of whirling disease on the production and population of fish in a given fishery: imagine how dramatically the NFL would be affected if the current system of college football were to be eliminated. That's something like the effect that whirling disease is having on trout fisheries.

MR. SLOAN: Right. Interesting. Dave, I know one of the challenges you face in raising money for the foundation is that you want to emphasize the seriousness of the disease, but you certainly don't want to give the impression that fisheries in all streams are going to be wiped out. Clearly, that's not the case; it is just that the young fish are having a problem, but you still have a resident trout population in these rivers that is so attractive to tourists, especially out West. I mean, we do not want to give folks the impression that they should just stay home. On the contrary, fishing is okay today, but the problem is a serious one that is affecting the recruitment for the future.

MR. KUMLIEN: That is exactly right. Getting that message out is part of my job and also our foundation's goal. We try to educate people and provide information, make people aware of the problem, but we try not to scare people. For example, the Madison River here in Montana has received the most publicity about whirling disease, and, while rainbow trout populations have suffered drastically in that river, it still remains a very good to excellent fishery. The Madison is still a world-class trout stream by any standard.

When I am not at the Whirling Disease Foundation offices, I run the Montana Troutfitters, a fly shop here in Bozeman that I've owned since 1978. I want to make sure that people understand that you can still have some outstanding fishing here and in other places where whirling disease is present.

MR. SLOAN: We have a caller on the line, Burt from Idaho Falls. Go ahead, Burt.

BURT: Thanks for taking my call. I listen to your program often at this time in the morning. Today, the subject of whirling disease caught my attention pretty quickly. Twenty-five years ago, I was a student in fish health. I remember that it became pretty apparent that whirling disease was going to ravage the trout populations and sporting industry if there weren't some pretty careful steps taken. I recall that a lot of the state fishery agencies were aware of the significance of the threat and tried to do something about it. But there was a lot of foot-dragging from the public because the public was not convinced that this disease was going to be so serious. Unfortunately, as in a lot of other similar situations, the public has to see the huge disaster before they believe the scientific facts.

MR. SLOAN: Well, in America, we are great at crisis management. We kind of invented and perfected it as an art form. I see that Idaho is on the list of states affected. Where do you go trout fishing?

BURT: I fish all around Idaho Falls, up in the North Fork of the Snake River, and on the South Fork. The North Fork is more appropriately called the Henry's Fork, but that depends on how long you've been here and where you were raised, I guess.

MR. SLOAN: Well, I was going to ask Tom and Dave to tell us a little bit more about the disease. For example, it's called whirling disease for a reason. I was also going to ask them to describe its symptoms. What happens when a fish gets attacked by the disease? What symptoms would somebody look for at streamside?

MR. ANACKER: Well, first of all, Steve, it's important to know that you're probably not going to see too many symptoms of whirling disease at streamside because the fish that have been infected by the disease significantly enough to be experiencing the clinical symptoms are not going to do very well out in the river environment. They are going to be subject to other predators.

What you may see in some of the fish affected by whirling disease are the deformation traits caused by inflammation and essentially failure of the skeletal elements to form over the top of the cartilage. Therefore, you might notice trout with curvature of the spine—called *scoliosis*—or cranial deformities. For instance, they may have a sunken or flattened forehead.

But the most obvious symptom of the disease to anglers is the tail-chasing pattern in which infected fish will swim. Remember, the fish has an organ that is essential to its equilibrium, and the swelling and inflammation caused by the disease puts pressure on this organ and causes the fish to be unable to swim in a straight line. When they are startled or when they attempt to feed, they exhibit a characteristic tail-chasing behavior, which is called whirling. They'll also move in a corkscrew-type motion through the water column. Both whirling and this corkscrew swimming motion serve as great big flags for any predator that there is a fish in trouble.

Another symptom that you can often see in infected fish is the interruption of the pigmentation of the tail. The tail and, in some cases, the entire back third of the fish will be blackened, resulting in them being what is commonly called "black tailed."

As I said earlier, most of these symptoms make it pretty hard for infected fish to survive in their environment for very long, although every now and then, somebody will catch a fish with a large deformity or a blackened tail.

MR. SLOAN: Is there any interaction between whirling disease and humans? Are there any risks associated with, say, handling or eating an infected fish, or drinking water that is infected? Burt, maybe you might know a little bit about it, since you also worked on it. Is there any correlation between human activity

—human waste, pesticides, run off, say—and this disease? Have we put a correlation together on this?

BURT: I think there's an indirect correlation. There is no direct correlation that I am aware of, except that just about anything you do to the stream itself could impact the fish in it. And, of course, anything that could have a detrimental effect on the fish population in general is going to have a significantly greater impact on a fishery that is infected with whirling disease because infected fish are more susceptible to infection by other agents. They're already stressed.

MR. SLOAN: Dave, what do you think?

MR. KUMLIEN: Well, one way that there is an interaction between whirling disease and humans is in the spread of the disease through equipment or fish that contain whirling disease spores. This spreading, of course, can be done advertently or inadvertently by humans; that is one thing that every informed fisherman has to pay attention to after a day of fishing.

MR. SLOAN: You mean in terms of being aware of how easily the disease can be transmitted?

MR. KUMLIEN: Exactly. There are simple steps that every fisherman can take to reduce the risk of spreading the spores to uninfected waters.

But, before I forget, I'd like to make one crucial point that came up when Burt called in. We should make it clear immediately this is not a disease that humans can get.

MR. SLOAN: Yes, absolutely. I wanted to make that clear, too.

MR. KUMLIEN: Maybe if it were a disease that humans could contract, people would pay more attention. You cannot get it from eating fish, but you can transfer it on your waders. Humans are very much involved in the transfer of this disease.

MR. SLOAN: For instance, I think I read somewhere that you could have been wearing your waders in an infected stream and subsequently wear them into an uninfected stream and inadvertently infect it with spores that may have clung to your waders. Is that scenario a possibility?

MR. ANACKER: Yes, it most certainly is. Fishermen transferring the spore on their equipment is a significant transmittal mechanism for this disease. That's why we counsel people to fish smart.

Rule number one is an obvious one: do not, under any circumstances, move live fish from one place to another; that is the single most effective way to transmit whirling disease. If you catch a heavily infected fish, you may be holding as many as a million whirling disease spores right in your hand, embedded in the spinal elements of that fish. So, the movement of even one live infected fish from one body of water to another is enough to thoroughly introduce the disease.

Secondly, if you are fishing where whirling disease is present in fish, be smart about it at the end of the day: rinse off and remove any film on your waders. Rinse off your equipment, and dry it out. The disease spore is microscopic; it can get into the scams of wading boots and waders. So exercise care by decontaminating all your equipment after you fish any infected waters. Our fishery resources are too important to accidentally introduce this spore around.

MR. SLOAN: Well, let me ask you this: would you recommend high-pressure spraying to wash off any potential spore? I'm talking about using a freshwater garden hose on your waders, or something comparable. Would that help?

MR. ANACKER: Well, what you're really concerned about is the spore form. We recommend that you rinse your equipment off at the stream before you leave, and then dry it out. For example, if I use my drift boat in an infected fishery, I will put it in the middle of my lawn, scrub it, and then hose it off. When I'm hosing it off, I let the rinse-water drain into the grass so that any runoff doesn't have access to the local sewer system, because these spores can travel through municipal sewer systems and remain viable. I always let the runoff go onto the ground.

MR. SLOAN: Well, Tom, how did this parasite get from only one or two states to twenty-two so far? What's the process here?

MR. ANACKER: There are several different factors at work, but primarily we believe whirling disease has spread through the movement of live fish transported from one state to another. Also, birds helped spread it. Migratory eagles or other fish-eating birds of prey, for example, can transport the spore.

MR. SLOAN: Sure. They may eat a diseased fish and then defecate in another stream, and a new area is infected.

MR. ANACKER: Correct. And it can be transmitted that way by other predators, such as an otter, for example, or it can simply move downstream with the current once an infection is established in upstream waters.

MR. SLOAN: Dave, do any states have a matching funds program to help with the research? For instance, if a listener sends in a donation to the Whirling Disease Foundation, can matching funds be obtained from corporate sources or other state programs?

MR. KUMLIEN: Well, certainly, those opportunities exist. Right now, we don't have the funds available for a matching program for contributions from our donors, but we are working on it through our executive administrator, Sue Higgins. Sue is an excellent grant writer and has been very effective at obtaining grants, and I'm confident we'll be able to obtain a funding source to match donor contributions at some level. As we hear of state or private matching fund programs, we'll certainly make our donors aware of them. They're a great way to magnify the impact of any donation.

MR. SLOAN: So you feel your donors are really getting a good bang for their charitable buck?

MR. KUMLIEN: Oh, absolutely. Every donor to the Whirling Disease Foundation needs to know that we put his or her money to good use for research. Research is our goal, and our mission for the foundation is to raise funds to support this research. We have the good fortune of having had a couple of very generous donors essentially underwrite our office operations; therefore, we are able to put every penny of each contribution we receive directly to work on research. Typically, up to 14 percent of donations to groups like ours gets spent on indirect costs associated with overhead. We're very proud of the fact that every dollar we receive goes right into the research program, which we feel is one of the most significant benefits of our organization. Donors could almost consider it something like a 14-percent match to their contributions.

MR. SLOAN: That's pretty impressive. So how do you put your donors' contributions to work specifically? What aspects of research are your main focuses?

MR. KUMLIEN: There's no question that the Whirling Disease Foundation has become the leader in coordinating research, but I want to point out that we don't do it ourselves. We are not a research laboratory; we are a foundation. We facilitate research by acting as a clearinghouse for information and helping researchers share information. We also have some other projects that we are looking at, such as a multi-media educational presentation that we want to put together. We have a Web site, of course, and we're always exploring ways to make that a more effective educational and research resource.

Of course, one of the most important things that we've done—and I think Tom would agree—is that we have established annual symposiums that serve as a forum to bring people who are interested in whirling disease together who had never gotten together before. These symposiums provide a forum for agency people, researchers, and biologists to share information. We would like to put two together every year. Our symposiums, really, are what have established us as the leader in coordinating research. Everybody involved in research on some aspect of the disease looks to us for direction. Anyone can call us in Bozeman at 406/585-0860 or fax us at 406/585-0863 and get the dates of our next symposium.

MR. SLOAN: Thanks, Dave. Those are good points. Tom, what do you think?

MR. ANACKER: I'd like to add that we have made a tremendous amount of progress since 1994, when we first started looking at whirling disease. It was really a black hole back then, as far as obtaining information and knowledge about this disease. So we started pretty much from scratch, developing baseline data and information. Initially, we did a lot of surveys to find out where the infection occurred, where the worm hosts existed, and then how bad the infection was in those places where it existed. And from there, a lot of work has been done to understand the disease's lifecycle and the factors influencing the various components of it.

For example, habitat conditions influence whether or not the tubifex worm is present. Any portion of a streambed that has breaks in the currents is likely to harbor tubifex worms. For example, we found a lot of tubifex worms below dams in most cases.

Many people wonder why we are so concerned about tubifex worm populations. The answer is simple: whirling disease is like a three-legged stool, with the tubifex worm, the fish, and the parasite each being one leg. If you eliminate the parasite or the worm, the stool is going to tip over, and you will have eliminated the disease. So, one of the current scientific approaches to managing the disease is to see whether there is a way to eliminate one leg. Of course, you don't want to eliminate the fish, but to eliminate the parasite or the tubifex worm from the cycle would then have a significant influence toward eliminating the disease.

MR. SLOAN: What about breeding disease-resistant trout? You had mentioned that browns are immune.

MR. ANACKER: They are, somewhat, and researchers are constantly looking for naturally resistant fish. While the brown trout has evolved toward some resistance, there are a few native fish species on the North American continent that do show some resistance mechanisms that are helpful. For example, the coho salmon, the grayling, and the bull trout all have different types of mechanisms that give them some resistance against whirling disease.

We are looking for life history advantages in certain species, too. For example, if a fish can emerge from the gravel and grow large enough before the fish-infecting stage of the spore is present in the water, that would be an advantage. Or in a species that spawns high up in tributaries, away from most of the infection in main streams, many times the fry can emerge and grow for months before moving downstream to the highly infected main stem of the river or stream.

MR. SLOAN: Does whirling disease affect other species, like chubs, shiners, dace, perch, sculpins, or forage fish?

MR. ANACKER: No, it infects trout and salmon only. It is a very specific and very complex organism, but it is specific for the salmonid species only.

MR. SLOAN: How far along do you think we are on the coordination of the research? Do you see a light at the end of the tunnel or have we still got some way to go?

MR. ANACKER: We do have a way to go, but I am optimistic. We are seeing some developments that are likely to be incremental at first. I think we will be seeing some improvements, some discoveries made, that will help fish survive while we seek a longer-term solution. Other organizations besides the individual states themselves have been supportive and are encouraging research. Trout Unlimited comes to mind immediately. We have a memo of understanding with TU, and they support the symposiums that the foundation has presented. Everyone has to realize that it is very important for the private sector to play a role in funding research. There are just not enough state or federal dollars available right now to do all the research that's needed.

Therefore, we need to encourage more of the private sector to work in partnership with the public sector on this. Because our foundation is a 501-[C](3) tax-exempt organization, all donations are tax deductible. We hope that all who care about the health of our fisheries will make an investment in good fishing for the future.

MR. KUMLIEN: Tom, I'd like to add just one thing. There is one other program that consumers should be aware of that the foundation has created: we call it "Buck-A-Product." Through Buck-A-Product, companies, primarily in the fly-fishing industry at this point, are inserting a card or a hang-tag on fishing products. The card contains information about whirling disease and the foundation, and it offers the consumer an opportunity to make a donation to the Whirling Disease Foundation for research. And in most instances, the manufacturer is matching and then contributing to the program.

So there is a way to forge this alliance between individuals and industry and work toward mutual goals in combating whirling disease. The companies participating thus far are Thomas & Thomas Fly Rods; The L.L. Bean Company, which is supporting Buck-A-Product with their Aquastealth boots; Cortland; Powell Rods; and Scott Rods. Also, The Orvis Company has been a strong supporter of the program, as well. FLY ROD & REEL magazine has followed the issue closely and has given us strong editorial support.

MR. SLOAN: Gentlemen, it has been an informative pleasure. I'd like to take just a moment to make sure that all who care about preserving trout fishing have your address so that they can send a contribution to help you continue your fight. Send your tax-deductible contributions to The Whirling Disease Foundation, P.O. Box 327, Bozeman, Montana 59771.

MR. ANACKER: Thanks, Steve. And thanks to all who can see fit to help out the foundation. We're counting on you.

MR. KUMLIEN: And your fisheries are counting on you. Thanks, Steve, for having us.

MR. SLOAN: My pleasure, gentlemen.

An Update on Whirling Disease, March 2001

Editor's Note: Mr. Kumlien was kind enough to provide the following brief addendum to his interview. Since the preceding interview originally aired more than three years ago, much has occurred in the battle against the disease. In the following update, Kumlien describes the progress that his been made to date in the battle against the disease. Kumlien continues to serve as the development director for the Whirling Disease Foundation. A twenty-year veteran of the fly-fishing tackle and outfitting business, he lives in Bozeman, Montana, with his wife, Karyn, and two sons, Kristopher and Kevin.

A great deal has transpired in whirling disease research since the first "Fishing Zone" show three years ago. At that time, not much was known about whirling disease, and research was focused on filling in the information gaps about the whirling disease parasite, the alternate host tubifex worm, and the susceptibility of the various species of trout and salmon to the disease. Since then, the amount of research into these areas has been quite amazing, and scientists have assembled a nearly complete dossier on the parasite, the worm, and the fish. With these information gaps filled, the focus has shifted to applying this newfound knowledge toward creating potential solutions that will eliminate this deadly threat to wild trout, salmon, char, and steelhead. Considering that as recently as two years ago, the talk around the water cooler at the annual Whirling Disease Symposium was not optimistic, this progress is remarkable.

At the Seventh Annual Whirling Disease Symposium, held in Salt Lake City in February 2001, several research presentations pointed toward the possibility of managing whirling disease. Findings from research at the University of California at Davis indicate that one strain of the alternate host tubifex worm is resistant to the parasite. When these worms are exposed to whirling disease spores, the worms do ingest the spore but do not produce the fish-infective TAM stage of the parasite. Prior to this research, it was believed that all tubifex worms would produce parasites, but the new findings indicate the possibility of biological control of the worm population.

One of the most interesting stories from the symposium was not from an actual research presentation. According to leading whirling disease researcher Dr. Mansour El Matbouli of the University of Munich, he has identified a strain of rainbow trout from a German trout farm that may be resistant to whirling disease. Apparently, this strain of rainbow has been in this particular German trout farm for 150 years. As rainbow trout are not native to Germany, they cannot be stocked into German waters but are raised in trout farms to be sold as food. In 2000, this particular trout farm imported some North American rainbow fry to raise and sell. When introduced into the hatchery, these rainbows immediately developed whirling disease and died. At about the same time, rainbows from South Africa were brought in, and they, too, developed a fatal whirling disease infection. In the meantime, the resident trout farm rainbows, swimming in the same "whirling disease soup," were doing just fine. These potentially whirling-disease-resistant trout are scheduled for testing in the lab of Dr. Ron Hedrick at the University of California at Davis. Should these rainbows prove to be whirling disease resistant, they will be tested for resistance to other North American pathogens, strength and performance, and other environmental capabilities.

In 1995, when the harsh glare of the national media fell on the announcement that a 90-percent decline in the upper Madison River's wild rainbow population was caused by a whirling disease infection, the upper Madison became the poster child for the effects of whirling disease. One could hardly read a story about whirling disease that wasn't prefaced with the statement, "Whirling disease, the cause of a 90-percent decline in rainbow trout in Montana's Madison River..." If you believed the news back then, you were left with the impression that there wasn't a trout left alive from Hebgen to Ennis! This was arguably the bleakest time in the battle against the disease in the Madison. Little did we know that some hopeful signs were not far off.

In 1998 and 1999, Mother Nature provided a temporary reprieve from a series of poor year classes. For two years in a row, the number of browns and rainbows were equal to pre-whirling-disease years. These fish, now approaching their second and third birthdays, have made it through their most vulnerable period for whirling-disease attack and will apparently live through a normal lifecycle to provide angling opportunities for the next three to four years. Why did this happen? After a careful analysis of the fish population data, Montana's whirling disease research director, Dick Vincent, thinks he knows the reason, and it could provide a partial solution to the upper Madison's ongoing whirling disease troubles.

In 1998 and 1999, during the critical period of rainbow fry emergence, the flows in the upper Madison were above normal. Through dilution, the higher-than-normal flows produced a milder whirling disease infection. The MacConnell-Baldwin scale for whirling disease infections uses the numbers 0 (no infection) through 5 (severe infection) to measure the severity of the infection. If the infection is above 2.5, mortality will occur. The upper Madison's infection score has consistently run in the 3.5 range, a level fatal to the river's rainbows. But in 1998 and 1999, the infection score fell below the 2.5 mark, producing very strong year classes of browns and rainbows.

Since the Madison is a dam-controlled river, there exists the possibility that flows in the river during the critical period of trout fry emergence could be manipulated to artificially provide the conditions that were provided naturally in 1998 and 1999. To test this hypothesis, Vincent has planned a project for the spring and summer of 2001. Structures will be placed in several side-channels in the Pine Butte section of the river to artificially raise their flows. This artificial flow increase is accomplished using essentially the same methods that irrigators use to divert water in their ditches: fence posts and plastic sheeting. The spawning populations in these side-channels will be carefully monitored to determine spawning success and survival.

Should this side-channel flow-management project prove effective, the next step will be to approach Pacific Power and Lighting (PP&L) Montana to provide the necessary flows to achieve the same effect in the Madison in 2002. Preliminary indications are that the flows that would be required are not that much higher than the flows the river normally produces. Instead of the average flow rate of 2,500 cubic feet per second (CFS), a flow rate of 3,000 to 3,500 CFS may be needed to dilute the spore concentration to a level that will ensure survival for the fry. This increased flow rate should still be a workable level for both PP&L Montana and the angler. However, it is important to recognize that in low-water years, it may not be possible for PP&L Montana to provide the water necessary to achieve the desired dilution rates. Still, Vincent feels that if this project increases the odds of trout survival to the point where strong year classes can be attained in five or six years out of ten, we will be way ahead of the one-in-ten-year average for above-normal flows that is likely to occur naturally.

The war against whirling disease is far from over, but it is clear that we are winning some of its important battles.

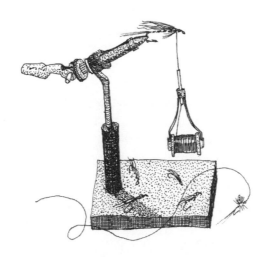

BILL LOGAN

on Fly Tying

An interview with preeminent fly tyer Bill Logan on his art, the apprenticeship and education of a fly tyer, and the value of taking a fish-eye perspective on the world.

*B*ill Logan is an artist. Perhaps better known to fly fishers for his exquisite, super-realistic flies than for anything else, Logan explains in this interview how his vocation as a sculptor influences his avocation as one of the world's preeminent tyers of flies. It's clear that Logan's mindset as a professional artist has a profound practical application. In his case, the old adage that "art imitates life" has never been applied more literally than in some of the streamside and stream-bottom life that he has created as art.

When Logan sat with Sloan, Logan spoke about his own experience as a sculptor and fly tyer and how he has taken a "fish-eye" perspective on the world to better understand some of the science behind his art.

MR. SLOAN: Bill, before we get started, I just wanted to share a little story with you that may be relevant to some of the issues surrounding fly selection that I hope we're going to discuss. I went up to the Catskill Fly Fishing Center and Museum for a benefit fishing tournament last week. While driving up to the Catskills, I had gotten on the telephone with Jack Samson, Lefty Krey, and Mark Sosin to ask them what kind of fly I should use.

MR. LOGAN: So what did you use?

MR. SLOAN: Jack Samson told me to use a Blue Damsel fly after he heard that the tournament was a "Peg-in-the-Ground" tournament. In this kind of tournament, the sponsor puts pegs in the bottom of the lake about every twenty feet around its circumference. Peg one is "beat" one, peg two is beat two, peg three is beat three, and so forth. You and your teammates then fish the beats around pegs one and two. Fifteen minutes later, you shift to three and four, and then to five and six, and so on. Eventually, you work your way entirely around the lake, and everybody has gotten a shot at the same spots.

MR. LOGAN: Wow; I've never heard of this. Does everyone use flies?

MR. SLOAN: Yes, it's a fly-tackle-only tournament.

Anyway, the fish are measured on a board before they're put back. The team with the most total inches at the end wins. We got to the lake, and I wore my tuxedo...

MR. LOGAN: A tuxedo? You were fishing in a tuxedo?

MR. SLOAN: That's right, a tuxedo, because years ago in England, where this started, people would dress formally. So, I got out on the lake in my tux. My teammate, Dick Despomier, and I were catching a small sunfish here, a perch there, and a trout every once in a while. We were pecking away, and with about a minute to go, we had a total of seventy-two inches. The first-place team had eighty-two inches. So, we needed to have eleven more inches to win.

Instead of casting out in the lake, I looked down, and there was this pretty good-sized largemouth bass just kind of finning itself in the rushes. I thought of Jack Samson's advice and dropped my Blue Damsel fly over him. I jigged it in front of his nose and, by God, he ate it. Just as he hit it, I hooked him, and the gun went off, signaling the end of the tournament. I had the winning fish on, which I landed.

MR. LOGAN: That's great.

MR. SLOAN: So, there you go: we won the tournament, the museum made some money, and we donated some back. It was a terrific time. If you ever want to do this to raise some money for a worthy cause, it's a lot of fun. We had bagpipes playing, dogs yapping, and kids running around. And I have a new-found respect for the Blue Damsel fly and really appreciated Jack Samson's advice.

MR. LOGAN: What a great story! As a matter of fact, I'm going to do a little fishing right after the show.

MR. SLOAN: Really? Where are you going?

MR. LOGAN: I'm going up to Esopus Creek, near Phoenicia, New York. A friend of mine has some property not too far from it, and I spend a fair amount of time up there.

MR. SLOAN: There was an article in THE NEW YORK TIMES a couple of weeks ago about you. It said Bill Logan had an art show with some flies in it down in New York City on Second Street. I went to see it, and I was just stunned with what I saw. Bill, I know you're a modest man, but I've got to say that I just cannot *believe* the flies that you made.

MR. LOGAN: Thanks, Steve.

MR. SLOAN: Bill, how many hours do you put in on a lifelike stone fly, for example? I mean, the ones I've seen that you've tied are even better than nature.

MR. LOGAN: Well, Steve, that's kind of you, but I don't think anything can be better than nature. I'm trying to get as close as I can, of course. I'm at the point now, I think, where the bugs are looking pretty good; they stand up. If you put a natural next to the realistic that I've tied, it's getting very, very difficult to tell the two apart.

MR. SLOAN: How many hours do you put in on one?

MR. LOGAN: I'd guess about a hundred and fifty hours. It depends on whether or not I've worked out the moves and researched the bug. If I haven't, it can take much longer.

MR. SLOAN: A hundred and fifty hours; that's incredible! You must have had quite an extensive fishing background. When did you start fishing?

MR. LOGAN: I don't remember when I started fishing. I was very young; I know that. I was a peewee. It was just one of those cases where my father started letting me tag along as soon as I could more or less keep up with him.

MR. SLOAN: Did he tie flies, too?

MR. LOGAN: Yes, he did. He was a great fisherman, but he was a very crude fly tyer.

MR. SLOAN: Crude by *your* standards, right?

MR. LOGAN: No. Actually, to be honest with you, crude probably by *anyone's* standards. The important point is that he caught a lot of fish with them.

MR. SLOAN: Now, what region of the country was this?

MR. LOGAN: I grew up in Colorado.

MR. SLOAN: So were these wet flies or dry flies that your dad was tying?

MR. LOGAN: He was tying a little bit of everything. It's funny when I look back on it: I'm about the same age now that my father was when I started fishing with him. In the last couple of years, I've realized that a lot of what he must have been going through and thinking of back then must be about what I'm going through and thinking of right now. It's kind of a revelation to me. Now, I realize he was still learning how to fly fish and had probably started not too long before I came of age. He learned to fish in a very traditional way. Consequently, I learned old ways first, such as wet-fly fishing, with two flies on a line.

MR. SLOAN: Right. Downstream then, basically.

MR. LOGAN: Exactly. It was a tradition that came from the English. It's very effective, by the way, yet, oddly, few people fish in this fashion today.

MR. SLOAN: Now, professionally, you are a sculptor, Bill. We're talking about fly tying as your avocation here—although spending a hundred and fifty hours tying a fly is awesome to me.

MR. LOGAN: My sculpting and fly tying are running neck and neck now between profession and avocation. In fact, fly tying is becoming as significant a part of my art as anything else. It all comes from the same place and feels the same when I'm doing it.

MR. SLOAN: How would you describe your sculptures? I saw the boat that you did. How do you categorize their style? They're not free form or ultra-modernistic at all. What's the best way to describe their style?

MR. LOGAN: My sculptures are kind of a strange mix. They're very representational, but at the same time they have some very strong abstract elements in them. The work that I'm doing now is primarily a cross between sailing ships and human bodies; it's almost as if the body were to turn into a sailing ship: it's fully rigged; it has sails; everything works.

MR. SLOAN: Interesting. The personification you describe is as old as the sea itself.

MR. LOGAN: Absolutely. A lot of cultures have contributed to that form of personification.

MR. SLOAN: Regarding fly tying, did somebody come along and take you by the hand and say, "This kid has promise; I'm going to teach him a couple of tricks," or did you just get it from watching people?

MR. LOGAN: I got it primarily from watching people. I guess when I was maybe twelve or thirteen, I was introduced to a man named Mike LaSalle. He was a Denver-based fly tyer and fly fisher—probably still is, although I have not heard of him in quite a while. Anyway, my dad sent me to some classes with him, and I learned a lot of good, basic stuff. I remember he was *very* fussy about the heads on flies being neat. Maybe that was my first introduction to an aesthetic in tying.

Most of what I learned, though, came from watching my father. When I was a little kid, fly tying was magical; it involved all this cool stuff. You know, it has occurred to me that my dad was very aware of my attraction to fly tying and of child psychology. I was probably six or seven. I'd watch him, and I would want to use his stuff, but he wouldn't let me. He'd tell me he was afraid I would lose a hook in the carpet or something. Now I realize I was being enticed. He was making me desire fly tying, making me really want to do it, so that when he finally gave me a hook, I was primed.

MR. SLOAN: Now, can you remember the first pattern you tied?

MR. LOGAN: Oh yeah. I've still got some of them. For the very first one, my father gave me a hook. Just a hook. It was a big, ugly thing—I'd guess about a number six. He said, "Here's the hook. Let's see what you can do with it."

MR. SLOAN: Did you put it in a vise?

MR. LOGAN: No, I didn't have a vise, and my dad wouldn't let me use his—or any of the rest of his stuff, for that matter. So, do you know what I did? I stole some thread from my mom's sewing box, and I yanked the yarn out of the fringe of my baby-blue bedspread and used that for the tail. I just sort of wound the thread on until it was kind of a bulging, lumpy, streamer-like thing.

MR. SLOAN: Did you catch a fish with it?

MR. LOGAN: No, I didn't. The funny thing is—and this is absolutely no claim to genius, believe me—those first flies looked like naked Woolly Buggers. Maybe I was on the right track. My dad and I had a lot of shop talk, and he kept giving me those hooks. I remember it as being a long time, but maybe it wasn't really all that long, before he started letting me use a tool or two, and then he showed me how to tie a hackle.

MR. SLOAN: What gave you the idea of tying a fly so natural that it even has tiny hairs on its legs?

MR. LOGAN: It was just one of those things. I think you hit the nail on the head a little earlier when you said my fly tying was more of an avocation than anything else. You see, my sculptural work is so long-winded; it takes between eight months and three years to complete a single piece. It's very intense. Strange as it may seem, I think that I just started tying super realistic flies as kind of a break from what I thought was my real art. Several years ago, I got a phone call from FLY ROD & REEL magazine. They wanted me to do a story on my version of fly tying. The story was so well received that it caused me to start taking the tying more seriously.

MR. SLOAN: I'd like to tell you about a little experience I had last week. I do not have the patience to tie my own flies, but I do know what I like. I have thousands of flies—far too many, really. I mean, the choices are too much. In any case, last week, I went into a great fly-tyer's shop, owned by Walt and Winnie Dette in Roscoe, New York.

MR. LOGAN: The Dettes? Oh yes.

MR. SLOAN: Yes, the Dette's shop. I was looking for some wet flies because I had tried a few, and they were successful. Winnie showed me some that had just been tied. The dressing and the way that they were put together were really superior to my eye. But I must admit that I really do not know very much about fly tying, except what pleases me.

What should somebody look for? When you go into a store and start looking at dry flies, wet flies, or nymphs, what are the good points to watch for? And of course, what are the signs of an inferior fly, the things to look for that should make you say, "Wait a minute. Maybe I shouldn't buy this one."

MR. LOGAN: First, you've got to understand that to begin with, the Dettes are incredibly good fly tyers. They would be an exception to some of what I am about to say, which is that many of the flies that you see in stores are tied as much to catch fishermen as they are to catch fish. When you are looking for flies, there are a lot of different theories. Basically, I'm going to share my opinions. They reflect the way I tie and what I believe.

I think that if you have a little wet fly or nymph, it should be something that is kind of fuzzy. Fly tyers for a long time have used body dubbing—fur that is twisted around the tying thread, which is then wound around the hook to make the fly's body. It used to be that dubbing was literally just fur. But nowadays, synthetic fibers like Antron, which I think was engineered by DuPont for the carpet industry, have become popular. If you look at some Antron fibers in cross section, you'll see that they're triangular, so they catch the light. A fly should have a little bit of glitter in it, some kind of sparkly fiber that gives the appearance of life. Remember, your fly is dead. It has a piece of metal that runs through its body. It can't wiggle and move. You've got to imitate that movement somehow. If a real bug becomes dislodged in the stream, it wiggles like crazy to get back under the rocks. It doesn't want to get eaten.

MR. SLOAN: Do you think some flies are too heavily dressed, that you should trim them a little bit?

MR. LOGAN: Oh yes. That would be something that you would definitely want to do. For instance, the flies that I tie are frequently very slim. The more bulk a fly has, the more resistance it offers to the current—especially if it's a fly that sinks. In that case, the fly is going to take much longer to get down. I think what you want is something that is fairly sparse. Most of the commercially tied flies that you see are not that way. Again, they are tied to be kind of big and very beefy looking.

MR. SLOAN: To catch your eye and get you to buy them, right?

MR. LOGAN: Probably.

MR. SLOAN: There are new flies coming out all the time, it seems: CDCs, parachute flies, the jassid patterns, and this, that, and the other thing. You also have the Muddler and the Muddler Marabous, then the Woolly Buggers.

MR. LOGAN: Actually, you've hit on two fundamentally different theories in fly tying right there.

MR. SLOAN: How so?

MR. LOGAN: Well, first, if you've got some of the jassids, the CDCs, and many of the parachutes, you're dealing with essentially on-surface flies, dry flies. They are for the most part more realistic, much closer in silhouette and body shape to naturals, than other dry flies. For example, a parachute hackle, for those who don't know it, is wound around a vertical hair post that sticks up, forming the wing of the fly, rather than around the hook's shank. This type of hackle is actually parallel to the water's surface.

Do you know what that does? As the fly lands on the water, those little hackle fibers, instead of sticking into the water, actually lie on top of the surface film, very much as a bug's legs would. What is presented to the fish is therefore a much more correct silhouette for a fly. All this reflects one way that fly tying is going: toward more effective reality.

Now, a fly like the Woolly Bugger is an altogether different story. It's a very generalized, impressionistic pattern that's meant to look a little bit like a lot of different things—minnows, big stone flies, crawdads, leeches. It covers a lot of ground, wiggles, and just looks tasty.

So let's see: you need to have something with a bit of sparkle that has more or less the correct shape. If it has some built-in wiggle to it, I think that's probably an advantage. It should have a little wispy fuzz, like marabou or ostrich herl. If the body is dubbed, it should be kind of fibrous. Oh, and it should have a color that looks pretty close, although you have to take into account its color when it's wet. Remember, it'll change when it gets wet. A lot of the commercially tied flies that you see are actually imitating "right color." While they look good dry, they get two or three shades darker when they are wet and become too dark.

MR. SLOAN: Do you believe fish can recognize color?

MR. LOGAN: Oh, yes; I'm sure they can. You know, scientific studies show fish have rods and cones in their eyes, just like we do. They have two different types of receptor cells: one sees light and dark, and the other distinguishes color.

MR. SLOAN: Maybe even, for their own world, their eyes are a lot more sophisticated than ours are.

MR. LOGAN: No doubt. Although a trout's eyes share all the same components of ours, the way they're put together is entirely different. They have permanent distance focus in their peripheral vision, but the central area of their vision lacks acuity. They are, in a sense, very near-sighted. Scientists do believe they have a fairly strong sense of color. They can see what's going on. And, of course, they have other senses that are highly developed, such as their lateral lines. Basically, even though they have a brain the size of a peanut, they are winners in the game of evolution. They would not have survived if they were not continually improving their senses.

MR. SLOAN: Bill, have you ever gone into a stream—say, taken a snorkel or scuba gear—and lain on your back and looked up at the surface?

MR. LOGAN: Well, I didn't do it in a stream, but I did do it in a hot tub. It was a lot more comfortable.

MR. SLOAN: What was the perception?

MR. LOGAN: It was interesting. The hot tub was not running, actually. It had been turned off, but the water was nice and warm. I just lay on my back, and I had a friend pitch dry flies in—literally, had him drop flies onto the water. Then we got some real insects, like a grasshopper and other flying bugs, and pitched them onto the water, as well. Aside from seeing movement, which is tough to get in a fly, when you are underwater and looking up at an insect that's riding on the surface film, what you actually can see is a lot different than what you'd expect.

Chunky bugs, like hoppers, float like little icebergs. On the other hand, lightweights, like mayflies or caddises, for example, hardly penetrate the surface film of the water at all. Wherever a portion of their abdomen, leg, or tail tip touches the surface of the water, they actually bend it a little bit rather than breaking through it. The water's surface will actually bend before it breaks.

MR. SLOAN: There's a scientific name for that: *meniscus*, meaning a concave or convex upper surface of a column of water.

MR. LOGAN: That's right. The fish will very clearly see any contact point. It's as if you watched someone press his or her face up against a piece of glass. Wherever it touches the glass, you would see an imprint, or an outline of a shape. The same holds true with a fly on the surface of the water. When a fish is looking up at a fly on the surface, it will first see the imprint of its body and legs, where they indent the surface. Then, as the fly floats overhead on the water's surface, the indented surface acts much like a lens that bends the light slightly, so the fish can see a fair portion of the fly's silhouette, too. If I had to guess, I'd bet that altogether there is about 270 degrees of visibility, if you count the fly's bottom and a good deal of both its sides viewed from just a slightly changing degree of angle.

MR. SLOAN: I suspect this is true of bass, panfish, and trout, right? I would think that any surface fishing that involves putting a fly out on top of the water would have this effect on fish. From what you've just described, I'm sure that's why when you throw out a little popping bug over bass or panfish, you don't even have to move it. If you let it sit there, and it kind of just wiggles almost imperceptibly, they'll hit it.

MR. LOGAN: That's right. If you ever watch insects in a lake, you'll notice that the ones on the surface are usually not moving a lot. However, let's compare that to a nymph in a stream. Most nymphs struggle to the surface through the current. Then they do their little shake-and-shimmy striptease out of their nymphal skin and emerge as, say, a mayfly. An entomologist once told me that the process of a nymph breaking through the surface film of the water is the equivalent of you or me being buried under three or four feet of earth and having to fight—literally push our way out—to the surface of the ground.

MR. SLOAN: Interesting analogy.

MR. LOGAN: We must understand the dynamics in insect terms. When an insect is in the surface film on top of the water, it is very much like being stuck on a kind of gooey trampoline. The insect will not sink, but it cannot really get out of it, either. Therefore, most insects that stay on the surface film for very long are pretty well exhausted. They are not going to wiggle very much or be very active; they will just kind of feebly twitch.

MR. SLOAN: Bill, what about wet flies? What would you see underneath the water? I would assume that for every fly we see on the surface, there must be thousands underwater.

MR. LOGAN: Yes. The largest percentage of any stream fish's diet is underwater life—nymphs, minnows, and such.

MR. SLOAN: The fish has got to make a much quicker decision than land predators.

MR. LOGAN: His meal is floating past him fast; he doesn't have a long time to look at the menu. If he's underneath the fly, I think as much as anything he's going to see a silhouette or the insect's body shape.

Again, color does some very strange things underwater. As pure white light passes through water, it's separated into colors that, in turn, drop away. The color is filtered out, basically. I think I've read that the color you can see farthest underwater is blue. Oddly enough, one of the colors that you cannot see very far in deep water is red. Red fish in deep water appear black. I thought that was very interesting, because a lot of fish tend to be red when they are in their spawning color. I don't know if that is a protective adaptation or not. Of course, stream fish don't live in terribly deep water, and the current itself carries a lot of particulate matter that reflects light. I'll bet they see red just fine.

When a fly is under the surface of the water and the fish is somewhere in the water column under the fly, probably the first thing that fish is going to see is some kind of a silhouette. They might see a little corona, or a sparkle or color around the edge of the fly, just like you or I might see if we were to hold a fly up in front of a light. If the fly is more or less at or below the fish's level in the water column, the fly appears more illuminated. Size, shape, and color all have a little bit more to do with their reaction.

MR. SLOAN: Bill, where can we see your fly-tying work?

MR. LOGAN: It's funny you should ask, Steve, because I have just come out of a period of frantic activity that was associated with the show in New York, which, sadly, has just closed. However, I'm writing a lot about tying now, primarily about the new *fishable* realistic patterns that I've been fooling with. Next year some of them will be offered commercially, and I'm excited about that. I'm being invited to speak more frequently, too. A couple of long-winded book projects are under way. I'd love to settle into one of those slightly quiet periods where I can get a bunch done on them and also maybe just sit down at the vise for a good bit.

MR. SLOAN: What about your sculptures? Where can people see them?

MR. LOGAN: I've been fortunate in showing my work, in getting it out for folks to see. I've been in several solo shows *and* about five other shows in San Francisco, New York, and all around the country. To be honest, though, I've got a hunch that bugs and tying will be taking over my life for awhile. The thought of it both amuses and fascinates me. I want to spend some real time on it.

MR. SLOAN: I'm sure everybody asks you this question I'm about to ask. You now put a hundred and fifty hours into tying a stone fly. You mount it as an art composition. But have you ever used one of these to go fishing?

MR. LOGAN: I have to admit that I haven't. But, you know, I will. I'm going to have to. Somebody told me that to really complete the experience, to go full circle, I need to use one of these things, catch a fish, release it, and then throw away the fly. I'm just not sure whether I can do that. I'm terrified that I'd hang the nymph on a log—probably on the first drift—after spending so much time making it. I would have to spend two days trying to get it back.

MR. SLOAN: Well, I have the answer to that: fish a smaller stream.

MR. LOGAN: *(laughing)* Something I can get to; good idea. You're right.

MR. SLOAN: I'll tell you what: I'm going to take you to Henryville. I promised you that.

MR. LOGAN: Yes, you did.

MR. SLOAN: I'm going out there today. So I'd like to announce that you and I are going to fish. We have a spot there with a bench, where you can watch the stream. It's very rustic—beautiful and bucolic. We'll have a little lunch, and you will tie a fly, and some of the members will come around. Then, we will let you go down and see if you catch a trout on one of your own creations.

MR. LOGAN: Oh boy, fishing with some pressure.

MR. SLOAN: Hey, this is the ultimate pressure. But it'll be fun, too.

MR. LOGAN: It sure sounds that way. I can't wait.

MR. SLOAN: Let me ask you one other thing. What's happening in terms of new materials, new things, new methods in fly tying?

MR. LOGAN: Oh boy, I'll tell you what...

MR. SLOAN: Is it a revolution?

MR. LOGAN: ...It is really kind of a continual explosion. There has been such an enormous growth of interest in fly fishing and fly tying, and with it has come a lot of product development. All kinds of new materials and new gear are being created for fly fishing. That's one thing that is very interesting about fly fishing in general: the people who are serious fly fishers tend to love equipment, new developments, and new fly-tying materials. These evolving products are all over the place; you cannot keep up with them.

MR. SLOAN: Well, Bill, let me tell you something: my money is on you. I'm sure you'll be continuing to lead the way in the art of fly tying.

ART NIERENBERG
on Fishing without Limits

———————

AN INTERVIEW WITH ART NIERENBERG ON WHY THE PHYSICAL LIMITATIONS OF ANGLING ARE REALLY MENTAL LIMITATIONS: A DISABLED ANGLER SHARES HIS EXPERIENCES.

Art Nierenberg is the founder of Breakthrough Disability, Inc., headquartered at 3915 Falls Run Road, Randallstown, Maryland, 21133. In his work with Project Access, a joint venture between volunteers and governmental agencies, Nierenberg is seeking ways to make fishing accessible to people with disabilities. When Sloan spoke with Nierenberg, they discussed some of the preconceptions and misconceptions about how the disabled view fishing. In addition to his assessment of the handicapped-accessibility of some of the most famous eastern and western trout streams —the likes of the Beaverkill and the Madison—Nierenberg speaks frankly about not only the physical limitations but the psychological barriers that are being broken between the world of the handicapped angler and his or her non-handicapped counterpart.

MR. SLOAN: Art, I'd like to take just a moment to introduce you to our audience, all right?

MR. NIERENBERG: Sure; go right ahead.

MR. SLOAN: Thanks.

Our guest today is Art Nierenberg. Art is involved in a campaign that is absolutely spellbinding. Now, Art is a disabled person. He was afflicted with polio at a young age, and he spent a lot of his life in a wheelchair. But he is crazy, absolutely nuts, about fishing, am I right, Art?

MR. NIERENBERG: Yes. Absolutely crazy.

MR. SLOAN: In spite of this disability—and we are going to discuss some of the ways we can get some of the forty-three million Americans who are disabled out fishing—you have fished some of the best fisheries in North America. That is a very worthwhile campaign. Art is one of the leaders in this country in demonstrating how limitations to what any individual can accomplish are far more mental than physical. For example, Art, you fished the Willowemoc, right?

MR. NIERENBERG: Yes.

MR. SLOAN: And the Beaverkill near Roscoe, New York?

MR. NIERENBERG: Right.

MR. SLOAN: And the Connetquot out here on Long Island?

MR. NIERENBERG: Yes, I fish that a lot. They have many stations for the handicapped. I've even helped design some of them.

MR. SLOAN: You've also fished the Madison River in Montana.

MR. NIERENBERG: Yes, we floated that.

MR. SLOAN: You *floated* it?

MR. NIERENBERG: Yes.

MR. SLOAN: Now, the Gallatin, in Montana, which is world famous: you've fished that?

MR. NIERENBERG: Yes. I've floated that, also.

MR. SLOAN: Of the two, which do you think is the better trout river?

MR. NIERENBERG: Well, I've had more experience on the Madison. That's where I learned to really fish out West with a Royal Wulff dry fly. I learned how to read a river from the different colors of the channels and drop the fly on the edge of that change of color. I learned that trout hang out in back of the rocks, out of the current. My best day on the Madison was ninety-seven fish.

MR. SLOAN: *Whoa!* Ninety-seven fish.

MR. NIERENBERG: That's right. I took them while floating down the river. On my office wall, I have a twenty-three inch rainbow that took me twenty minutes to land that day. He took the fly line off the reel, all the way through the backing, twice. That's the only fish I have ever had mounted.

MR. SLOAN: Now, Art, you did all of this as a disabled person from a wheelchair?

MR. NIERENBERG: Oh, yes. In fact, the guides were terrific. I had a special chair made that used to clamp in the johnboats used for drifting. The guides would just pick me up from the van or the car and carry me down the bank and heave me into my chair. Once I was in my chair, I was as good as any other fisherman floating and fishing down the river.

MR. SLOAN: Wow.

MR. NIERENBERG: I learned to fish on the Madison. You know, as the river curls downstream, the wind keeps shifting. First it's in back of you, next it's in front of you, and then it's on the side of you. You just have to keep fishing if you want to catch a lot of trout there. There was wonderful fishing on the Madison.

On the Gallatin, I had a different invention. We could not get the usual johnboat, and I had an unusual guide. He fixed up this rubber or plastic raft for us to use. We tried to tie my chair into it, and then he hooked himself to the raft. He was weighing down the platform, and I was floating. We got into a very bad spot with some really severe white water and rocks. He said, "I cannot hold you; I have to let you go." So he let me go, and he had tied me into the chair, which was tied into the raft. The raft hit some rocks, and I figured I had better untie myself. I thought, "I'm going to go over." But we did not go over. The current finally pulled me around the rocks.

It was really scary, but it was exciting. It's not the first time I've been in water like that.

MR. SLOAN: Now, wait a minute. He had to let you go, and you and your wheelchair just roared down the river?

MR. NIERENBERG: No, there was no wheelchair in the raft. I was just in a special chair that a friend of mine had designed that was tied into this raft. When we tied it in, the raft was no longer flat.

When you push up against some rocks, the tendency would be for the raft to tip and for me to turn over with the raft on top of me, upside down. So, I untied myself. But the water did not turn me over, and I floated free.

MR. SLOAN: Were you wearing a vest that popped you up?

MR. NIERENBERG: For years, I had one of these stupid belts that's supposed to be a lifesaver. I never tried it. So, I never knew if it would work or not. I will tell you this much, though: this experience was one of my greatest fishing times, and I wasn't even fishing.

MR. SLOAN: I'll say. It sounds more like a near-death experience than a fishing experience.

MR. NIERENBERG: *(laughing)* I guess you could say that. My guide had finally run along the banks to fish me out of the river. You had to see him—just crazy, running in the wake of the raft, trying to keep up with me free floating. He eventually got to a spot where he waded into the river and caught me.

Later that evening, he heaved me up on the bank, and I was just lying on my back and watching the stars, a great sky full of stars that you can only see out in Montana, that you cannot see around the big cities.

MR. SLOAN: The Big Sky.

MR. NIERENBERG: Yes, The Big Sky. I was just lying on my back and looking at those stars. I was one very happy guy.

MR. SLOAN: That is some story. I think I see why your foundation is called Breakthrough Disability, Inc. It sounds like there aren't too many barriers that you haven't broken through.

Art, you not only fished the Gallatin, where A RIVER RUNS THROUGH IT was filmed, but you also fly-fished for largemouth bass in Florida. Where was that? On the west coast, or the east?

MR. NIERENBERG: Neither; it was in the swamp, the big swamp, part of the River of Grass, on Lake Okeechobee. My daughter lived there, and I went out fishing one day when I was down visiting her. They told me it was not the good bass season, that it was an off time of year. Yet, I kept raising and catching bass, and we released them all. I had a great time. And it was a good workout for me, casting a big minnow-type fly.

But some of the greatest fishing I had was up in Maine, where I caught my first salmon.

MR. SLOAN: Really? In Grand Lake?

MR. NIERENBERG: Yes, in the stream right near the dam. Again, that was the place where their idea of fishing was having the guide take you to a little lake, you put a minnow on, and you sit there with a sinker and soak it on the bottom. My guide's name was Hazen Bagley, and he was close to seventy years old. He was tall, rangy, and very quiet. He was watching my face. We were out in this boat, drowning minnows.

Finally, he said, "You don't like this fishing, do you?"

I said, "No. I'd rather fish with a fly."

He said, "Do you trust me?"

I said, "Sure, I trust you."

He said, "Then we're going to quit this. We'll eat lunch on the bank, and then I'm going to take you to a special place."

So after lunch, we begin by riding around in his old Ford. He drives for a little while, and we get to a place with a high bank. He stops the Ford, takes out my wheelchair, and disappears down the bank. The next thing I know, he's back. He tells me to put my arms around his neck. I do, and he picks me up.

I'm watching this tall, rangy, weather-beaten guy, with his shoes untied and the laces hanging out, carrying me down this steep bank. We were heading for the river. I looked down and saw little round boulders about twelve feet down at the edge of the river.

I said to myself, "Oh, I'm going to get killed." My mind kept seeing a vision of the two of us rolling down among the boulders.

He couldn't even see where he was walking because he was carrying me across his arms in front of him. Somehow we ended up getting down the bank; how, I do not know. The next thing I see is my wheelchair in the middle of the stream on a sandbar. The seat is covered by flowing water. He starts clumping through the current with the water up to his knees.

MR. SLOAN: Still carrying you?

MR. NIERENBERG: Yes, still carrying me. Then he puts me in the wheelchair. The course of the water floats my legs out to one side. He takes out what looks like an old piece of canvas. It must have been the first fly-fishing vest ever made—it was a rough, brownish-orangy-red canvas—and he puts that over my shoulder. He told me there were plenty of flies in the patched-up pockets. I told him I had my own, and I tied one on and began to cast.

So, I had his flies, and I had my flies. I was sitting in my wheelchair, concentrating on my casting, when he disappeared up the bank and back to the car. I am all alone.

I began casting my fly across stream, up a bit, getting a nice drift. I notice it is twilight and getting dark quickly. Just before it gets black, I start hearing slams, as if somebody were taking a canoe paddle and smacking the surface of the water with it.

I tried to peer through the diminishing light, and I can barely see some white shapes jumping out of the water and then falling back. My heart starts pounding.

"What is this?" I asked myself.

"This is why I came here," I silently answered.

I didn't know what to do, really. I kept hearing those splashes. A tiny black fly, about a number 18, landed on my hand. I figured this was a sign from the Lord, some sort of unusual form of divine communication. I knew I didn't have any number 18 black flies.

I started rummaging through the pockets of the old canvas vest and found a box of tiny black flies. I put one on. I could not reach the section of the river where I was hearing the vigorous splashes. But I cast as far as I could, slightly up and across the stream, feeding and meting out line. I felt that perhaps I could get the fly to the rising fish. The line straightened out as I reached the spot.

Man, I had a terrific hit, and I hooked the fish. My hair stood up. Then I realized I didn't have a net. I was very tender playing that fish. I didn't want to lose it. I started yelling and screaming, "Hazen! Hazen! Hazen!" as loudly as I could. Finally, he appeared and said, "I hear you."

I screamed, "I have a fish on. We need a net!" He had no net, he said; he had left it in the boat on the lake. I hear him start clumping toward me. I get the fish close to the wheelchair. In about ten minutes, I get the fish where I can see its huge form. It was a terrific fighter. Hazen gets in the water and starts walking toward the fish. Of course, when the fish hears that clumping, he wants to take off, and I have to give him line because I don't want to break the leader.

I want to make sure I don't pull the tiny fly out of his mouth, either. Finally, Hazen gets on the other side of the fish, bends down, and, with two hands, scoops up the fish and throws it toward the bank. If I had not let slack line out, the fish would have broken off.

It landed on the bank. He picked up the fish, then he picked me up out of the wheelchair, and we started to climb up these rolling rocks. He got me in the car, and then he went back to get my soaking-wet wheelchair.

MR. SLOAN: What kind of fish was it?

MR. NIERENBERG: It was a landlocked salmon and measured twenty-three inches.

MR. SLOAN: A landlocked salmon. *Wow!*

MR. NIERENBERG: When we got back to the lodge, we met the other fishing parties. They had all the latest Abercrombie & Fitch equipment. All their rods, reels, and equipment matched. Everybody came over to see the fish. The hook, which was still in the fish, was bent at a right angle to the shank.

One of the guests was the vice president of some Virginia railroad. He looked at me in amazement. Nobody there was catching any salmon on flies in a stream. This was the time of the year they all went salmon trolling in the lake, apparently.

MR. SLOAN: Using those Gray Ghost streamer flies?

MR. NIERENBERG: Exactly. This old gentleman, a dignified old fly fisherman, said, "That is one of the finest landlocked salmon I've ever seen." Apparently, nobody was catching anything. None of them was fly fishing.

MR. SLOAN: Art, I've got to tell you that that is one heck of a story, but when I think that you were fishing from a wheelchair in the middle of a stream, it is a fantastic story. It's really an inspiration for people. Now, what can we do to help the other tens of millions of Americans who would like to fish and are somewhat physically handicapped or disabled?

MR. NIERENBERG: Project Access.

MR. SLOAN: Project Access, your program for providing fishing access to folks with physical disabilities? Art, what gave you the idea for that? You also fished in Utah, Idaho, New York, and Maryland. It's obvious from the way you describe your fishing adventures that you are as mad about it as I am.

MR. NIERENBERG: Yes.

MR. SLOAN: Well what gave you the idea of starting a program for access for people who have a disability or handicap? How did that get started?

MR. NIERENBERG: Well, you know, Steve, wherever I was fishing, I was always struck by the look on peoples' faces when they saw me in a wheelchair, casting. I got the distinct impression that people felt I was not supposed to be out

71

there. I got the sense that nobody had ever seen anything like this before. It was like they must have been thinking, "Oh my God, look at that. Look at what he can do."

To me, of course, it was exactly the opposite; it seemed like the most natural thing in the world. I just love fishing like anyone else. Whenever I had a chance to work it out, I went fishing.

I would do things that people did not think of as possible because I loved it. Then it dawned on me that there were other handicapped people who might love it, too. For instance, I know that kids loved fishing.

I once took a group of handicapped children down to catch fish at Connetquot, Long Island. The other fishermen there looked at us in wonderment. I remember one little boy in the group who had severe cerebral palsy with spasms and difficulty with his speech. When we took him fishing at Connetquot hatchery, I directed the counselors to take this little boy, who was spastic, and lay him on his stomach on a little footbridge over the stream.

I told them to put a fly on his fly line and put the line in his hand. This kid was lying on his stomach, and as he held the line—of course, he was moving it because he was spastic and therefore twitching that fly on the water—bang, he would get a fish. They would run over as he pulled in the fish, and they would take it off of the hook for him. He would put the fly back, and bang, he would get another fish. The way he was moving the fly was what every fly fisherman tries to do: move the fly in a natural manner so the fish would hit it. That kid was having a ball—an absolute ball—even though he was lying on his stomach.

MR. SLOAN: Art, that was an inspiring story about an untapped segment of the fishing market. There are forty-three million people in the United States who are handicapped or disabled in some way, right?

MR. NIERENBERG: That's right, forty-three million. And don't forget the elderly. As people get older, they cannot do the things they could do when they were younger. For example, they cannot wade rivers, so they give up fishing.

But the sad thing is that they don't have to give up fishing. When I saw the joy on these handicapped children's faces while they were fishing, I got this idea—to answer your original question—that there is something special when disabled people are in the outdoors and fully participating in recreational activities. As I said earlier, many people look on as if it is very, very unusual—as if to say, "You know, these people are not supposed to be able to do that."

Yet, Project Access, which started in New York with Joan Stoliar, who initiated the Trout in the Classroom program *[This program provides trout eggs and aquariums for inner city classrooms. Students and their teachers hatch trout and then release the fry into the wild. The program's founder, Joan Stoliar, passed away in August 2000. See "Joan Stoliar on Trout in the Classroom" on page 197.—the Editors]*, back when I was on its board, has made it possible for anyone to enjoy fishing.

By the way, Project Access is on the Internet. You can learn about Project Access at www.projectaccess.com. Their site has loads of information, and you can learn about the organization and find out what places have become accessible in the State of New York. TROUT magazine also covered Project Access in a story published in the Autumn 1996 issue. They ran a picture of me with the story and did a good job of discussing how Project Access is becoming a movement that is working all across the country. A video was also made that is really very good. The video introduces the Trout Unlimited chapters in many states that have programs and will help interested parties get into the program.

To me, Project Access is a bridge. Fly fishing, being outdoors, seeing disabled people or the elderly on crutches or in wheelchairs being able to fish and enjoy it turns me on. I watched a guy who had such a bad heart that they used to have to pull the van right up next to the stream at Connetquot. His helper would put out a beach chair for him because this guy could only walk about ten feet because he had such a bad heart.

MR. SLOAN: Yet, he went fishing.

MR. NIERENBERG: He went fishing, and he knew how to handle a fly rod. He had that joy of being outdoors. Even I was impressed at his perseverance.

You see, Steve, I learned from my own experience. The fact that I am in a wheelchair does not mean I do not have some of the same feelings and senses toward disabilities that other people do. People forget that.

I saw that we could break the mold of thinking about what disabled people could and could not do.

MR. SLOAN: How did Project Access get started, Art?

MR. NIERENBERG: It started when I went to the local community after I had moved to Maryland. I told people I had no place to fish. This was in Randallstown, Maryland.

MR. SLOAN: How far from Baltimore is that, Art?

MR. NIERENBERG: Oh, about twenty minutes, twenty-two minutes to be exact, northwest. Anyway, they suggested I speak to the Maryland Trout Unlimited chapter. TU told me they would help me. TU helped build a handicapped access station. The community supported it, too, at my urging.

Unfortunately, the access station was washed out in a terrible storm. That one storm just destroyed all the good work that had been done by volunteers. Fortunately, the State of Maryland committed to rebuild almost immediately. Local business owners and private citizens also chipped in. When we got finished, we encouraged people to come down to this gorgeous fishing platform that we had built. Kids, parents, and members of two Trout Unlimited chapters were always ready to come down with their fishing gear and teach and work with handicapped people.

We got another idea: we realized we needed an educational center, a place to study how to get people into and out of the river, to design and use ramps, and to build a platform in the water. We needed to know what kind of davit, with or without a sling, would work. We investigated what kind of floating devices could work that would be safe. We needed a place to experiment. I took the entire conceptual plan for the educational center to the State of Maryland's Department of Natural Resources. They loved it and Trout Unlimited loved it.

Right now, we are studying, preparing, and beginning to take Project Access to Gunpowder Creek, one of the most famous fly-fishing tributaries in the East. It will soon become well known as one of the better handicapped access fishing spots.

MR. SLOAN: Now, how far is the Gunpowder from Randallstown?

MR. NIERENBERG: It's about twenty-five minutes, in the other direction.

MR. SLOAN: Which direction?

MR. NIERENBERG: I go up Route 83, to Monkton. It is then about five minutes further to the Macemore section, which has a controlled level of fishing from the dam. It is gorgeous. I had a guide take me in a wheelchair and pull me a half mile through the Gunpowder to fish one day—another great experience.

MR. SLOAN: Art, do you think it would be possible to have some type of mat that had, for instance, rails or ridges that would hold a wheelchair or other seating device to help the handicapped obtain access? The mat would have stabilizers on it somehow, so it could be moved on a level plane. You could unfold it in front of you to get in the track and get access down to these streams.

MR. NIERENBERG: That sounds like another great idea for our research center. This is exactly what we are going to do at the Gunpowder Center for Environmental Accessibility—the study of environmental accessibility. Plans are in the works to provide a place for handicapped people to visit and stay over. The whole center will be handicapped accessible. Bathrooms, showers, all of it would be accessible, and one would be able to go fly fishing for a couple of days.

And it would not be just for the physically handicapped in wheelchairs, either. We are going to find out how to allow the blind to enjoy the environment. We are even going to set up campsites, so you can do overnight camping with accessible tents, and establish the center as a resource for information on how to achieve handicapped access for every part of the United States.

MR. SLOAN: Well, Art, I can help you a little bit on your efforts with the blind.

MR. NIERENBERG: That's great.

MR. SLOAN: We have had on the show, and have also helped financially, a club called the Helen Keller Fishing Club for the Blind, out of Sheepshead Bay, New York.

MR. NIERENBERG: That's terrific.

MR. SLOAN: They take blind people out fishing on party boats. I've been invited to give a lecture at the club, and they have about thirty men and women who are blind but love fishing. I'll get you in touch with them. I'm sure you can get some ideas from them.

MR. NIERENBERG: See, all of this can be pulled together. We have many different people, special people, who believe that we handicapped can go anyplace, can do anything. We should be seen; disability has to be seen.

There has to be a bridge from this world of disability, of non-empowerment, of saying, "Well, we just cannot do this." We do not want disabled kids sitting in front of the boob tube and vegetating. They have enough to cope with with their disability. They do not have to sit there and have all their ambition and energy go to waste.

MR. SLOAN: Art, one hour of fishing is worth twenty-four hours in front of the tube.

MR. NIERENBERG: Exactly. We have to encourage and educate the parents. One of the reasons I used to take the kids with their parents was with the hope that the parents would continue to take their child to these places like the Connetquot, which has more than twenty stations that are handicapped accessible.

MR. SLOAN: That is remarkable.

MR. NIERENBERG: Yes, it is part of the environment in handicapped-accessible places like Connetquot. In those places, it's not at all unusual to see somebody who is seriously disabled fishing.

For example, I fished with a blind fly fisherman. I tied his flies on. I referred to the face of a clock to give him casting directions. He knew how to cast. I think he had become blind later in life. He came back to fly fishing. You should have seen this guy when he caught his first fish.

MR. SLOAN: That is another remarkable story among many remarkable stories you spoke about today.

MR. NIERENBERG: We handicapped belong in the world of non-disabled people. We have the same loves, the same desires. I want to create this bridge to make it possible for the disabled to join the non-handicapped in enjoying fishing. Fly fishing can be an example of one part of that bridge. That bridge is what we need.

MR. SLOAN: Well, I hope our discussion today will help build that bridge. Art, I would be proud to fish with you any time, any place. Until then, tight lines, a good drift, and take care. And thanks so much for coming on.

MR. NIERENBERG: Thanks for helping to get out the Project Access message.

FEN MONTAIGNE
on Fishing in Russia

AN INTERVIEW WITH FEN MONTAIGNE ON HIS BOOK, *REELING IN RUSSIA*, A FIRSTHAND LOOK AT THE FORMER SOVIET UNION THROUGH THE EYES OF A FISHERMAN.

*I*n his recent book, REELING IN RUSSIA, Fen Montaigne chronicles his seven-thousand-mile journey across the newly awakened Russian republic. As one would expect from a reporter for THE PHILADELPHIA INQUIRER, Montaigne brings an investigator's instinct to the reporting of his travels. But beyond the pursuit of facts, of course, was the pursuit of fish, and it is through Montaigne's sensibility as a fisherman—albeit, a not very good one—that the reader comes to understand the transformation that glasnost has brought to post-communist Russia. Montaigne found the very qualities that define angling—patience, perseverance, ingenuity, and resourcefulness—reflected in countless ways throughout a broad cross section of the Russian people.

Montaigne's journey started in Moscow and ended, more than 100 days later, on the Bering Sea. In those 100 days, the author used fishing to come to know the Russian people, their society, their environment, and their prospects for the future. The angling *community has often been a microcosm for socio-political understanding since Walton's time, and Montaigne's understanding of this fact enables him to reveal a unique and hidden perspective on both the transformation of Russian society after seventy years of communism and the enduring qualities of the Russian spirit that persist today. And while Montaigne by his own admission may not have been particularly effective at catching fish, REELING IN RUSSIA reveals that the author caught and shared something far more valuable: a glimpse of a country and a people at a unique time in their history. Montaigne sat with Sloan for an extended interview that amplifies many of the themes discussed in his book.*

MR. SLOAN: I am pleased to have with me today Fen Montaigne, who wrote a book called REELING IN RUSSIA. That's kind of a pun, isn't it?

MR. MONTAIGNE: Yes, it is sort of a triple *entÉndre* or pun. It means I was reeling in fish, although not that many.

MR. SLOAN: So I noticed.

MR. MONTAIGNE: It also means that that country is reeling after seventy years of communism. And finally, it means that I and some of the characters in the book were reeling from too much vodka.

MR. SLOAN: True. We are going to cover all of that, Fen, but let's start at the beginning. You were a reporter for THE PHILADELPHIA INQUIRER and you were in the former Soviet Union during the period of *glasnost* and *perestroika*, right?

MR. MONTAIGNE: Exactly. I was there from 1990 to 1993—during the tail end of the last two years of Gorbachev and during the collapse of the Soviet Union. I just fell in love with the place as I was covering it. When I got back to the United States in 1993, I was soon hankering to get back to Russia.

MR. SLOAN: You speak Russian fluently.

MR. MONTAIGNE: I speak it pretty well, yes. I speak it well enough to communicate quite well with people.

MR. SLOAN: Now, the name "Montaigne" is French, isn't it?

MR. MONTAIGNE: It is. I do not have a drop of Russian blood in my veins. And although I'm not Russian, I found that the Russian people are extraordinary—so tough, resilient, and hospitable. They have suffered so much in this century. I think that is one of the things that drew me to Russia and its landscape.

MR. SLOAN: Could you explain the terms *glasnost* and *perestroika* to our audience and how they provided a kind of backdrop for this trip?

MR. MONTAIGNE: Well, *glasnost* literally means sort of "the opening up of the voice," or "freedom of speech." *Perestroika* means "restructuring," and that is exactly what Gorbachev did in Russia. He gave people a voice after seventy years of being silenced under communism, and he tried to restructure the Soviet communist system, which did not work. Of course, the whole system wound up being swept away.

MR. SLOAN: You are a fly fisherman, correct?

MR. MONTAIGNE: Yes, I'm a fly fisherman, but if you read this book, you'll see that I am an extremely mediocre fly fisherman.

I am not a good fly fisherman. I have gotten a little better since I wrote the book, but as I wandered across Russia—fishing from one end of the country to the other, from the Atlantic to the Pacific—I had quite a lot of bad luck. There were a lot of fish I did not catch.

MR. SLOAN: Well, let's start the journey. You were in Russia for three years. Then, you got an idea that you would like to start basically at Moscow and go up north and back down south, and then all the way east to the Kamchatka Peninsula, which is at the end of Siberia, and the Bering Sea.

MR. MONTAIGNE: Exactly, yes. I wound up covering about seven thousand miles.

MR. SLOAN: How long did that take?

MR. MONTAIGNE: It took about three and a half months. Sometimes I spent a couple of weeks in one place, and sometimes I would travel twenty-five hundred miles in two days on a train. In the book, I write about how at one point, when I was still in western Russia, I spread out my map of the country. When I looked at it and realized that I had so much territory to cover, I was almost overcome by a sense of panic.

MR. SLOAN: Well, give us an idea in American terms of just how big Russia is. In the first place, I think you mentioned that it has ten time zones. Of course, we only have four.

MR. MONTAIGNE: Russia is about two and a half times the size of the continental United States. You can board a plane, take off from Moscow, fly eight and a half hours to the east to Vladivostok, which is on the Pacific Coast, and never leave Russian air space. Russia is an enormous country. Just crossing it was an ordeal in itself.

MR. SLOAN: It certainly sounds that way.

MR. MONTAIGNE: My first real fishing stop was on the Kola Peninsula. I wanted to start on Kola for the very simple reason that this is the Shangri-La of Atlantic salmon fishermen of the world now. As you know, Russia has the world's largest population of wild Atlantic salmon, an estimated two-hundred thousand. At least two-hundred thousand still run into Kola's rivers because these rivers are still largely un-dammed, most of them are relatively unpolluted, and the poaching hasn't been too great—although it has been intensifying of late, which is worrisome.

I set a goal in Kola. As you know, western anglers will pay five thousand to nine thousand dollars *per week* to fish these Kola rivers. Of course, that was about my budget for my whole trip. So, my plan was to fish with the Russians and on the cheap, which is what I did.

MR. SLOAN: I found several interesting sub-themes in your book. The first was the unbelievable amount of poaching that went on throughout your seven-thousand-mile trip.

MR. MONTAIGNE: Yes. I was fully expecting to see some poaching, but I saw more than I had ever expected. On the Kola Peninsula, I fished three rivers, the Kola, the Umba, and the Varzuga. Basically, as much as fifty percent of the salmon running up those three rivers is poached out. They are taken by people with nets.

I remember visiting the Umba River, where there is one of these swanky western angling camps. I was just visiting for the afternoon to say hello to people. The anglers there were lovingly catching and releasing these beautiful salmon, which had completed this epic migratory journey.

About ten miles downstream that evening, about midnight, I stood on a bridge. Of course, it was summer there and it was still light because the white nights keep it light twenty-four hours a day. Anyway, I stood on this bridge over the Umba River and watched three groups of poachers either stringing their nets out or collecting their nets that had a good number of salmon in them.

MR. SLOAN: So enforcement is really at ground zero.

MR. MONTAIGNE: Enforcement is at ground zero for a lot of reasons. To understand the major reason, you really have to understand one of the basic differences between Russia and the United States. Seventy years of communism have led most Russians to believe that only fools obey laws. Under communist rule, there were so many stupid laws that everyone tried to find a way to get around the system.

The Russians had this wonderful little aphorism about life under the communist system. They would say, "The government pretends to pay us, and we pretend to work." Everyone was sort of getting it over on everybody else. That attitude created a sense of lawlessness.

You also have a problem that we had a century ago, which is that there really is no sense of conservation. That is partly because people do not have full bellies. Many of them are poaching for subsistence. But a lot of the poaching is also attributable to that same feeling that our forefathers had about the United States: that the resources of Russia are inexhaustible. So many Russians just think they can take and take and take.

Poaching is quite pervasive. While it's true that not everybody poaches and there are some people who care about conservation, I would say that conservation-minded Russians are in the minority. At this point, it's kind of every man for himself.

One of the other non-fishing themes that comes across in the book is that you now have this post-Soviet society, a society in which the once-strong communist social safety net is gone. People have sort of been left, particularly in the countryside, to fend for themselves. One of the strongest impressions I had as I crossed Russia was of the countryside in the rural areas being one vast potato patch or vegetable garden. I realized that because people have to grow their own vegetables, their own potatoes, they probably also have to do subsistence fishing to survive.

There is a great old Russian proverb that goes, "God is a long way up, and the czar is a long way off."

MR. SLOAN: The czar *is* a long way off. That is absolutely correct.

Now, you write about another experience in the book that was most interesting. As you went north of Moscow, up toward the peninsula near Murmansk, you came across the first gulag that Stalin had used. It was a monastery.

MR. MONTAIGNE: Exactly. This was a place that was on my route to Kola, called the Solovetsky Islands. It is a beautiful archipelago of a half-dozen islands. On the islands are these lovely fifteenth- and sixteenth-century monastery buildings.

81

Stalin used those buildings as the first prisons for the so-called "enemies of the people." The islands had a lovely northern landscape, with boulder-strewn shores, pine trees, and beautiful buildings. But the old monastery buildings all have bars over the windows, and everywhere you look are the old signs of the prison.

In fact, many of the gulags had this slogan painted over the entranceways to the prisons: "With an iron hand we will drive humanity to happiness." The irony of seeing it written on a prison door really summed up the communist philosophy for me. That was their point of view.

MR. SLOAN: Fen, after the Kola Peninsula, you were not doing very well fishing. I mean, it wasn't your fault. It sounds like things just did not get glued, that's all.

MR. MONTAIGNE: Well, I got to this beautiful river on the Kola Peninsula called the Varzuga, which held a fair number of salmon. But it turned out that in order to fish there, I needed the permission of the boss of the whole river. He owned the river; he had the rights to it. He also owned a big North Atlantic troller fishing fleet.

MR. SLOAN: That was Mr. Mikhailovich?

MR. MONTAIGNE: Yes, this was Mikhailovich—a big burly guy with a Fu Manchu mustache. Anyway, when I arrived at the Varzuga, he was away in Murmansk. I had to sit there and wait three days. Finally, he came back. He was a real character, a real czar. With reluctance, he gave me permission to fish. I did catch one salmon.

Now, my American fellow anglers who are flown by helicopter into these beautiful, remote rivers like the Penoit often are catching seven or eight salmon a day. So I did not do nearly as well, but I did get a good look at Russia itself.

MR. SLOAN: You were really right on the White Sea then, up on the far northern shores of Russia, right?

MR. MONTAIGNE: Exactly.

MR. SLOAN: Now, you describe Mikhailovich as the boss. Did you get the feeling he was the boss because he had the power? Or was he the boss because he really owned things?

MR. MONTAIGNE: I think he had gotten permission from the powers that be on the Kola Peninsula to really run that river, and he certainly had the respect and fear of everyone on the whole tip of the peninsula. He was known throughout the entire Kola Peninsula. He was, as that Russian slogan put it, someone "with an iron hand." Russia is a country with no tradition of democracy. The Russians respect strong authority.

MR. SLOAN: Tell me, Fen, what did you mean by the statement, "This country is under narcosis"? You were quoting another Russian, I think, with that statement.

MR. MONTAIGNE: Yes.

MR. SLOAN: What did the speaker mean by that?

MR. MONTAIGNE: Well, the quote is attributable to a Russian boat captain, actually, who had tried his hand at a number of businesses in the post-communist era. He had a terrible problem with drunken Russian workers. Indeed, in rural Russia, there is an incredible amount of drinking. He was very discouraged by it.

I remember clearly how he delivered the quote I attributed to him. I was sitting on his boat on a rainy day. We were docked in the White Sea, and he just looked at me and said, "The country is under narcosis. It is under vodka narcosis."

You really do come to appreciate what a tremendous problem alcoholism is in Russia. I certainly do not want to convey the notion that the country is full of drunks, but when you get out into the rural areas, it sometimes seems like half the male population is either drunk or hung over.

MR. SLOAN: I recall your describing the various ways you traveled over there—in trucks, on trains, and on boats. I remember especially well your account of being on a boat on the White Sea and how the guy who took over on the second watch was absolutely loaded to the gills. He was responsible for everybody's safety. They must have an unbelievable accident rate over there.

MR. MONTAIGNE: I think they do, yes. I think on the major transportation modes, the trains and the planes, the folks are sober, but you are right. The event you referred to from the book actually occurred on Lake Baikal, which I was travelling on during a big storm. The first captain, who was on duty for eight hours, was great; he was stalwart and sober. When he went to bed, the second captain came up. He had apparently been drinking heavily and then had slept for a few hours, but you could still smell the fumes.

MR. SLOAN: Fen, to Americans, the name "Volga" is familiar in song and dance, and even in references to the Volga boatman. Describe the Volga River as you saw it when you tried to fish it. What was it like?

MR. MONTAIGNE: The Volga is a beautiful river. It is very wide. It is reminiscent, I think, of the Mississippi, both in terms of its physical appearance and also in terms of the central cultural role it plays in Russian lore and life and history. It has bluffs on one bank and is forested and has fields on the other side. It is a beautiful river.

I had this hilarious experience fishing on the Volga for pike—an experience that was sort of classically Russian. It showed me how much the Russians put up with in their day-to-day existence, how tough and annoying life can be, but how the Russian people always seem to overcome it.

I went fishing with a guy named Lev Bobilev, whom I had met through a friend. We went out on the Volga on this beautiful weekday evening, a lovely summer night. Lev is a big, strapping guy. He is a security guard. He has gold teeth. He's wearing a white pith helmet. I do not know quite why he had a white pith helmet on, but he did.

MR. SLOAN: He saw GUNGA DIN once, that's why.

MR. MONTAIGNE: Anyway, he was a wonderful character. We get into his boat, which is a very cheap little metal blue boat that the Russians affectionately refer to as "a soap dish." We are ready to take off in his little soap dish, and I notice that he has these two really old and terrible-looking motors on the transom. I believe I described them in my book as looking like 1940s blenders.

To make a long story short, we fished for a day, and those motors must have been broken 95 percent of the time. The poor Russians: so many Russian fishermen put up with this terrible equipment that's always breaking down, but somehow they always manage to fix it.

We went down to a houseboat where a captain entertained us for the night. The next morning, we caught some pike and perch. Poor Lev spent the entire day on the dock of this houseboat, taking apart this stupid engine. At one point, he literally seemed to have the whole motor spread out in pieces in front of him.

MR. SLOAN: It has also made the Russian population self-sufficient, in being able to fix things over and over again. They cannot afford to replace them, right?

MR. MONTAIGNE: Exactly. They have to make do with what they've got. I will tell you that I came away from my three-and-a-half-month trip through Russia with such incredible respect for the people, with how much they have had to put up with in this century, and with an appreciation for how much they really can do by themselves. They can solve almost any problem.

There is a wonderful line from a French traveler who traveled through Russia two centuries ago. That Frenchman said, "If you get lost in a Russian woods with a Russian and you have to spend the night there, do not fret. Within an hour, that Russian will have built a house for you." It really bears out what I saw in terms of just how ingenious and hard-working many Russians are.

MR. SLOAN: From there, you took an extended train trip all the way to Novosabersk. Then, you went back and forth a little bit down south, almost to Mongolia.

MR. MONTAIGNE: Yes; exactly. I was in search through much of Siberia for a legendary Eurasian fish called the *taimen*—a fabulous salmon-like fish. It generally is a landlocked fish that lives in big rivers. It used to be found from the Danube all the way to the Pacific coast.

MR. SLOAN: I think it's the largest salmonid known, isn't it?

MR. MONTAIGNE: Yes, it is. In fact, the record taimen in Russia was 240 pounds.

Steve, these taimen are so big—and this is the truth—that the Russians used to fish for them by catching a squirrel, trapping a squirrel...

MR. SLOAN: ...Now, wait a minute. You mean you take *the fur* from a squirrel and tie it on a fly, right?

MR. MONTAIGNE: No; you take the *whole live squirrel.* You then take an enormous hook. You thread the hook through the back of this poor squirrel.

MR. SLOAN: PETA [People for the Ethical Treatment of Animals] would be cross-eyed about this.

MR. MONTAIGNE: I'm sure they would. PETA would not have fun in Russia.

But let me tell you the rest. They would then toss this hooked squirrel from their boat out into the current, and this poor squirrel would skitter around on the surface of the river. These big taimen would come up, grab the squirrel, and get hooked. The fishermen would then eventually fight the taimen to the surface and shoot it so that they could land it.

MR. SLOAN: *Shoot* the hooked fish?

MR. MONTAIGNE: That's right. Taimen are so big that they used to shoot them before attempting to land them.

Now, of course, I was thinking, "Oh, my God. I've *got* to try to catch something like that."

I went all over Siberia looking for a taimen fishery, and literally everywhere I went, people told me the same thing: "You should have been here five years ago. You should have been here ten years ago. You should have been here fifteen years ago." Because they are so big, very tasty, and pretty easy to catch, their populations have been hammered almost everywhere there had been any population.

I must have tried finding taimen on, I don't know, five or six rivers. I think if you could get in a helicopter and fly in to some of the really remote rivers, which I did not want to do because I always wanted to fish with Russians in populated areas, you could probably find them. In fact, I know you can still catch taimen in Siberia.

MR. SLOAN: Fen, when you say that you've been all over Siberia, I think people need to appreciate that this is not at all like the American concept of getting in your car for a little two-hour drive to your favorite trout stream or bass lake.

MR. MONTAIGNE: No, it most certainly is not. Siberia is a big, big place—every bit as big as the United States without Alaska. I did a lot of hitchhiking there.

MR. SLOAN: Fen, you described how you went after taimen by first catching some grayling, which used to be very popular in the western United States. In any case, you caught some small grayling and put them on sets off of planer boards and trolled with them. I understand that you did get a strike from a taimen.

MR. MONTAIGNE: Yes, we did. Not a big one. I would say it was probably a two-footer, which is not a big taimen.

MR. SLOAN: About four or five pounds, maybe?

MR. MONTAIGNE: Yes. Maybe a little bigger than that. It spit out the grayling and the hook.

MR. SLOAN: But I want you to know that that method is used all the time for coho and other salmon in the Great Lakes, especially in Lake Ontario, where they put a planer board out with anywhere from three to five swimming plugs off of it.

MR. MONTAIGNE: Interesting. Well, I could see why it would be an effective method.

I never saw anyone land a taimen, which was unfortunate. We did catch some grayling when I was near Mongolia on a river called the Beas. I was with some fishermen who would literally hook, land, and keep, say, a three-or four-inch grayling. We caught bigger ones as well, but no matter how small it was, they put it in the creel.

MR. SLOAN: Nothing went back?

MR. MONTAIGNE: Nothing went back. And if you try to explain to them that if they release it, it will grow and get bigger and they will have something better to eat at a future day, they're just not interested. Again, this is that sense of conservation we spoke about earlier that just is not developed. One Russian told me, "Look, conservation is for people with full bellies, and we do not have full bellies. So it's going to take a while here."

MR. SLOAN: Well, you wound up at Lake Baikal, although not after some unbelievable adventures on the train ride there, including almost being drugged by a couple of ladies who were after your pocketbook and God knows what else.

MR. MONTAIGNE: Yes. It is a tough story to summarize quickly on the radio, but you've touched on the high points of it. Some women aboard the train had some sort of very strong anesthetic, which they were attempting to use on people. This is done to foreigners sometimes on trains and in restaurants in Russia. Anyway, read the book for the complete story. You will see I could tell they were up to something. I finally did not drink what they offered.

MR. SLOAN: You outwitted them.

MR. MONTAIGNE: Yes. Then I got to Lake Baikal.

MR. SLOAN: Could you describe the lake for us?

MR. MONTAIGNE: It is a remarkable lake. It is a marvelous aquifer for the entire region where it is located. It holds more water than any other lake in the world. In fact, Baikal holds 20 percent of the world's aboveground supply of freshwater. The lake is up to a mile deep, which makes it the deepest lake in the world, and about three- or four-hundred miles long and about forty miles across. Baikal is surrounded by nine-thousand-foot snow-capped peaks, particularly on the eastern shore. It is truly one of the natural wonders of the world.

I spent two weeks on Baikal, and you can drink right out of the lake. It is the clearest water I have ever seen. I had some fabulous fishing in some of the rivers that feed into Baikal. I caught some wonderful arctic grayling, some very big ones, and a local fish, called a *lenok*, that is like a cross between a char and a trout and inhabits these beautiful, deep pools on the rivers. To catch lenok, you cast what they call "a bomber," or a skating pattern; it is a floating lure that skitters on the surface. The lenok then torpedo up from the bottom and grab the bomber right on the surface. It is a tremendously exciting way to fish.

MR. SLOAN: Fen, when you whipped out your fly rod in areas of Russia that have never seen one, what was the reaction of the local population? They must have been stupefied at first.

MR. MONTAIGNE: People were fascinated. They first of all remarked at how pretty it was. Fly fishing is so little practiced in Russia. When I was travelling across Russia two summers ago for this book, there probably were no more than three- or four-hundred fly fishermen in the whole country. In my book, I describe how I carried thousands of dollars' worth of rods and reels and flies and extra waders because there would have been nowhere to get anything replaced or repaired if I had needed it.

The Russians have a great expression for fishing with a fly rod: they call it "fishing with a buggy whip" because that's the closest comparison they can draw. As you can imagine, I was quite an oddity. But some of the locals I fished with were curious about fly fishing, so I showed them how to do it. When there were a lot of fish around, they caught fish. I also introduced these fishermen to the principle of catch and release, which they really loved. They really understood the point of it and seemed eager for their country to get to the point where it would be possible to start doing more of it.

MR. SLOAN: I wrote down some of the species that you fished for. You fished for grayling and salmon. I also have down herring. You fished for herring?

MR. MONTAIGNE: That's right. I fished for herring in the White Sea. I didn't catch any.

MR. SLOAN: Then, you fished for something called a "canal trout" up near Murmansk.

MR. MONTAIGNE: Right. A canal trout is a trout that was introduced on the Solovetsky Islands by the monks centuries ago. I saw a couple of canal trout, but I never caught one. They're pretty small.

MR. SLOAN: Then Atlantic salmon, taimen, pike, perch, and lenok.

MR. MONTAIGNE: Yes, I had wonderful experiences fishing for all of those. But it was the travelling in between the fishing that was really fascinating.

I hitchhiked for about fifteen hundred miles through the most remote region of the Russian far east, a region that had been the center of the old Stalin-era gulag, where hundreds of thousands of people died digging gold. They actually have ruined so many streams there, but are still digging for gold today. The Russian gold-mining technique basically tears up streambeds and riverbeds. As I traveled through this area, which is called Kolyma, a beautiful mountainous area with birch and tamarack on the hillsides, I saw heaps of tailings and waste rock piled up next to the streams for literally hundreds of miles. I flew only about three hundred miles on my whole trip as I crossed Russia overland. I remember that I could see this destruction from the air, and I got a first-hand look at it as I drove alongside it. It is the worst destruction of any waterways I saw in all of Russia.

MR. SLOAN: What would this area be comparable to in American terms? Montana and Idaho, circa 1850?

MR. MONTAIGNE: Yes, once you get away from the cities, it is like travelling back in time, and the nineteenth century American frontier is an apt comparison. People live in log huts. They draw water from wells. They use outhouses. They rely on their gardens and subsistence fishing. They are just as tough as the old folks, as our pioneer ancestors.

When I hitchhiked through Kolyma, I got to know this new breed of capitalists, if you will, in Russia: long-haul truckers. Truckers were the ones who always picked me up when I was hitchhiking over these terrible roads with no service stations, or anything at all, for that matter. Roads would go a hundred, a hundred and twenty, sometimes a hundred and fifty miles through Kolyma without any town or even any rest stop. The roads are just dirt roads, full of holes. We averaged about fifteen, maybe twenty, miles per hour.

But these truckers who picked me up were terrific. In my book, I describe how one of them worked when our truck broke down. The weather was cool; it was already September. I said to this trucker, whose name was Vova, "Vova, what happens when you break down in the winter, and it is fifty degrees below zero?" Vova described poetically how you step out of your truck in the middle of winter, and the *taiga*, or the forest, is literally humming with the sound of frozen branches and trees sort of crackling in the hard frost. He talked with pride.

MR. SLOAN: We're talking thirty or forty below zero now, right?

MR. MONTAIGNE: Oh yes. Easily. I mean, we're talking fifty degrees below zero *centigrade*, which is like seventy degrees below zero Fahrenheit. Vova told me that if you do not get your engine fixed in the first five or ten minutes, you must light a fire under it, either with tires or with wood, or you and your engine will freeze up solid. He was a great guy.

I fished for arctic char in that area. I visited an old survivor of Stalin's gulag who had lived for forty years deep in the forest as a kind of a hermit and trapper and hunter. I spent three wonderful days fishing for arctic char with him.

MR. SLOAN: Yes, I enjoyed your description of him. This fellow, who was basically in the gulag and then wound up in a cabin in a sort of self-imposed exile, never wanted to go back to civilization again. He came across as a very intelligent man who had a kind of uncanny understanding of what you were trying to do. It was an amazing portrait.

MR. MONTAIGNE: He did have a very deep understanding of my goals. You know, this was someone who even knew about the greenhouse effect. He spoke poetically to me about how much warmer his winters had become. He lived on this beautiful lake called Sunny Lake, which is not all that far below the Arctic Circle. He talked at length about how much warmer it had become and about how the autumns there used to be so clear and were not that way anymore. Yes, he was a wonderful, almost poetic, character.

MR. SLOAN: You know, Fen, we had Pete Soverel on the program, and he was describing a trip to the Kamchatka Peninsula, basically to preserve the wild steelhead there, but you had some pretty good fishing when you were there, did you not?

MR. MONTAIGNE: I did, yes. Kamchatka was beautiful. That was the one point on my trip where I broke my rule: I hopped in a helicopter because I was part of an expedition to tag and scientifically track the last strain of wild steelhead trout, and we flew to some gorgeous tundra rivers. I describe in the book how we arrived right at the tail end of the salmon run, and all these dead and dying spawning salmon were floating downstream. The banks of the river were just stamped throughout with huge bear tracks. It was really wild. I had a great experience.

I was standing at this beautiful pool with a Russian friend of mine. We were going for a steelhead, and we could see him porpoising in a very long pool below me. To my left was a smaller pool—I don't know, about twenty-five or thirty feet in diameter. I was standing there casting to the steelhead, and I heard this big splash to my left. I looked over, and I saw that the water was roiled up in this deep green pool.

All of a sudden, I looked across the pool, and I saw this lemming or mouse swimming frantically across the current. Just as I am looking at this mouse, wondering what in the world is going on here, a huge rainbow trout comes up and devours it. Well, I had been carrying these mouse imitation flies across all of Russia. I had never used them, and I got pretty excited at the prospect of using them then. I said to myself, "I have got to get one of these."

I ran back to the gravel bar and tied on my mouse imitation fly. This was one of the few times on my trip when everything worked perfectly. I cast this deer-hair mouse imitation, and on the third float over this pool, a big rainbow trout, probably three or four pounds, struck the fly, and I caught it. It was quite a thrill. As I joked in the book, I was matching the hatch.

MR. SLOAN: Match to hatch with a lemming.

MR. MONTAIGNE: Exactly. It was really quite something.

MR. SLOAN: Now Fen, if somebody reads your book and decides he or she would really like to visit Russia to fish, what would you suggest? Clearly, you cannot do it all. How would one get started? What would be the first move? Whom would one contact?

MR. MONTAIGNE: There are a number of ways to make arrangements to fish in Russia. If you want to go to the Kola Peninsula, you should find one of the reputable outfitters who guide trips to a really wonderful river like the Penoit. For the Kamchatka, you've got Pete Soverel's Kamchatka steelhead project.

But, if you want to go on your own, that's possible, too. You wouldn't want to repeat my trip because you'd need language skills, and it really is a pretty tough trip. The one place you would not want to miss, if you are a freelance angler, is Lake Baikal. You can stay in Irkutsk, which is a beautiful city with nice hotels, about thirty miles from the lake. Then, you could find yourself a translator and a captain and fish the lake and some of those rivers flowing into it. Lake Baikal is really a doable trip—one of the few fishing trips that you could do on your own in Russia.

MR. SLOAN: How many air hours is it from Moscow?

MR. MONTAIGNE: I think Irkutsk is probably five or six, certainly no more than that.

MR. SLOAN: So, New York to California, or vice versa, basically?

MR. MONTAIGNE: Right, which is not too bad in Russia. As I said, Irkutsk really is a beautiful, beautiful city that still has a lot of its old architecture left. And Lake Baikal is really something worth seeing. I tell people it truly is one of the wonders of the natural world.

MR. SLOAN: I'd like to close with one brief quote from your book. You wrote, "Fishing is drinking with hip boots on in Russia."

MR. MONTAIGNE: Yes; that's a Russian joke. It often seems that it is true. I met guides who would take a case of vodka on a fishing trip. They would drink the entire twelve-bottle case, two or three guys, and then they would start fishing.

MR. SLOAN: Incredible. And somehow they live to fish again.

Fen, thanks for joining us.

MR. MONTAIGNE: Steve, I really enjoyed it. Thank you for having me.

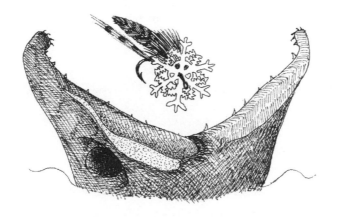

JOSEPH HEYWOOD

on THE SNOWFLY

An interview with Joseph Heywood on his novel,
THE SNOWFLY.

*I*t's in some ways telling that the first three pages of the following interview with novelist Joe Heywood are devoted to that author's most recent fishing experiences rather than most recent novel. One senses not exactly reluctance as much as something akin to resignation when the author is finally brought around to discussing his novel. With Heywood, it's always clear that fishing is never too far removed from his writing. Heywood is not a writer who fishes; he is a fisherman who writes. As the following interview reveals, that sensibility permeates his latest work, THE SNOWFLY, a novel published by The Lyons Press.

Heywood was born in Rhinebeck, New York, and graduated from Michigan State University with a bachelor's degree in journalism in 1965. After graduation, he served in the United States Air Force from 1965 through 1970. Heywood has worked as a firefighter in the Air Force, a rent-a-cop, a public relations executive, and a university professor. He is the author of four novels—TAXI DANCER, THE BERKUT, THE

DOMINO CONSPIRACY, and THE SNOWFLY—and is just completing work on a fifth, ICE HUNTER, which was published in June 2001 by The Lyons Press. Heywood is an avid fly fisherman and can often be found ranging along the Pere Marquette and Au Sable rivers in Michigan.

When Heywood spoke with Sloan in the following interview, he explained much of how his fisherman's mindset contributed to the creative task before him with THE SNOWFLY. From the Native American vision quest, to Ishmael's quest in MOBY DICK, to the hidden allegory of Walton's COMPLEAT ANGLER, Heywood reveals how THE SNOWFLY taps and builds upon a rich tradition of narrative art that has relied upon angling for successful metaphors for some of the larger issues of life.

MR. SLOAN: I'm pleased to have with us today Joe Heywood, author of a new novel from The Lyons Press called THE SNOWFLY.

MR. HEYWOOD: It's a pleasure to be here, Steve.

MR. SLOAN: What's up in the Upper Peninsula?

MR. HEYWOOD: It's cold. They've already had some snow up there. And I'm sorry I didn't get back to you right away when you called. In fact, I was salmon fishing on the day you initially called to invite me here today.

MR. SLOAN: How was the fishing?

MR. HEYWOOD: We had four runs. It's a little early for them actually; they're pretty skittish right now. They're not settled on the bed. But we had four fish.

MR. SLOAN: Is this stream fishing?

MR. HEYWOOD: Yes. We were on the Muskegon River.

MR. SLOAN: Oh yes, the Muskegon. And were these coho or Chinook?

MR. HEYWOOD: Actually, we call them king salmon up there, but they're the same as Chinook.

MR. SLOAN: Kings? Oh, God almighty.

MR. HEYWOOD: There are some huge ones in there.

MR. SLOAN: You can say that again. I've caught about four of them: two in Alaska and two out West. They are just so strong.

MR. HEYWOOD: It's hard to keep them on your tackle this time of year because there's still a lot of piss and vinegar left in them. On two good hookups we had, they just took the fly, swam about a hundred yards, popped the leader, and that was that.

MR. SLOAN: How big a fish? Forty, fifty?

MR. HEYWOOD: No, not forty or fifty. I'd say the big ones are twenty to thirty pounds. Most of them are probably around twelve to seventeen.

MR. SLOAN: Where is the Muskegon River exactly? How far up?

MR. HEYWOOD: It's north of me about an hour, about thirty miles or so north of Grand Rapids. It's a big tailwater fishery—beautiful, beautiful water.

MR. SLOAN: Now, what do they hit up there? Mostly egg pattern flies?

MR. HEYWOOD: Well, we hit one with an egg pattern and one with a freshwater shrimp with a green cat body on it. I picked up some rainbows, too—some of the big ones. It was a cold day.

MR. SLOAN: Yeah, I'll bet.

Joe, by the way, I just picked up a copy of Bob Linsenman's MODERN STREAMERS FOR TROPHY TROUT *(See "Robert Linsenman on Streamer Fishing" on page 113)*. Hearing you mention those streamers brought his book to mind. I just got it.

MR. HEYWOOD: Oh, did you? Great.

MR. SLOAN: I just thumbed through it last night. I got it yesterday afternoon. I happen to love streamer fishing, I really do.

MR. HEYWOOD: I'll tell you something. As far as the streamer fishing business is concerned, Bob's the man. I was out with him last week for two days, and we caught thirty trout in our two outings, six of them between twenty-three and twenty-five inches.

MR. SLOAN: Geez.

MR. HEYWOOD: Major fish.

MR. SLOAN: Well, let's face it: a big fish is going to eat something big.

MR. HEYWOOD: He's going to eat other fish.

MR. SLOAN: Exactly. He's going to eat a lot of protein in one gulp.

MR. HEYWOOD: That's right. The number of fishermen that you talk to who've caught big trout with other trout sticking out of their mouths is pretty amazing.

I probably know a dozen guys who've caught twenty-four- or twenty-five-inch fish that way. In fact, the day before I went up to fish with Bob last week, one of his friends hooked a huge brown trout. He hooked about a twelve-incher, and some bigger fish came and took it off the end of his line.

MR. SLOAN: I've had that happen several times, where I caught a small fish and this big thing came out of the pool and just nailed it.

MR. HEYWOOD: They're very carnivorous.

MR. SLOAN: You know, it's funny, one of the best flies I used earlier this spring, into about June, was a bead-headed streamer. They call it a Badger Honey, or a Honey Streamer. The wing of it was a honey color with a black line in it. I'm sure it ends up looking like a small trout to bigger fish. Without a doubt.

MR. HEYWOOD: Yeah, I think it would. I think the whole use of color in a streamer is hard to figure out, though.

MR. SLOAN: I think a lot of it has to do with the character of the light coming into the water.

MR. HEYWOOD: That's what I think, too.

MR. SLOAN: Sometimes you put a White Marabou on and, as you wrote in your book, it's a "flusher-outer." You just use it to find out where they are. Fish don't nail it, but they turn on it.

MR. HEYWOOD: That's right. I think the time of year has something to do with it, too. For instance, are there lots of smelt in the river at a certain time? If that's true, then a certain color streamer, like a large, white one with a flash in it, is going to reflect in a certain way and be productive because it resembles the smelt that are present in the river at that time. The rest of the time, I think it's the shape of the streamer that matters.

MR. SLOAN: What fishing is coming up next in Michigan? Steelhead fishing?

MR. HEYWOOD: Salmon has started right now, and they'll be in until late October and during the fall steelhead run. Some of our rivers are open for trout all winter.

MR. SLOAN: How big do the steelhead get?

MR. HEYWOOD: Steelhead generally run between five and fifteen pounds up here.

MR. SLOAN: That's a good-sized fish.

Joe, I feel like I could talk fishing with you all day, but I'd like to get to the real reason I asked you to join me today, and that's to talk about your new book. It's clear to me that this book could not have been written unless you were a superb fisherman. So give us a little background about some of your other fishing activity.

MR. HEYWOOD: Well, Steve, first let me finish laughing from hearing you say that I'm a superb fisherman. I'm not. I am a fisherman, and a friend of mine says I'm serious about fishing because I try to figure it out all the time.

MR. SLOAN: To figure out fishing? Well, that's okay.

MR. HEYWOOD: But I'm not a great fisherman. I'm pretty average. In fact, I thought sometime I'd write about the theory that 5 percent of the fishermen account for 95 percent of the fish that are caught. I thought I'd write a book for the other 95 percent of us who insist on trying to catch that remaining 5 percent. That's what I know best.

MR. SLOAN: Well, you know why I think people like fishing, especially trout fishing? Because it's problem solving all the time.

MR. HEYWOOD: Absolutely.

MR. SLOAN: It really is.

MR. HEYWOOD: Yes, it's a little way of solving life's mysteries.

MR. SLOAN: Well, tell me, Joe, how did you get the idea to write THE SNOWFLY?

MR. HEYWOOD: That's a really good question, Steve, and there isn't a simple answer to it. I didn't sit down to write this book. In fact, I was playing with the idea for something else, and two years ago this October—in fact, today—I sat down one morning to piddle with something else, and the prologue to this book just popped out. And I thought, "Gee, this is pretty interesting. I'll see where it goes." And over the next six weeks, I wrote the book. I have no idea where it came from. I suppose it was because I was enmeshed in fishing and sort of fascinated with the whole thing.

MR. SLOAN: Joe, one of the scenes I recall most vividly from THE SNOWFLY— and our talking about salmon fishing a minute ago just brought it to mind—was that scene when your protagonist was at the mouth of that lake and the anglers were in a frenzy of snagging the big salmon. That scene was almost unreadable for me. We get snaggers up in the Salmon River, in upstate New York. Even when it's against the law today, you see guys who are looking right at the fish, trying to get their fly right near the mouth, and giving the rod a big jerk.

MR. HEYWOOD: Around here, they used to fish with these little chunks of lead with three big hooks. They're called spiders.

MR. SLOAN: Yeah, miniature gaffs.

MR. HEYWOOD: I think they hooked each other more than they hooked the fish.

MR. SLOAN: This is true. And there was a great controversy about snagging because the salmon die anyway after the run.

MR. HEYWOOD: It *is* a tremendous controversy, but snagging is outlawed here now.

MR. SLOAN: Same here.

MR. HEYWOOD: I think practices like snagging are what happen when people chase big fish. The salmon-snagging frenzy on Thompson Creek described in that scene is an example of what happens when you use a snowfly.

MR. SLOAN: Exactly. Joe, I'd like to know what the largest hatch you ever saw was. I mean, other than a snowfly, what's the largest insect you ever saw hatch?

MR. HEYWOOD: I think it was a hex fly.

MR. SLOAN: I'll tell you what happened to me. The summer before last, I was fishing the Ausable, in upstate New York, and I had a guide with me, a nice guy who runs the Hungry Trout shop up there. He took me on a cascading, downward part of the stream where you had terraces of water running down. The stream was very low, and at about 7:30 at night I saw these flies come out of the woods. They were about four inches long, had two sets of wings, and were orange. They dropped like bats out of the sky onto the water, and a couple of large trout nailed them.

MR. HEYWOOD: A salmon fly, perhaps?

MR. SLOAN: No, it was a stone fly.

MR. HEYWOOD: It was a stone fly? Okay. Yeah, there are some huge ones.

MR. SLOAN: Huge. I never saw a fly that big in my life.

MR. HEYWOOD: The hex flies generally tend to be larger.

MR. SLOAN: Really?

MR. HEYWOOD: Yeah. I think they're the largest fly we know about.

MR. SLOAN: We ran and looked for anything in our fly boxes that could compare in size, but no luck. Matching the hatch failed that night.

Now Joe, why don't you describe a snowfly for us, if you can.

MR. HEYWOOD: Sure. A snowfly is a very big bug that hatches once every seven to ten years and only once on a river. And as a result, there's no predictable hatch. So in my novel, I have people going out to hunt for it—at least hoping to find it in the course of their lifetime.

MR. SLOAN: And it's about as big as the palm of your hand, right?

MR. HEYWOOD: That's right; it's about the size of the palm of your hand. It's definitely huge, and it tends to hatch in winter. As you know, most of the flies that hatch in the winter are midges and tricos and blue-winged olives. Primarily, they're small flies.

Big fish really don't pay much attention to them. Big fish will feed on other fish and basically are lethargic in the wintertime. But if you have a huge fly that suddenly hatches in the winter—think of a hex fly hatching in winter—imagine what that would do to fish. And that's essentially what a snowfly would do.

MR. SLOAN: Now where did you hear about the snowfly legend?

MR. HEYWOOD: I didn't.

MR. SLOAN: You didn't?

MR. HEYWOOD: No. It came out of my twisted mind. In a sense, it's sort of an outgrowth of thinking about what happens when people get big-fish madness. We were just talking about the Thompson Creek salmon-snagging episode and how people go crazy over big fish. They go to the ends of the earth to chase them, to places like Russia and Iceland, so I just got to thinking to myself, "What if there were a fly that hatched in the wintertime, when nothing else is coming up, and it brought out these huge fish?" And the story just sort of flowed from there.

MR. SLOAN: Boy, it really did flow. THE SNOWFLY starts in the Upper Peninsula of Michigan, with the Rhodes family. Bowie Rhodes, the protagonist in your novel, goes to Michigan State University and hears about the legend of the snowfly and discovers a box that has a couple of snowflies in it.

By the way, is the name "Bowie" synonymous with James Bowie, the famous hunter and defender of the Alamo, the inventor of the Bowie knife?

MR. HEYWOOD: No. It's not synonymous with anything. I just liked the name.

MR. SLOAN: Really? You're putting me on.

MR. HEYWOOD: I'm not putting you on. It's fiction, remember? I can give my characters any name I like.

MR. SLOAN: Who were your favorite American authors?

MR. HEYWOOD: My favorite American authors? I think the best book I've read in years and years and years was Larry McMurtry's LONESOME DOVE. It's the greatest American novel that's been published in the last twenty-five years—a wonderful story. I also like Jim Harrison very much and Tom McGuane. I read some mystery writers that a lot of people probably haven't run across: Stewart Kiminsky, who writes about a Russian investigator based in Moscow; a Dutchman named Vanderbett, who writes about the Amsterdam police; and a lot of different writers.

MR. SLOAN: Maybe I'm overdoing it and becoming so enthusiastic about this book that I believe it is written on many levels, like MOBY DICK. I don't know if anybody ever told you that, but my daughter, who is one of the most literate people I've ever met in my life, read it and loved it. She got excited about it, and we discussed it. She would like to know whether Melville is a hero of yours.

MR. HEYWOOD: I've read MOBY DICK, and I heard it described one time as "all you wanted to know about whales but didn't want to ask."

But don't get me wrong: I love Melville. I think he's a great example of somebody who really received very little acclaim in his lifetime but slaved away at his work and wrote great things.

MR. SLOAN: Well, how about the MOBY DICK theme of Calvinism versus Puritanism? A good God versus an angry God? This is the symbolism that many have seen in MOBY DICK. There's so much symbolism in your book. I don't know if you intended it that way, but it's there.

MR. HEYWOOD: I'd like to say that I did, but I can't. There are a few things in there that readers will seize on, I suppose. But I really am of the school that believes that most writers tell a story, and I don't think they're really aware of the symbolism of the story that's coming out of their subconscious and conscious mind.

Hemingway was the one who was always being asked, "What does the story mean?" He would reply, and I'm paraphrasing here, "Well, the story is the story, and whatever else you take from it is really a reflection of your mind and your psychological makeup rather than the author's." Readers will find symbols in THE SNOWFLY, probably, but a lot of them are not intentional.

MR. SLOAN: Did you serve in Vietnam?

MR. HEYWOOD: Yes. Well, I served in Thailand. I consider that Vietnam.

MR. SLOAN: I would, too. So that chapter about Rhodes fishing in Vietnam is very real to you, I take it. Don't worry; I'm not going to give the plot away. Suffice it to say that you had fishing experience in Vietnam, and Rhodes' profession is a reporter. Rhodes goes out on some of the trips with the troops, special combat troops, and the story that unfolds from it is spellbinding—absolutely fabulous. The quest for the snowfly continues, and, believe it or not, it's found in a certain place in Vietnam and under very extenuating circumstances.

MR. HEYWOOD: Very extenuating.

MR. SLOAN: Right. And from there, Rhodes gets involved in Russia, and the snowfly reappears there.

MR. HEYWOOD: It would make sense that if there were a fly like this, people would chase it everywhere. Therefore, people who were serious about fishing or addicted to chasing big fish would know about it and continue the quest.

MR. SLOAN: Yes, they would, and a lot of us have. I'm guilty of that. I don't know if you should have a guilt trip about pursuing large fish, but I would rather catch a large trout and work on him and be satisfied I caught that one fish that day than catch a dozen average-sized trout. Fortunately, I have the opportunity to do it out at Henryville, Pennsylvania.

MR. HEYWOOD: I don't think there should be any guilt attached to the quest for big fish, Steve. I think fisherman go through phases. I've read this a number of times. When you first start out fly fishing, you want to just catch fish—any fish. And then you go to the next phase, when you want to catch a lot of fish. At some point, a fly fisherman will progress to a phase where he wants to catch big fish. I think it's a natural progression.

MR. SLOAN: Tell me, Joe, have you read Fen Montaigne's book, REELING IN RUSSIA?

MR. HEYWOOD: Yes, I have. It's a very good book.

MR. SLOAN: It sure is. Montaigne was on this program. I found his book very interesting. *(See "Fen Montaigne on Fishing in Russia" on page 77).*

MR. HEYWOOD: His was a real adventure, wasn't it?

MR. SLOAN: It sure was.

MR. SLOAN: It's a wonderful book and is really more about the Russian people than anything else, I think. Montaigne uses his six- or seven-thousand-mile journey as a wonderful backdrop for describing Russian life as well as fishing.

MR. HEYWOOD: I agree. Don't you think that most fishing books end up being really less about the technical how-to and more of a travel memoir of what life was like?

MR. SLOAN: Sure. By the way, Montaigne and I went fishing out in Pennsylvania. He's a damn good fisherman.

I'd like to return to your book for a moment, Joe, and specifically, I'd like to ask you about the vision quest in THE SNOWFLY. What happens? Was it a conscious decision on your part to depict it this way?

MR. HEYWOOD: Absolutely, absolutely.

MR. SLOAN: That's what I figured. Did you have exposure to any Native American culture?

MR. HEYWOOD: Yes. I wrote a book for Random House called FORCE OF BLOOD, which my editors objected to spiritually. They thought it was too spiritual because it dealt with a lot of Indian beliefs and Indian rituals. I did a lot of research on Indian beliefs in the course of writing that book. It's a pretty good piece of work, I think, but it never saw the light of day.

MR. SLOAN: Getting back to THE SNOWFLY, Joe, Rhodes is your hero, the protagonist of your novel. After coming out of Vietnam, he returns to the United States before he winds up in Russia. In between, he has what is known as a vision quest, which is a part of Indian lore. Is it more than lore? Is it really a practice? What exactly *is* a vision quest?

MR. HEYWOOD: In many Indian tribes, as the young men or boys—adolescents, really—get ready to go into manhood, they are expected to go out and search their souls for a period of time to find out where their inner core is. Sometimes they call this soul-searching process a vision quest; sometimes they call it something else. But the practice is generally the same.

They usually fast for a period of days, isolate themselves to try to achieve a trance-like state, and have some sort of dream. From the dream, they then interpret something about themselves as it applies to their lives. This is the process that Rhodes undergoes in THE SNOWFLY. He doesn't seek the experience; instead, he is sort of induced to a vision quest by people he becomes involved with.

MR. SLOAN: I see. But at the end of the vision quest, your life is revealed to you and it predicts what your future will be, right? Is that part of it?

MR. HEYWOOD: I don't think it predicts your future as much as it gives you a sense of what your center is and who you are. The vision quest provides a way of looking at yourself that will sort of dictate how you comport yourself over the rest of your life.

It's very much akin to other common facets of Native American religions. But you also find aspects of the vision quest in other religions—for example, the idea of taking solace in the wilderness and trying to come to grips with yourself and life. These practices tend to be human activities, and even though they're not always formalized, the concept is still there. It's a form of prayer, if you will.

MR. SLOAN: Yes. And you conveyed that clearly. So Rhodes gets put into this vision-quest condition. I won't reveal how because it's exciting in itself, and he's left alone for a couple of days, just to the point where he actually breaks. He hallucinates. But he sees his life unfold, and, sure enough, the vision quest did happen.

MR. HEYWOOD: Yes, it happened. It's very real. When I was in the Air Force, we all went through survival training, which included practicing how to stay alive and escape-and-evasion training. One of the things that you learn in training for a prison camp situation is that when you're isolated from others and surviving on small rations for a long period of time, your mind begins to play tricks on you. I think the Native Americans and other aboriginal societies around the world have always known this. Some of them also employ drugs to enhance or stimulate this effect. But in THE SNOWFLY, drugs were not necessary for Rhodes. If you isolate yourself long enough and you don't have enough food, your mind *will* begin to play tricks on you. So I suppose I was using a little bit of my personal experience in the book.

MR. SLOAN: Now, Rhodes winds up in Russia, and I'd like to talk about that in a moment. But first, is there any significance to the name Fire Heart?

MR. HEYWOOD: Fire Heart? No. Only as it relates to what he's told about himself all through his life. And this is something he has to balance. People who have fire in their hearts have to learn how to temper it.

MR. SLOAN: Absolutely, and the quest for the snowfly leads Rhodes into some very interesting places, including Russia. Now, you said you've been to Russia.

MR. HEYWOOD: That's right. I've been there three times. I was there once before the so-called "fall" and twice afterwards.

MR. SLOAN: Interesting. I've actually been invited to the Kamchatka Peninsula to fish at one of the places that Montaigne described in REELING IN RUSSIA. Do you know about that wild salmon center that he wrote about?

MR. HEYWOOD: I do. You should go.

MR. SLOAN: I think I will. Have you been there?

MR. HEYWOOD: No, I've not been to Siberia, but I actually have a novel in the works that is set in that area of Russia.

MR. SLOAN: Right. Now, somehow Rhodes gets into Russia and then gets out, under some rather interesting circumstances, comes back to the United States, saves his life, and the quest goes on for the snowfly.

I'd like to shift gears somewhat and talk a little bit about the Cold War setting for your book and some of the insight that setting provides. You very poignantly describe a Canadian uranium-mining area in THE SNOWFLY. Have you been there?

MR. HEYWOOD: Yes, I have. In fact, I spent about ten days up there going through what's left of the uranium mines. They're all closed down now, but you can see how they once operated. They polluted a lot of waters, and the Canadians are trying to do remediation and restoration now. But visually, the area looks pretty terrible. It's in the Elliot Lake area, which is about a hundred miles east of Sault Ste. Marie, Ontario.

MR. SLOAN: When you stepped on that Canadian uranium-mining land, did you get a strange feeling that you were walking on a polluted wasteland—similar to the feeling that you describe Rhodes as having had in your book—that everything is poisoned, that the poison is invisible, that you can't see it but you know it's there? Was that your basic feeling?

MR. HEYWOOD: That's exactly the way I felt. It was funny, but it reminded me of being back in the Strategic Air Command from my Air Force days. I had been in the refueling part of SAC, but I can recall thinking of the B-52s on the base and our big stores of H-bombs in the munitions area there, knowing that all of that explosive power was always nearby.

In some ways, visiting that Canadian uranium-mining area felt like that. It's a feeling that makes you want to say to yourself, "I know this poison is here." You can't see it at all, but you know it's there and you know it's lethal. It's a spooky sort of feeling.

MR. SLOAN: Do you think that land can ever be remediated?

MR. HEYWOOD: I really don't know. I think that what we consider to be remediation now will be changed into something else down the road. That seems to be the pattern. And, of course, this current problem in Canada really came about because the United States was looking for sources of uranium for its nuclear arsenal. That's how this whole mining area developed. Then, after a few years, somebody got to thinking, "Well, that's Canada, and we really ought to have our own national source of uranium." The big uranium rush then began in the United States. We opened our own mines, abandoned the Canadian mines, and left the Canadians with the mess. That was the decision by the United States government, and that's the backdrop against which Rhodes is working.

MR. SLOAN: But Rhodes' quest went on for the snowfly, right?

MR. HEYWOOD: That's right. I think that early on, Rhodes hears about this legend when he was a young kid, eight years old. He then first hears about the snowfly when he's working for the Forest Service in Idaho, and then it just seems to pop back into and out of his life. He tries to ignore it, he chases it for a while, and then he goes on to do other things. But the snowfly keeps coming back. Finally, he succumbs to it and attempts to discover it.

MR. SLOAN: A lot of things popped in and out of Rhodes' life, including the women and his first love.

MR. HEYWOOD: That's right. She had been his best friend when he was a kid.

MR. SLOAN: And she weaves in and out and throughout this story, appearing and then disappearing. Finally—and I won't tell about her end—in the true quest for the snowfly, something happens to her. Other women weave their way in and out, as well, including the one whom Rhodes marries and loves, and then, unfortunately, something happens to her.

MR. HEYWOOD: Don't you think that's the way life is, though? People come in and out of our lives?

MR. SLOAN: Yes, they do.

MR. HEYWOOD: We live life sequentially. Some people stay in it in little bits and pieces for all of our lives. Others are at the center of our lives for a while, and then they're gone. I believe that's just the way life is. And I tried to write it that way.

MR. SLOAN: I think the hardest thing to have is a true friend for a full lifetime. It's very difficult to maintain such a friendship in the course of human relationships, including the ladies. I've been married forty-three years to the same lady; I'm very fortunate. But I know that that is something exceptional. I'm talking about friends now: they come, they go, certain things develop, you lose confidence in them, they lose confidence in you. Whatever. It's just very difficult to maintain a friendship for a lifetime. You're right: friends do come in and out as we live our lives.

MR. HEYWOOD: I think that happens with Rhodes, too. I mean, he's looking for a home, which is a place where there are friends. I think he finds that home, but in a place where he didn't really expect to find it.

MR. SLOAN: I'd like to talk about the epilogue to THE SNOWFLY for a moment. In it, you write, "Do what's inside you, and let God keep score." Does this reflect a pantheistic philosophy that you might have—that God is omnipresent and you might find him in a trout stream or in the ocean or certainly fishing?

MR. HEYWOOD: I think there's something to that. To me, a river with trout in it is a sort of church. It's a place with quiet, beautiful, natural music, a place with a beautiful setting and colors. For instance, right now our fall colors are just starting here in the Upper Peninsula, and the river is absolutely gorgeous. It's a place for contemplation and a place to get back to a simple center that we have.

MR. SLOAN: This is true, and how very well said. A cathedral for you is a trout stream. How marvelous.

MR. HEYWOOD: I think trout fishing is a kind of a church, a place for contemplation, an opportunity for solving some of life's little mysteries. Because most mysteries we can't solve, fishing at least provides us with some that we can. I think there's a tremendous power to that. I think people who go out and chase fish or chase anything—the snowfly can stand for anything—are making accomplishments that fulfill a need. It's funny that they are finding them in the least possible places. But the looking, the searching, the seeking—those are the really important things.

MR. SLOAN: I find God in the ocean; I really do. I mean, I've taken people for eight hours of trolling. "We didn't see a thing," they say. I say, "No, you missed the whole day."

MR. HEYWOOD: I think people find it sometimes, and it's interesting when they do. People find it in water. I think that water is the life substance. We'll find it in all sorts of ways, whether it's a cottage on a lake or sailing on the ocean or fishing a stream. Water is an important life source, the well spring.

MR. SLOAN: Well said. Joe, you also mention that every time you catch a trout, it gets a little smarter. Do you think that's true?

MR. HEYWOOD: Well, I have read many, many accounts saying that the reason it's so difficult to catch a trout in England is that over generations, millennia really, they've become smarter genetically because they're fished so hard. I'm sure you've heard this too, Steve. The idea is simply that it takes a lot to fool smart fish that have been fished so hard. So I don't know whether it's true or not, genetically or biologically, but it certainly is true in a practical sense. There are some places where the fish are damn difficult to catch, and other places where they're not so difficult to hook.

MR. SLOAN: I'll tell you what Ernie Schwiebert said about that when I asked him *(See "Ernest Schwiebert on Trout Fishing" on page 23)*. He said that there's another side to it. Brown trout, he said, had interacted with human beings for a long, long time over in Europe, so they don't get as nervous when humans show up. But Schwiebert also says that browns have also seen a lot of the different lures that we've presented in trying to catch them, so they're much wilier than, say, our native brookies. I've certainly found that to be true out in Pennsylvania. He said that because brook trout never interacted with anybody till two hundred and something years ago, they're not as smart.

MR. HEYWOOD: Well, they had interacted with the Indians in pre-Colonial times but had not been exposed to the kind of fishing that we do until about two hundred years ago. And I think it's interesting that if you go into northern Canada, for example, and fish for brook trout, they're pretty easy to catch because they've never seen *anything* before.

MR. SLOAN: Exactly.

MR. HEYWOOD: But if you go up to Michigan's Au Sable and fish the holy waters, there are lots of big fish. Or if you fish the South Platte west of Denver, you'll see huge fish holding the water. But in either case, you'll find that they just don't want to come to anything. So I don't know whether they pass knowledge on through their genes or what, but there are some places where fish are very, very difficult to catch. Nick Lyons talks about fishing spring creeks in Montana and how difficult it is and how smart the fish are—how wary they are, I should say.

MR. SLOAN: That's true.

MR. HEYWOOD: God gave humans the brains to fish, but it doesn't work all the time.

MR. SLOAN: That's true. After reviewing the stocking log at Henryville, I figured out that we put in about six hundred fish a year to mix with the wild ones that are in there, and there are a lot of wild ones. But if you total up the annual catch recorded in the log—and remember that it's all catch and release up there—they catch and release about forty-five hundred to five thousand fish a year. So some of them have got to be caught what, two, three, or four times? You know, perhaps we are getting smarter, too.

MR. HEYWOOD: Could be.

MR. SLOAN: Joe, if there's a snowfly legend, does the quest for it, the discoveries along the way, exact a price? The book seemed to imply as much. Rhodes sets out on the trail and really tries for something and discovers things. It seems that he also learns that there's a price to be paid.

MR. HEYWOOD: I think so, Steve. I remember that when we were talking the other day, you asked, "Is there a snowfly within all of us? Is this symbolic of something?"

It is, I think. Everybody is trying for some kind of accomplishment. And it can be fairly modest, or it can be fairly outrageous and really ego-driven. Perhaps the snowfly is just another attempt at finding immortality. To chase and find something that nobody has gotten to—I think that that sort of individual pursuit is within all of us, that we want to be immortal in some way and accomplish something that we'll each be remembered by. And so the snowfly is representative of that sort of quest.

MR. SLOAN: Well, this is true. I wanted to be the first man to catch a sailfish on two-pound line.

MR. HEYWOOD: Well, then you will be.

MR. SLOAN: I did it. And I thought it would live forever, but it didn't. Somebody broke the record, you know.

MR. HEYWOOD: It's Olympics time; all records are made to be broken.

MR. SLOAN: This is true. But I remember thinking to myself, "My goodness, nobody's ever going to do this again." In the first place, it was so hard. Secondly, I had been lucky because the fish just jumped in the shallows and thrashed around, instead of going into deep water, and we were able to land it. Hey, you're entitled to that kind of break sometimes, too.

MR. HEYWOOD: Well, luck is a great part of it, isn't it?

MR. SLOAN: It sure is. Joe, how many times have you hooked a big trout and had it go around a log or some obstruction? And you said, "Oh, oh. That's it." And somehow it got free, and away you went with landing it. I mean, it happens all the time.

MR. HEYWOOD: Right. But not just a big trout—*any* trout. Most of mine, it seems. Some of them seem to have an innate sense for seeking cover—similar to certain gamebirds, like ruffed grouse, which always find a way to get a tree between you and them when they flush.

MR. SLOAN: True.

MR. HEYWOOD: I think that trout are like that too, sometimes.

MR. SLOAN: Well, a smart one that has lived a while knows the territory he's in, and he's going to take every advantage he can from it.

MR. HEYWOOD: Absolutely. They very much know the territory. The big ones, like big browns, are the kings of the river. They're not afraid of anything. They may be a little leery of birds—big birds of prey like bald eagles and ospreys and the like—but by and large, if it swims in the water, they're not afraid of it. Big trout go where they want and do what they want. But they're also very careful about where they go, keeping themselves in cover, and working as little as they can—all traits for which I admire them greatly.

MR. SLOAN: I know what you mean. By the way, before we wrap up, I wanted to bring up one other item that you might find interesting.

I had James Prosek, who wrote THE COMPLETE ANGLER: A CONNECTICUT YANKEE FOLLOWS IN THE FOOTSTEPS OF WALTON, on the program recently *(See "James Prosek on Izaak Walton" on page 11).*

MR. HEYWOOD: I read it. I know Jim's work.

MR. SLOAN: He's a terrific young man. And he is a *young* man—he hasn't reached thirty yet.

MR. HEYWOOD: He's very mature. When I was that age, I didn't know half of what he knows.

MR. SLOAN: Exactly. And I've fished with him a couple of times. He's a very good fisherman. But one thing that really jumped out of his book was an amazing statistic on the ranking of the most popular books of all time. The Bible is number one, and Shakespeare's plays are number two. But the third most popular book of all time is Walton's THE COMPLEAT ANGLER. Now, that's saying something.

MR. HEYWOOD: It sure is. That's interesting.

MR. SLOAN: So here is a fishing book that, along with the dialogue and discourse on fishing and Cotton's addendum to it about fly fishing, has survived for more than three hundred years and wound up to be number three.

You see, THE SNOWFLY is in a great tradition.

MR. HEYWOOD: I sincerely hope so.

MR. SLOAN: I'm serious, it is.

MR. HEYWOOD: Thanks, Steve. And that's an interesting point that you're bringing up, too, because Walton's work is considered a code and an allegory.

MR. SLOAN: Exactly. When Prosek visited, we talked about that in Walton's book. The word "angler" was really a code word for "Anglican."

MR. HEYWOOD: That's right: the Complete Anglican. Walton was writing while a civil war was going on, with the Royalists being persecuted.

MR. SLOAN: Right, with Cromwell. And in reading THE SNOWFLY, I couldn't help but notice that you've got a key in your book, too.

MR. HEYWOOD: You're right. THE SNOWFLY relates very much to Walton's COMPLEAT ANGLER.

MR. SLOAN: Absolutely. I noticed that as Rhodes' life unfolds and as his quest continues for the snowfly, M.J. Key and codes become one of the focal points of the novel. By the way, M.J. Key is a great name because it suddenly conjures up questions like, "Is this the key to life?" or "What became unlocked because of this quest?" With the quest for the snowfly, there's a written document about it, and this document appears, disappears, reappears, and then disappears again. But the key—and his name is M.J. Key, and I'm sure you selected that name on purpose—is related, I'm sure, to some of the keys that went back to Walton's time when he said he used the code word "angler" for "Anglican," trying to get around Cromwell's troops, who didn't want anyone practicing that kind of religion.

MR. HEYWOOD: That's correct. It's M.J. Key. I was looking for something that I could base in historical fact. I figured that during the war a spy who was used to talking about fishing could use an open text as a good way to transfer code. And then I discovered that scholars believe that Walton's COMPLEAT ANGLER is actually a code and an allegory, and that the phrase "compleat angler," as I mentioned earlier, really refers to the "complete Anglican." At the time that Walton wrote his book, Royalists were being dispatched in large numbers in the English Civil War. Walton refers frequently to "the brotherhood of the angle," which some scholars believe refers to Anglicans who unjustly lost their parishes—or some of them their lives. This, of course, sent others with their beliefs underground.

Further, there were references by Walton to foxes, which was the code word of the day for Roman Catholics. Walton also wrote about otters, using the creature as a metaphor for those in his day who jumped from political camp to political camp in hope of ending up in the right camp in the civil war. My point was that using my SNOWFLY manuscript as the holder of code was supported to some extent by history and could be where M.J. Key got his idea for what he did. It was a nice precedent. And in fact, maybe there's even a code embedded in the plain language of the novel, as well.

MR. SLOAN: Maybe. Well, I'll have to read it again and see if I can figure it out.

MR. HEYWOOD: There could very well be a code in there.

MR. SLOAN: Okay. Thanks for the tip.

MR. HEYWOOD: It's unbreakable, Steve; M.J. Key gave me his keys.

MR. SLOAN: Oh, okay. You have M.J. Key's keys, so you've got a head start. That's unfair.

MR. HEYWOOD: That's true. It goes a lot easier if you have the code. If you haven't seen the code, it's a lot harder.

MR. SLOAN: This is true, this is true. It reminds me of when Ken Schultz came on this program. Ken wrote this new book, KEN SCHULTZ'S FISHING ENCYCLOPEDIA AND WORLDWIDE ANGLING GUIDE, and he said that if anyone could guess the number of species of game fish in North America, he or she would win a week's vacation in Mexico with him bass fishing. So I don't know. I took a guess, but I don't know how close I was. I think it's way up there in numbers.

MR. HEYWOOD: I think it's way up there, too.

MR. SLOAN: He said between one and 999, if that's any help.

MR. HEYWOOD: The real key to that particular question is the definition of "game fish."

MR. SLOAN: No, I think it's just a way to sell his encyclopedia, because he knows that it's all in his book. That's what I'm getting at.

MR. HEYWOOD: Oh, there's nothing wrong with plugging one's book.

MR. SLOAN: That's right. But if you tell me there's a code in the book, by God, I'll read it again and again. I'll find that code one day.

MR. HEYWOOD: I guarantee you it's impossible to find.

MR. SLOAN: Well, you know, Joe, we'll have to leave it with that challenge. Thanks a million for coming on.

MR. HEYWOOD: My pleasure.

ROBERT LINSENMAN

on Streamer Fishing

AN INTERVIEW WITH THE AUTHOR OF *MODERN STREAMERS FOR TROPHY TROUT* ON HIS NEW, AGGRESSIVE APPROACH TO STREAMER FISHING FOR BIG TROUT, HIS FAVORITE STREAMER PATTERNS, AND SOME RECOMMENDED WATERS FOR THE SERIOUS STREAMER FISHERMAN.

*R*obert Linsenman claims to wear three hats: fly-fishing guide, author/ lecturer, and literary agent. Actually, he wears four, as is evident from the following interview: Bob is an inventor. By his own admission, he fishes two hundred days each year, sixty to seventy of those as a guide for trout and steelhead on the Au Sable River in Michigan's Lower Peninsula. It would take someone who has extensive experience studying fish, especially large browns, steelheads, and rainbows, to have invented a new method of streamer fishing. Bob has that experience, and his new approach to streamer fishing has therefore undergone extensive hands-on testing. When he's not after his real love—trout and salmon—Bob also likes to fish saltwater for tarpon, bonefish, striped bass, and bluefish.

In the following interview, Bob describes his new methods of fishing streamers— techniques that have led many anglers to rethink their entire approach toward streamer fishing. After reading his book, MODERN STREAMERS FOR TROPHY TROUT, *many anglers make a streamer their fly of first choice, not their fly of last resort.*

Immediately after graduating from Oakland University in 1965, Bob spent eight years in the book-publishing industry and another ten as a computer software executive before becoming a literary agent in 1983, a profession he continues to practice. Bob has been an avid fly fisherman since age ten and has fished extensively throughout North America, but he has always found a strong pull to the trout streams of Michigan. Bob's articles and stories have been published in FLY FISHERMAN, AMERICAN ANGLER, WILD STEELHEAD & SALMON, SPRING CREEK JOURNAL, FLY FISHER, and MIDWEST FLYFISHING magazines. In addition to the aforementioned MODERN STREAMERS FOR TROPHY TROUT, Bob's other book titles include MICHIGAN TROUT STREAMS: A FLY ANGLER'S GUIDE, GREAT LAKES STEELHEAD: A GUIDED TOUR FOR FLY ANGLERS, THE AU SABLE RIVER, and many others.

In addition to fishing, guiding, and writing, Bob is an avid upland bird hunter as well as a staunch conservationist who releases all of his and his clients' catches.

MR. SLOAN: Today, we're going to talk about big trout—I mean *whoppers*. We'll be talking about consistently catching trout of twenty inches or more in streams and rivers that you might fish. Our discussion will start with a new book called MODERN STREAMERS FOR TROPHY TROUT, written by Bob Linsenman and Kelly Galloup. I'd like to welcome Bob to the show.

MR. LINSENMAN: Thanks, Steve. It's a pleasure to be here.

MR. SLOAN: Bob, I'll have you know that I did a little trout fishing yesterday. I'm up here in the Catskills right now for the Hall of Fame induction at the Catskill Fly Fishing Center and Museum.

MR. LINSENMAN: Wonderful.

MR. SLOAN: And we took in some of your friends last night—Vince Marinaro, Charlie Fox, George Harvey, and Joan Wulff.

MR. LINSENMAN: Those are some pretty prominent people who contributed a great deal to the sport.

MR. SLOAN: They certainly did. Today, I'm going to go fish the Delaware, the big Delaware, from a guide boat. So I'll be using some of your techniques.

MR. LINSENMAN: I hope they work for you, Steve.

MR. SLOAN: I hope so, too. I really enjoyed your book, MODERN STREAMERS

FOR TROPHY TROUT. It made me wonder where you gained your experience. Where *do* you fish?

MR. LINSENMAN: Well, I fly fish pretty much throughout North America, Steve, but my home rivers are in the northern Lower Peninsula of Michigan. I fish Michigan's Manistee and Au Sable rivers most prominently.

MR. SLOAN: What kind of streams are they?

MR. LINSENMAN: They're both classic ground-spring rivers—highly productive in terms of growth rates, and very fertile in terms of food forms. Just to give you a feeling for the size of these rivers, when we fish them they flow at a rate of anywhere from about a thousand to fifteen hundred cubic feet per second. So they're sizeable, but they're not large in terms of rivers like the Delaware, for example, or some of the western rivers.

MR. SLOAN: Bob, what was the old way of fishing these rivers with streamers?

MR. LINSENMAN: Well, typically what I did, and I think what most people have done, is treat streamer fishing as an afterthought. Most of us go out to fish a given hatch. We focus on fishing the hatches of the Hendricksons, the caddises, the March browns, or the green drakes. We've only reached for a streamer, whether it was a Woolly Bugger or a Mickey Finn or a Muddler, to pass the time when fish weren't rising to the hatch. The way we fished streamers was a very passive approach. Basically, we cast the fly across the stream, or across and slightly downstream, and let it swing. I remember when I was a kid and was first reading about streamers—that's pretty much how we were told to do it.

MR. SLOAN: I think that was prevalent advice in Joe Bates's book, STREAMER FLY FISHING IN FRESH AND SALT WATER, and Joe Brooks's book, THE COMPLETE BOOK OF FLY FISHING, too, wasn't it?

MR. LINSENMAN: Yes, it was. But we've come to find out over the past few years that the fish just don't respond that well to those techniques—particularly the really big fish that are fairly sophisticated and critical about how bait and forage fish move and swim. It wasn't until one day when I was fishing with Kelly Galloup and saw him working streamers very aggressively that I understood there was an alternative. Watching how Kelly fished streamers was just an eye-opener for me. I later teamed up with him to write MODERN STREAMERS FOR TROPHY TROUT.

MR. SLOAN: He was fishing on a very short leader, too. About four feet, right?

MR. LINSENMAN: That's right. We typically fish with leaders that are about four feet long—three and a half to four and a half feet is the range. We also use full-sinking lines. The full-sinking line is used not so much to get the fly down to great depth but rather to control the fly so that it swims at the same depth in the water column all the way through the retrieve. You can manipulate and control the depth by the speed of the retrieve.

MR. SLOAN: Why do you think that short a leader helps you so much?

MR. LINSENMAN: I think it helps for a couple of reasons. First, when the fish are really aggressive and they're moving after a big fly that appears to be acting naturally, they don't see the leader at all. They don't see it because they're reacting to a bulky fly that's moving quickly. But if you're drifting a nymph or floating a dry fly, it's moving naturally with the current, and there's no movement of the fly itself. Therefore, the fish has a considerable amount of time to see whether there's something large attached to that fly—and to take notice of a leader that's too big or too thick.

MR. SLOAN: To notice something unnatural to him.

MR. LINSENMAN: Exactly. So while a short, heavy leader would unnaturally affect the drift of a dry fly or a nymph, it does not impact the presentation of a big streamer. But the most important thing we found is that our presentation had to be very aggressive and high energy when we fish these streamers.

MR. SLOAN: You describe it as an "active hunt."

MR. LINSENMAN: That's right; it's a high-energy way of fishing. I guide a bit, as does Kelly, and we found that some of our repeat customers who are serious about catching big trout actually go into training for about two weeks before they come up so that they don't wear out. But the essence of it, Steve, is a cast across to the bank if you're fishing from a boat, or to the center of the river if you're wading. We want to swim that fly in, say, fourteen- to eighteen-inch pulses or jerks, back to where it's in a perpendicular position to the water flow. You're working with a fourteen- to eighteen-inch twitch, basically. The fly jumps that distance and then pauses. When it pauses, it looks like it's wounded and can't quite get away. That's when it's time for another fourteen- to eighteen-inch jerk.

The key to succeeding with this kind of presentation is to move the fly with the rod tip. We pulse the streamer with a sweep of the rod tip, then we strip with our empty hand to take up the slack, and then we repeat the process.

MR. SLOAN: I've done that a lot in saltwater fishing but not much in freshwater. I haven't tried it, but it sounds good.

MR. LINSENMAN: Well, it really does work. I've seen a lot of people try to effect that motion with a straight strip—strip, strip, strip—but without moving the fly with the rod tip. But in flowing water, like in a river current, it just doesn't work as well when you try to do that. The most important thing is to move that fly with the rod tip—with a pause, then with another move with the rod tip, and then again with a pause. This movement makes your streamer look like a bait fish trying to escape: it swims fourteen to eighteen inches and stops, as if to say, "Oh, oh, something's wrong. I don't feel good." It then kind of flutters and swoons, and that's very often when the big fish will hit it.

MR. SLOAN: Now, you're talking fourteen- to eighteen-inch sweeps. In the world of trout-fly retrieves, that's a lot. That's a big pulse.

MR. LINSENMAN: It's a big pulse; you're darn right. But remember that we're fishing flies that are two and a half to four and a half inches long. And we're trying to mimic the action of a sizeable injured bait fish, whether it's a sculpin or a dace or a shiner. We want to give the impression that the cripple has wandered into the territory of a big fish, and it's really motoring trying to get out of there. And that short pause, which is effected in essence by stripping and gathering up the slack, makes the bait fish look like it's wounded.

MR. SLOAN: Interesting.

MR. LINSENMAN: What this retrieval process does, Steve, is trigger one of two responses from your quarry. If the fish is hungry, all is well and good because it's going to come after it as its next meal. If it's not hungry, this presentation tends to make the fish react in an aggressive, territorial way. So we're appealing to two basic instincts here. It works extremely well either way.

MR. SLOAN: What I find most interesting here is that it's all very logical. But I'm getting a vision now of making eighteen-inch pulses all day long while I'm floating or wading a river. I'm going to be pretty tired at the end of the day. So perhaps your suggestion of training is pertinent. Of course, you'll forget you're getting tired if you nail one of those lunker trout every now and then.

MR. LINSENMAN: That's for sure.

MR. SLOAN: Are there any specific exercises you recommend for training?

MR. LINSENMAN: Those little hand-grip exercisers are very good. So is squeezing a tennis ball. In fact, when I have a day off, quite often I'll go fishing with a buddy who's a guide and we'll take turns fishing just so we can keep the fatigue to a minimum.

MR. SLOAN: Bob, I'd like to talk for a moment about the behavior of these large trout. You said that a big fish can go anywhere he wants, anytime he wants.

MR. LINSENMAN: Absolutely: they're the alpha predators in their ecosystem. Particularly under clear water, big trout will be sensitive to wading anglers and boats, and maybe they'll be on the lookout for an eagle or an otter. But other than these threats, they're not afraid of anything. We've caught really big fish on bright, sunny Saturday afternoons in shallow water, with recreational canoers all over the place. The fact is, if you only fish where you think big fish ought to be, you're missing a beat. You need to cover as much water as you possibly can.

MR. SLOAN: A lot of that is what I call "river reading" or "stream reading." You've got to approximate where you think one of these big fish might lie and then go to work. But you seem to say that they're in spots that you wouldn't even believe they'd be in.

MR. LINSENMAN: That's true. Particularly at certain times of the day.

Also, there's no such thing as a bad cast.

MR. SLOAN: Really?

MR. LINSENMAN: Absolutely. I believe that if a cast hits the water, fish it.

MR. SLOAN: You make me feel a hell of a lot better this morning. So, even if your cast smashes down and flops, just keep stripping?

MR. LINSENMAN: Keep stripping. Keep pulsing your streamer with the rod tip, and you'll be pleasantly surprised.

But you're quite right on your other point about reading a stream: there are preferred lies and holes and types of water where big fish are more likely to be found. But, as I started to say, most people believe the best time for fishing is at night. Most people think that big trout, particularly big brown trout, are most active at night. Yet most studies that we've done here in the State of Michigan and through the universities indicate that the fish move and are more active at dusk and dawn than they are at night. Remember that they can be just anywhere.

MR. SLOAN: That's interesting because, as you know, fishermen like Joe Humphreys and George Harvey are great proponents of night fishing for big fish.

MR. LINSENMAN: Yes, but what I'm describing is a little different.

MR. SLOAN: You seem to describe a very good life for one of these big fish. He's off the current in a spot that allows him to look and rest, and if he sees something coming down, he can dart out and nail it.

MR. LINSENMAN: That's right.

MR. SLOAN: So, you're talking about good cover. For example, the spot behind a rock or a log would be a good one because it cuts the flow of the current down.

MR. LINSENMAN: That's true. We've gotten pretty sophisticated about streamer fishing as we've been applying it more and more over the years. Your point about good cover is most true in high-gradient streams—those streams with a severe hydraulic gradient, where the current is fast. But if you have a gently flowing river with a very moderate current, rocks—particularly rocks—are much less important in terms of a current break than they would be, say, in the Delaware in New York or on the Madison River out in Montana.

What we found is that the place most preferred by big fish, the most consistent place to find them, is at a depth change where a gravel bar drops off into a deeper riffle. So we look for color changes where the light sand of the shallow water shows through and then drops off to, say, a darker blue or gray. We also look for shelves. These are the places where we consistently find most of the big fish.

MR. SLOAN: Interesting. That is fascinating.

Tell me, Bob, what's the typical streamer-fishing tackle like now? This is a new way of fishing, using short leaders and actively hunting for huge fish. Tell us a little about the equipment you use.

MR. LINSENMAN: Most people come under-gunned. I carry five streamer rods strung up on my car all the time. I like a nine-foot six-weight rod with a pretty stiff action. I guess in today's nomenclature, Steve, they'd be called moderately fast actions. I use a full-sinking weight-forward line. I prefer Scientific Anglers' lines, but all the lines are good, Cortland and the others. I use a single-action disk-drag reel with quite a bit of backing. On this last point, most people will repeat the conventional wisdom—which is that brown trout don't run and take much line so you don't really need backing. Let me tell you that the conventional wisdom is dead wrong on this point. It's just malarkey that you don't need backing line when you're streamer fishing for browns.

MR. SLOAN: I'm glad you've debunked that myth for us.

MR. LINSENMAN: It's absolutely false. There are plenty of old wives' tales about fly fishing that need to be debunked, and that's one of the biggest ones. We've hit fish close to thirty inches—we're talking ten or twelve pounds, Steve—that just burn line off the reel like a steelhead. You have no chance of landing a fish like that without the right equipment. The six-weight rod allows you to cast pretty much all day without too much fatigue. And it also gives you enough power to lift and turn a really good fish so that you can land it, resuscitate it, and release it before it's totally exhausted and while it's still got a good chance for survival.

MR. SLOAN: You mentioned disk reels a moment ago. Now, this is different from a reel that has just the click pawl to serve as a drag?

MR. LINSENMAN: Well, the reel still has a disk drag. I mean, a lot of them do have an outgoing click drag, just so that you can hear it. But I find it easier and more consistently helpful to have my clients fish a disk-drag reel because I can set the drag at a proper tension and then not worry about it. I mean, a highly skilled angler can certainly use just a click-and-pawl drag reel, like the old Hardy Perfects and Hardy Lightweights, and do the job. But most people aren't that skilled, and since a fish like the ones we're seeking will be a fish of a lifetime, I want to load up the odds in my client's favor as much as I can. So a properly set disk-drag reel is what I try to put in their hands.

MR. SLOAN: Bob, I love streamer fishing. I stumbled across an upstream method where I could fish very light leaders out in Henryville, Pennsylvania. As you know, that area is fished a lot. We've got some big fish up there, but it's hard to come up with presentations that the fish haven't already seen. One technique I tried was that, as the streamer came downstream and swung deeper in the water column, I moved my hand right to left and got the head of it to move, like a minnow that was knocked goofy. I had some good success with that technique.

MR. LINSENMAN: Well, you know, another reason you had good success with that retrieve is that the fly was swimming with its head pointed downstream.

MR. SLOAN: Right.

MR. LINSENMAN: Most people don't realize how significant that downstream head direction is. They're jerking streamers upstream against the current, but a fleeing bait fish *never* swims upstream. Bait fish swim across stream or they swim downstream, the paths of least resistance. A big twenty-five-inch brown trout knows that—particularly in heavily fished waters. If the fly is acting strangely, they're going to say, "No thanks; I don't think so." It's like if you or I sat down for a pork chop dinner, and our pork chops crawled off our plates. We'd say, "I don't think I'll eat that one."

MR. SLOAN: Right. That's true. And if a fish is wobbly or hit or wounded, it's going to go downstream, not upstream.

MR. LINSENMAN: Absolutely true.

MR. SLOAN: I mean, it may go two feet up, but eventually it's going to be heading downstream.

MR. LINSENMAN: Right. The fish knows it can't fight the current and flee at the same time.

MR. SLOAN: Exactly. So this method takes advantage of that theory.

Bob, Joe Heywood was on this show a couple of weeks ago *(See "Joseph Heywood on* THE SNOWFLY" *on page 93)*. He was talking about his new novel, THE SNOWFLY, which we love.

MR. LINSENMAN: It's a great book.

MR. SLOAN: I really feel there'll be an explosion of trout fishing once people start reading it, especially if it's made into a movie. It would make a great movie, don't you think?

MR. LINSENMAN: Yes, it would. Let me share a little story about Joe.

Joe is a friend and a client of mine, and we fish together five or six, maybe seven, days at different times each year. Two weeks ago, Joe and his good friend Godfrey Grant were up to fish with me, and they'd booked a day specifically for streamers. We've had drought conditions here, and for several days in advance of his arrival it had been bright and sunny. I told Joe, "Pray for rain. Pray for clouds. If we get clouds, we'll do real well." The conditions, I have to admit, were very good because we had clouds and drizzle, it was a dark day, and a lot of people decided not to fish. I think we were one of only two boats on the river. But it was fabulous fishing. Joe is a guy who has been fly fishing for seven or eight years, I'd say, and he has a moderate to high-moderate level of skill. But on this day, everything worked. We caught sixteen fish over eighteen inches.

MR. SLOAN: *Sixteen trout over eighteen inches.*

MR. LINSENMAN: That's right. But wait until you hear the rest. Five of those fish, Steve, *were over twenty-three inches.* The biggest fish was twenty-five and a half inches, and Godfrey caught that. We lost three other fish that we just could not control, and each of these was bigger than Godfrey's twenty-five-inch fish. It was honestly one of the very best days I've ever had guiding.

MR. SLOAN: Here's the good news, folks: all of these fish were released.

MR. LINSENMAN: Oh, absolutely. Joe took some pictures, and I'm sure he would be happy to send you some.

MR. SLOAN: I'll bet he would, after a day like that.

Bob, I'd like to tap your brain a little bit further for the benefit of our listeners. I'm going to name some of the natural foods trout eat, and you tell me what fly you would use to imitate it. Okay?

MR. LINSENMAN: Sure.

MR. SLOAN: For example, how about a dace, the black-striped dace?

MR. LINSENMAN: Well, there are several dace patterns that are workable. We typically use some bicolors, like the Black and White, and some tricolor patterns. The dace is not a real big bait fish.

MR. SLOAN: So how big a fly are we talking about? Three, four inches?

MR. LINSENMAN: About three inches.

MR. SLOAN: Okay. And what kind of material is it made of?

MR. LINSENMAN: Usually hair. Bucktail. We'll layer it. We call it a Tricolored Bucktail. We'll use black, white, bluish-green, or other light colors like that.

MR. SLOAN: All right, now how about a sculpin?

MR. LINSENMAN: Sculpin are one of the most prevalent food forms in our rivers here in Michigan and, in fact, all across the country. You just about can't go wrong if you fish a sculpin pattern.

MR. SLOAN: Is this fish a high-protein food for trout?

MR. LINSENMAN: Oh, it is; it really is. The fish actually go and hunt them, the big fish do. I have two favorite modern patterns for sculpin. One of them is called the Zoo Cougar, and the other one is called the Woolly Sculpin. They're both featured in the book; there are color photographs of them. They each provide a lot of built-in action and a lot of wobble. And when you pause after the strip—we talked about that fourteen- to eighteen-inch pulse and then the pause—the fly actually swoons and quivers like it's really hurt. They're almost impossible to fish incorrectly. So, as a guide, that's one of the reasons I really like them.

MR. SLOAN: Well, the interesting part, too, is that sculpins usually live under rocks, so if one is out in the open, boy, he's fair game.

MR. LINSENMAN: He sure is.

MR. SLOAN: Okay, what about your favorite fly to imitate crayfish?

MR. LINSENMAN: Yes, crayfish; they're another very popular food form that we find in a wide variety of waters. Big trout just love crayfish. Take the Woolly Bugger, for example. A lot of people have said, "Well, gee, what does a Woolly Bugger look like? A leech, a stone fly, a nymph?" Well one of the things it resembles most closely if it's tied in the right color—say, a brown or an olive—is a small crayfish. And the Woolly Bugger is impressionistic, so it's a good fly to use for crayfish patterns.

Another good crayfish pattern is called the Trick or Treat, which is a little more complicated to tie. It has rubber legs and is fairly busy looking, but the fish really seem to like it. Another fly, which is fairly easy to tie, is called the Madonna.

MR. SLOAN: And these are all crayfish imitations, right?

MR. LINSENMAN: That's right.

MR. SLOAN: Well, you can find all these patterns at the back of Bob's book, MODERN STREAMERS FOR TROPHY TROUT, if you like to tie flies.

Now Bob, we've been talking about the natural foods that are imitated by flies. I'd like to turn to the places where these flies are going to be fished. What are some of the best streamer waters you've fished? Where would you say someone who was interested in streamer fishing might start? Maybe you could describe a couple of your favorite streamer-fishing rivers; you mentioned a few in your book. What would you say would be the best waters?

MR. LINSENMAN: From east to west? You want me to list them that way?

MR. SLOAN: Sure.

MR. LINSENMAN: Well, certainly the Delaware.

MR. SLOAN: Really?

MR. LINSENMAN: Oh yes. The Delaware would be right up there.

MR. SLOAN: I'm going to be there in about an hour.

MR. LINSENMAN: Well, good for you. Take along some sculpin patterns, and fish them in the way that we've been discussing here. I think you'll be pleasantly surprised.

MR. SLOAN: Okay.

MR. LINSENMAN: I've done very well on the Delaware. Years ago, I used to live in Connecticut, I worked in New York City, and I fished the Beaverkill a lot. Classic places like Barnhart's Pool, areas that you think of as purely dry-fly water, can give you a real surprise if you go into them and fish streamers the right way. Down at the Acid Factory, still in the no-kill water there on the Beaverkill, streamers also work very well.

Moving westward, we'll just jump over to my home waters. I think the Au Sable and the Manistee are far and away the best rivers in the upper Great Lakes area. Moving westward, I'd include the Big Horn. There's a river in Montana called the Stillwater, which is not fished nearly as heavily as some other Montana rivers, in which streamers work extremely well. But probably my favorite Western river is the Madison. A stretch that I really enjoy fishing on the Madison is right below the Madison Dam in the town of Ennis, in the upper Bear Trap Canyon.

That's just a brief overview of some of my favorites.

MR. SLOAN: And what about the Nipigon?

MR. LINSENMAN: Yes, the Nipigon is on the north shore of Lake Superior. It's a Canadian river, flowing in from Lake Nipigon in northern Ontario. The Nipigon is an incredible body of water; it's vodka clear and flows at about fifteen thousand cubic feet per second. You could drop the Delaware, the Beaverkill, the Au Sable, and the Manistee into it and never find them again.

MR. SLOAN: Really?

MR. LINSENMAN: It's a huge river, and it holds huge, huge brook trout, lake trout, and rainbow trout.

MR. SLOAN: What do you mean by "huge" brook trout? A couple of pounds?

MR. LINSENMAN: No. I'm talking six, seven pounds.

MR. SLOAN: Wow!

MR. LINSENMAN: In fact, a world-record brook trout—fourteen pounds—was caught in the Nipigon River. I've fished it four or five times, and I think the *smallest* brook trout I ever caught up there was about fourteen inches. An average Nipigon brook trout is nineteen or twenty inches long, and they're incredibly thick and heavy.

MR. SLOAN: That's fabulous. And that fishery is as viable today as it ever was?

MR. LINSENMAN: Oh, absolutely. In fact, I would highly recommend that your listeners who might be interested in fishing the Nipigon contact a young guide up there named Scott Smith. He's a police officer in the Thunder Bay Police Department in Ontario, and he is a very knowledgeable guide on the Nipigon and the surrounding waters up there.

MR. SLOAN: Fabulous. Now, how do you get there?

MR. LINSENMAN: From where I live, Steve, in northern Michigan, I drive up to Sault Ste. Marie, Ontario, which is just about a two-and-a-half-hour drive for me. Then, I fly from Sault Ste. Marie to Thunder Bay, Ontario. The flight costs about a hundred dollars Canadian, which is only about sixty dollars American, so it's hardly worth the driving. But if you do decide to drive it, you're in for a treat. If you drive the Trans-Canada Highway, Route 17, along the north shore of Lake Superior, it is probably one of the top two scenic drives in all of North America. It's spectacular. You're up on big hills and cliffs overlooking Lake Superior, with islands and waterfalls. It's just spectacular.

MR. SLOAN: Well, that sounds like a fabulous tip.

Meanwhile, we'll keep stripping fourteen to eighteen inches. We've got a new way of fishing streamers. Thanks a million for coming on the show and telling us about it.

MR. LINSENMAN: It's my pleasure, Steve. Have good fun up on the Delaware later today.

MR. SLOAN: You bet. I'll let you know how we do.

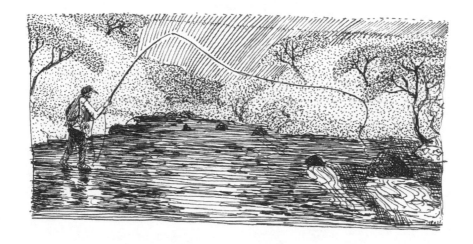

JOSEPH HUMPHREYS
on Nymph Fishing

AN INTERVIEW WITH JOE HUMPHREYS, MENTOR TO THOUSANDS
OF FLY ANGLERS AND A PUPIL OF GEORGE HARVEY, THE
CREATOR OF THE FIRST ACCREDITED COLLEGE CURRICULUM IN
FLY FISHING, AT PENNSYLVANIA STATE UNIVERSITY.

*I f you had to name the top ten trout fishermen of all time, certainly the name Joe
Humphreys would be among them. In his landmark book, JOE HUMPHREYS'
TROUT TACTICS, Humphreys mentions the name of his mentor George Harvey no
fewer than nineteen times. This is no accident because Harvey himself belongs near the
top of the aforementioned top-ten list. The story of Harvey and Humphreys fishing
together is the story of a master and his pupil, sharing and learning together, united by
the first accredited college classes ever taught for fly tying and fly fishing. Harvey
taught, Humphreys learned, and then Dan Shields, author of PENN'S CREEK, and
Greg Hoover, author of GREAT HATCHES, GREAT RIVERS, joined Humphreys as
acolytes of Harvey and each other.*

*Since 1934, when the first Harvey class began at Penn State University, hundreds
of men and women have taken up the art of fly fishing under Harvey's tutelage,
including Humphreys. The resulting Penn State fly-fishing order has thus grown over*

the years, and its most ardent fly-fishing missionaries—Harvey, Humphreys, Shields, and Hoover—have proselytized us all. They have shared their lives and thereby their fishing experiences with us in their simple, direct, and honest way. They themselves live simply, directly, and honestly, and we who have learned from them are the beneficiaries of their knowledge.

When Humphreys sat down to talk with Sloan, he looked back fondly on his career as an educator in the art of angling, touching on everything from how water temperature and time of day influence fish activity, to the details of his techniques for fishing nymphs deeply, to George Harvey's formulas for leader construction.

MR. SLOAN: I thought that we would open this year's trout season by introducing you to one of the really great trout fishermen in the United States. He is a fellow who not only fishes but teaches fishing at Penn State University in State College, Pennsylvania. He is a disciple of the great George Harvey. We are going to learn something this morning about why trout take a fly and what you should do to get ready for the trout season.

Today, around the New York area, it's going to be about fifty to fifty-five degrees and probably a little cooler in the suburbs—a kind of ideal temperature for opening day of trout season. Usually when I go out at this time of the year, it's around twenty-eight degrees and both the water and I are near freezing.

MR. HUMPHREYS: Good morning, Steve.

MR. SLOAN: Good morning, Joe. I first read your book, JOE HUMPHREYS' TROUT TACTICS, a few years ago, and then I just read it again recently. It was just as good this time as the first time.

MR. HUMPHREYS: Good. It did not change, did it? You know, I revised it in 1993.

MR. SLOAN: No, the plot did not change. Here we are, on the first of April, and it is going to be chilly around here. In reading your book, one of the first things that struck me was something my mother would say: "You do not look very good. You've got a fever and a chill. Go take your temperature."

MR. HUMPHREYS: Exactly.

MR. SLOAN: Tell us about your stream temperature theory.

MR. HUMPHREYS: A trout's life revolves around temperature. Trout move and feed according to the temperature. They migrate according to temperature, and they feed with relative changes in temperature. An ideal water temperature for a trout might be sixty to sixty-one degrees.

The other factor relative to temperature is called "conditioning." In the winter, spring, or fall, trout can condition and feed in temperatures just above freezing. Their metabolism slows down, but they still feed. When water temperature first drops or rises suddenly—say, five degrees or more—fishing really can shut off with a drop or turn on with a rise. Even stocked trout can back off their feeding with a temperature drop. Once they are caught up in that sudden temperature drop—for instance, the water temperature is fifty-five degrees one day and drops overnight to forty-eight to fifty—trout will really get turned off. But once those new temperatures hold steady for a period of time, then they can get conditioned, or acclimate and become active and start feeding again. Your tactics might have to change a little bit to compensate for these temperature changes. You might have to slow down your drifts, and, if you're nymphing, slow it down even more and really work the bottom for them.

MR. SLOAN: So the scenario goes something like this: you get to your stream at daybreak, and you really should carry a thermometer with you...

MR. HUMPHREYS: You bet.

MR. SLOAN: ...Now, say the sun is low and the sky overcast; it's a very chilly day, and the water temperature is forty-eight. If you don't wish to really work for your trout, you recommend just biding your time until the water warms up, say around eleven or twelve o'clock, right? In your book, you have a clock illustration that shows how rapidly the water will warm up once the sun hits it.

MR. HUMPHREYS: Surely it does. A temperature rise of just a few degrees will start the fish feeding. But don't forget that this holds true more so with native fish than with stocked ones. Stocked fish can react a little bit differently; they were fed every day by hand or by machine at the hatchery, so when they are put in a stream, they can become active in a hurry. They are still looking for food pellets; they have been put in this stream, which is completely foreign to them, and now they're looking for their regular diet of food pellets. For these newly stocked trout, it's not a bad idea to fish with wet flies. Those hungry stocked fish often come right up through the water column for wet flies while your natives will not and are remaining down on the bottom. But remember, stocked trout condition themselves to the food chain rapidly, which can have a big impact on bottom feeding. And, of course, stocked trout can rapidly react to temperature changes just like natives.

MR. SLOAN: I guess one should check with the local conservation agency in whatever state you're in to find out when the fish were stocked. I have observed over the years that many anglers just like to get out opening day to do a little "subsistence" fishing. They like to take a few trout home, and then when things settle down, the serious anglers come in after the crowds have dissipated to really work on the trout with a fly and be creative with their equipment and tackle.

MR. HUMPHREYS: Yes, the rush is usually over after the first couple of weeks, and it's then time to settle down and use your tactics and go after bigger trout.

MR. SLOAN: Now, what about the reverse scenario of what we were just talking about regarding temperature? For example, if you have a hot, sultry day in June and July, you point out in the book, you would like to fish early in the morning, when the sun has not yet had a chance to warm the water. The water then is a little cooler, instead of in the middle of the day when it is going to warm up again.

MR. HUMPHREYS: This is very true. But remember, when the water temperature reaches seventy degrees or more and holds at that temperature for four to seven hours, trout will migrate to colder waters. They've got to have oxygen, and colder water is where they'll find it.

MR. SLOAN: The evening is productive, too. Now, Joe, you describe in your book your experiences with night trout fishing.

MR. HUMPHREYS: Yes, I do.

MR. SLOAN: I wonder if you could give us some ideas about night fishing, a couple of rules for success, some tips on what you should wear and what to look for. I would assume that you'd only want to night-fish a stretch of water that you're familiar with, so you don't stumble all over the place.

MR. HUMPHREYS: That's the big thing; safety can't be stressed enough. One of the important tactics is that you really know your water and where the big fish will hold in pools. Some pools seem to almost be devoid of life, but don't be discouraged by this when you encounter it. It is often a good sign that you might have a monster in there that is pushing everything out.

MR. SLOAN: So in other words, if you come to a pool and you know it looks fishy but you cannot raise anything, chances are good that something else is probably in there, eating?

MR. HUMPHREYS: That's often true. You've probably got a heavyweight in there that has taken over.

MR. SLOAN: So when the sun goes down, you would go revisit that pool? Is that the idea?

MR. HUMPHREYS: That's exactly the idea.

Here's another tip: when fishing at night, I fish with big wet flies and fish slowly. You do not want to be in a hurry at night because it takes time to connect with the trout. Although trout have excellent vision, their feeding window of opportunity is not that great at night. Their viewing window is smaller. You have to really slow your presentation down and take your time. One tactic is to fish big wet flies and fish them down and across.

You can also nymph at night. Most anglers do not realize that you can use nymphs at night for trout, with their small window and good visibility. I have picked up fish in pitch darkness. I have picked up fish at night on number 12 and number 14 nymphs.

MR. SLOAN: Wow.

MR. HUMPHREYS: Most people just do not believe or understand that fish can be caught at night, but it does work that way. Night fishing is particularly effective when you have hatching activity. You have a lot of fish moving into feeding stations in the darkness. Once it gets really dark, many anglers go home because they cannot see well and lots of times they feel that the fishing has really slacked off because the surface activity has slowed. But those fish are still really nymphing on the bottom. This can be one of your best times.

MR. SLOAN: Joe, on the back dust jacket of your book, there is a picture of a huge brown trout. You are kneeling, and you're holding this trout in your arms. How big was that fish?

MR. HUMPHREYS: That is still Pennsylvania's record trout caught on a fly; it was sixteen pounds, a thirty-four-inch fish.

MR. SLOAN: Oh, my goodness.

MR. HUMPHREYS: That fish was taken at night, on a big wet fly. When I am after a trophy fish, I use 1/0- and 2/0-size wet flies because these big fish do not like to expend a lot of energy when they feed. They may trap a ten-inch sucker, knock off another nine-inch fish, and then have three sizable crayfish for an evening's meal. They want a high-caloric mouthful, so that's why I go after them with a large wet fly.

MR. SLOAN: You have fished in streams near Penn's Creek, Spruce Creek, and a lot of others down around State College. I was most intrigued by the notion that you "stake out" a really large fish. In other words, you might see a large trout coming off an early-morning feeding and then say, "Okay, I'll take the lay of the land, and then I'll come back at night and see what I can do." Is that somewhat of the process?

MR. HUMPHREYS: That is the process I use. But I also ought to mention that it is possible to encounter trophy fish unexpectedly. For instance, if you are working a piece of water at night and you hear an explosion of water, you know a big fish is there. When fishing the hatches into darkness and even in pitch darkness, you may hear a big fish feeding; this is another good way to locate them. The record fish, the sixteen-pounder we were just discussing, I stalked for three years before I finally took him. It was difficult each time because he lived in a large pool. That pool presented a lot of water to cover, and you may have to go down through such a pool several times in one evening to even raise a fish. Not only that, but when a fish like that feeds in a pool, it can feed maybe at the tail, or he may come up into the riffles to feed, to find a sculpin, crayfish, suckers, dace, or a mouse. Remember that crayfish and sculpin are nocturnal.

MR. SLOAN: Sure.

MR. HUMPHREYS: So there are two places to look. You never know when a fish like that is going to feed. He may feed for a half an hour at 10:00 P.M. and be done for not only that evening but a couple of days. Big trout fishing is a game of patience; you have got to stay with it.

MR. SLOAN: Absolutely. Well, that was a heck of a fish, a sixteen-pound brown trout out of a stream, on a fly. How old would you say a fish like that was?

MR. HUMPHREYS: Some scientists sampled that fish's scales, which they can read like the rings on a tree. They figured that fish was about eleven years old— quite a bit of longevity in today's heavily fished streams. That fish really did dodge the bullet, and he got big because he was strictly a night feeder.

MR. SLOAN: Joe, you have made some professional videotapes. What are the titles of these videotapes?

MR. HUMPHREYS: I've made two: "A Casting Approach to Nymphing Tactics" and "A Casting Approach to Dry Fly Tactics in Tight Brush."

MR. SLOAN: Joe, in the book you describe a "tuck cast" for nymph fishing and presentation. Could you explain this casting method a little bit? Maybe you could explain how you tuck cast and why you think it is so much more effective.

MR. HUMPHREYS: Well, when you are nymphing, Steve, what you want to do is get the nymph down to the trout as quickly as you possibly can. In using the tuck cast, you stop the rod directly overhead during your back cast, and you have to wait until you feel the pull of the weighted nymph as it transmits to the rod tip. Then you can make a forward cast while gripping the rod handle with just a squeeze and your thumb forward. Your casting stroke should be just a squeeze, and this takes the fly line over the rod tip and causes the fly to tuck and enter the water first. This makes the nymph drop deeper into the stream's pockets or runs. The nymph fly is therefore on the bottom sooner and with a better drift. You then will be fishing that run completely on the bottom for the entire length of the drift.

MR. SLOAN: That is the key to nymph fishing, correct?

MR. HUMPHREYS: That's it: to get it down there. I use split-shot weight adjustments on my nymph leaders. You can use weighted nymphs and perhaps additional weight on the leader. I do all this so I can have those nymphs productively down there as long and naturally as possible. When correctly presented, nymphs are just bobbing and bouncing along on the bottom in a natural manner, and you are giving those trout plenty of time to find them on the bottom.

MR. SLOAN: You really should feel the bottom now and then, right? Isn't it true that if you are not feeling the bottom occasionally, you are not doing it right?

MR. HUMPHREYS: That is true. It is just good common sense that you should keep adjusting your split-shot weights. If you are hanging up on the bottom too much, you have too much weight on. On the other hand, if the nymphs are coming back to you too fast, you do not have enough weight on. You have to stop and take the time to put split-shot on and off and to adjust the weight and work with it.

MR. SLOAN: How about mending line a little bit so you slow down the line if it is coming too fast?

MR. HUMPHREYS: I do not mend that much when I am working. Preferably, if I can, I like to work upstream and be in contact directly from rod tip to nymph throughout the drift. When you are on larger streams and it is too deep to wade in certain areas and in large pools, you may have to mend some line—yes, that is true.

MR. SLOAN: Joe, do you use this new clear monofilament fly line for fly fishing?

MR. HUMPHREYS: No, I use the line that Cortland has developed for me for use in real deep water; it is a line that is 0.022 inch in diameter. Cortland calls it the "deep nymph floating line." It is a very thin diameter, and you have the weight on the business end of the leader. The fact that the diameter is so small makes the line drop and sink very fast. It is like a telephone wire; you have real good communication and you can really feel the bottom in night fishing with this outfit. I have even felt big fish mouthing a big wet fly when using it.

MR. SLOAN: Really?

MR. HUMPHREYS: That's how sensitive it is.

MR. SLOAN: Cortland makes it?

MR. HUMPHREYS: Cortland makes it. It is a level line that has a fly line laser finish. It shoots very well. It is an excellent way to go after trout in real deep, heavy water.

MR. SLOAN: Of all trout-fishing methods, I happen to love nymph fishing best. I liked it best once I learned how to do it correctly. It really does catch trout—and bigger fish, too.

MR. HUMPHREYS: Right. And 90 percent of the time, trout are feeding on the bottom. So fishing the bottom is often your best bet.

MR. SLOAN: Your book is chock full of drawings that describe how to cast, tuck cast, and roll cast. I take a lot of friends of mine out to Henryville, Pennsylvania. Some of them are pretty good trout fisherman. I notice that even these pretty good ones seem to love to make many false casts, and it drives me crazy. I know all they need is one or two casts, if they are doing it right. You do not have to whip the fly line back and forth. In the first place, it spooks the fish. Secondly, you can make mistakes—slap the water or hang up in a tree, for example. Maybe they think it's good form. To me it is not. One back stroke and in is my philosophy. Keep fishing; you are much more productive that way.

MR. HUMPHREYS: You false cast, basically, to line up your distance and ensure accuracy. You may take a false cast or two when dry-fly fishing to dry the line and the fly out for a good float presentation. Steve, you are correct: basically one cast is all you need.

MR. SLOAN: I notice that you have some illustrations in the book showing a two-fly setup of a dropper fly and how to rig that up. It is a wonderful method and catches some large trout. Joe, on page sixty-five, you have a picture of the basic hand-and-twist retrieve. It is like a weaving figure eight that loops in your hand. A lot of people do not realize it, but this is the way to keep your fly line from going around your feet, your ankles, and other places that can hang it up. It is also a way to keep you in direct control of your line and fly.

MR. HUMPHREYS: That's true, Steve, and with the hand-and-twist retrieve you can stay in touch from your rod tip to the nymph, wet fly, or streamer. For instance, if you are fishing wet flies and they are swinging down and across the current, you can stay right with the movement of the fly with that hand-and-twist retrieve and lead your wet flies through the drift. Sometimes while nymphing in somewhat faster water, it is a little better to strip the line in with small loops and have the loops in your free hand. So it depends, again, on the speed of the water.

MR. SLOAN: The book has some illustrations showing that two-fly dropper method with split-shot weights. You point out that the closer the split-shot is to the two flies, the better it ensures that one fly will be closer to the bottom, where the presentation is going to be more productive for both. The farther away the split-shot is from the flies, the higher in the current the flies will ride.

MR. HUMPHREYS: That is true. Anglers may not realize that the farther you pull your weight back away from your nymph or wet fly, the higher the fly will rise—particularly if the nymph is not weighted itself. But you must remember that you do not want to put your weight too close to the nymph. The correct measure is about twelve to fourteen inches away from your bottom fly, which will make it drift naturally. If the weight or split-shot is too close, it may drag the flies unnaturally on the bottom, so I do not put my weight any closer than about ten inches to the fly to get the desired drift and presentation. I keep adjusting the weight placement according to the depth and speed of the water and where I want my fly to be in the water column.

MR. SLOAN: Joe, do you have any prejudice against the dropper for the second fly being tied to the shank of the hook of the first fly and separated from it by about twelve inches of 5X or 6X leader material?

MR. HUMPHREYS: That system originated in the West, and it is acceptable and it does work. I am just an old-fashioned man, and I like the dropper off the leader. Here's a tip: if you are going to use that dropper, the length of the dropper should be no more than four inches. Four inches is what I use. If it is five inches or longer, it wraps around the leader. If it is too short, say only two or three inches, then the trout cannot put it in its mouth. Trout do not grab nymphs or aquatic insects; they inhale them and have to suck things in.

The other point to remember about droppers is that when nymphing, you are fishing two different levels: you have a bottom nymph, and your second nymph can rise higher. With the weight adjusted on both nymphs, they will roll the bottom, and you are covering a lot more stream bottom using the two nymphs with adjusted split-shot weights. Your chances rise for attracting that fish in fast water.

MR. SLOAN: Joe, please explain this to me: when fishing wet flies, is it true that you want to keep the rod at a ninety-degree angle to the line as you go through the riffle?

MR. HUMPHREYS: That's right. What happens is if you drop that rod tip and the line is straight from the rod tip down to your flies, the trout cannot inhale the fly. They cannot pull your fly in because there is no give in that position. When you use the ninety-degree angle, there is enough slack in the line so that the trout can really pull that fly into its mouth. Basically, what they then are doing is hooking themselves.

MR. SLOAN: I discovered that by accident one day. I went through a pool, and I didn't get anything. So I just tied a streamer on, and instead of fishing downstream with it, I fished it directly upstream.

MR. HUMPHREYS: Exactly.

MR. SLOAN: Trout porpoised on that streamer immediately. This occurred in pools that I had struck out in when going down and across with my fly. I also discovered you could fish very light tippets, 4X or 5X, and get a hook-up there because there was no drag against the leader and fly line. Trout just suck it in.

MR. HUMPHREYS: That is exactly it.

MR. SLOAN: Joe, describe your leader system that you and George Harvey and a lot of your disciples in State College use. I know you take this leader system very seriously, and I believe it is all part of the presentation that you like to achieve.

MR. HUMPHREYS: Well, Steve, George Harvey's leader formula really changed my dry-fly fishing and catching approach. This is the way it works: the leader butt begins at 0.017 inch and sometimes even a smaller diameter, say 0.015. George then tapers the leader down every twenty inches, reducing each twenty-inch section by 0.002 inch, the length with the tippet being between nine and a half and ten feet overall. He graduates the leader diameter down from 0.015, to 0.013, to 0.011, and, finally, to 0.009 inch. Remember, we are talking about thousandths of an inch, and that final 0.009-inch-diameter length of leader is equal to 2X.

The final section before the tippet may be only eighteen inches long. Now, most of these lengths are twenty inches, and until he gets down to 2X—and that can be about a foot long—he will have another eighteen inches of 3X or 4X when he's using all soft monofilament and if he's using 5X for the tippet. A variation is if the fly is a number 12, a heavily dressed fly, or a number 10, in which case the tippet will not be as long—say, twenty-four to thirty inches—because of the air resistance of the fly. On a smaller fly, let's say you're working number 16s or 18s, your tippet lengths could be of 4X or 5X. And George does not go to 6X; he doesn't usually drop down less than 5X. But then it could be longer, say thirty-two to thirty-six inches for number 20 to number 26 flies. One example of this leader-tying method is illustrated in my book. *[Some examples of George Harvey's leader-tying formulas for nine- and ten-foot leaders have been reproduced by Mr. Humphreys in the following table—The Editors.]*

George Harvey's Leader Formulas							
Nine-Foot Leader							
Line Diameter in Inches (Weight)	0.015	0.013	0.011 (0X)	0.009 (2X)	0.008 (3X)	0.007 tippet (4X)	
Section Length in Inches	20	20	20	20	18	22 to 36, depending on the density of the fly	
Ten-Foot Leader							
Line Diameter in Inches (Weight)	0.015	0.013	0.011 (0X)	0.009 (2X)	0.008 (3X)	0.007 (4X)	0.006 tippet (5X)
Section Length in Inches	20	20	20	20	12	18	24 to 36, depending on the density of the fly

MR. SLOAN: Well, I notice that from 0.017 tapered to 0.009 really ends up giving you more than nine feet of stiff mono, and then from 0.008 to 4X to 5X is soft. However, I'm told that George Harvey recently has gone to using all soft monofilament.

MR. HUMPHREYS: Yes, the business end of the leader is soft.

MR. SLOAN: Now, that entails using two different types of leader material, right?

MR. HUMPHREYS: Yes, George is experimenting more and more. Sometimes soft mono will work very well on the butt section. I like stiff mono myself when I am fishing in the bush because it turns the fly over much faster in a very tight area. But still the last segment of the leader is soft material, yes.

MR. SLOAN: Joe, does it bother you that you have knots in the surface film a lot?

MR. HUMPHREYS: Knots in the leader? No, not at all.

MR. SLOAN: I don't know. Maybe it is psychological, but it bothers me. I use only knotless leaders. Most do not have a stiff butt section.

MR. HUMPHREYS: Steve, having knots in your leader should not bother you. The only part of the leader the trout sees is the tippet, anyway. Your presentation should have those "S" curves. If you are dry-fly fishing, you get those good, soft S curves right up at the fly by shocking, or checking, your forward cast. To check your forward cast, you simply stop your rod tip abruptly at the 12:00 o'clock position and then drop your rod tip before the fly enters the water. Then you are going to get those S curves knocked off without any bother at all. The leader make-up I just described will help you and not spook the fish.

MR. SLOAN: Well, Joe, you may not believe this, but you have shocked us all with some great fishing tips and techniques.

MR. HUMPHREYS: Okay, and good luck this season.

⚜

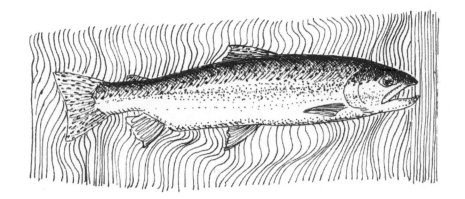

VALERIE HAIG-BROWN

on Her Late Father, Roderick Haig-Brown

An interview with Valerie Haig-Brown on the legacy of her father and some reflections on her own life as an environmentalist and biographer in *Deep Currents*.

*V*alerie Haig-Brown is a writer and editor who lives and works on the eastern slope of the Canadian Rockies near the Montana border. She was brought up on Vancouver Island and has lived in Vancouver and Toronto, where she has held editorial positions in both print and educational television, and returns frequently to those two cities for further projects. She has edited several collections of work by her father, Roderick Haig-Brown—among them, the recent To Know a River, now in paperback. She is a co-editor of a collection of pieces arising from the Waterton-Glacier International Writers' Workshop, Voices in the Wind. She has also written a biography of her parents, Deep Currents: Roderick and Ann Haig-Brown, and is currently writing the script for a television biography of her father. She travels frequently to England and, lately, Morocco "in search of more mountains," she says.

MR. SLOAN: I'd like to welcome our listeners to the show today and take just a moment to provide a bit of biographical information on our guest. Valerie Haig-Brown is the daughter of Roderick Haig-Brown, one of the great, great writers of our fishing world. If you were creating a bibliography of the literature of fishing, or if you had to pick five of the best all-time fishing writers, he would certainly be one of them.

MS. HAIG-BROWN: I have to agree with you there.

MR. SLOAN: No doubt about it. Now, Valerie, your dad wrote in what era?

MS. HAIG-BROWN: His first book was published in 1931, when he was still living in England, and his last book was published in the late 1960s.

MR. SLOAN: Your dad passed away in what year?

MS. HAIG-BROWN: He died in 1976.

MR. SLOAN: And what a tremendous body of work he left us. Here's a list of some of his essays: "The Art of Fishing," "Spring Defined," "Figures and Definitions," "Fry Imitations," "Early Cutthroat Lakes," "The Maculate Purist," "The Unexpected Fish," "Putting Fish Back," "Local Knowledge," "The New Rod," "Fly Lines," "A Boy and Fish Pole," "Northward Geese," "Stone Fly Imitations," "The Secret Life," "Boats and Fast Water," "On Wading," "Fishing and the Common Man," " When Is a Rainbow?," and "Leave the Guns at Home"—just to name a few.

MS. HAIG-BROWN: Yes, those are all essay titles in FISHERMAN'S SPRING. Oh boy, you're testing my memory!

MR. SLOAN: Well, it's important. Now, the reason we have Valerie on is that a new book of her father's work has just been published by The Lyons Press. It's called THE SEASONS OF A FISHERMAN, and it contains some of the writings of your late father

MS. HAIG-BROWN: Some.

MR. SLOAN: Yes, just some. As we were saying, he was quite prolific.

MS. HAIG-BROWN: He wrote four separate books called FISHERMAN'S SPRING, FISHERMAN'S SUMMER, FISHERMAN'S FALL, AND FISHERMAN'S WINTER, and those four are collected in this Lyons Press anthology.

MR. SLOAN: Right.

MS. HAIG-BROWN: It's more than an anthology. It's a—what do they call it?—

a retrospective? A compendium? It's the four complete books all in one.

MR. SLOAN: What are some of his other books?

MS. HAIG-BROWN: His most famous works were the fishing books, particularly the fly-fishing books. He wrote novels, as well, and books for younger readers, but the most famous fishing books would probably end up being a toss-up between THE WESTERN ANGLER, A RIVER NEVER SLEEPS, and RETURN TO THE RIVER.

MR. SLOAN: Tell me about the Campbell River, where your dad lived.

MS. HAIG-BROWN: My dad's house is very much still there and maintained in the same way it was when we *did* live there, my mother and father and the four of us children. We lived on a little farm of twenty acres. When I was very young, we had chickens and cows and all of the rest of the components of subsistence agriculture, to keep food on the table while the writing went on. Farming became less and less important as the writing got more important. But what's still there is a lovely twenty acres with a little stream running through it, and then the big river, the Campbell River, at the foot of the lawn.

MR. SLOAN: Right. And the Campbell runs from where to where?

MS. HAIG-BROWN: It's an eastern Vancouver Island river, and eastern Vancouver Island rivers flow from the center of Vancouver Island toward the east coast of the island. The Campbell flows through a chain of lakes that starts in Strathcona Provincial Park, a big park in the center of the island, where, incidentally, they've named a mountain after my mother and father. There's an Ann and Roderick Haig-Brown Peak up there in the center of the island, and the actual Campbell River...

MR. SLOAN: Talk about immortality!

MS. HAIG-BROWN: That's right.

MR. SLOAN: I mean, even statues get worn out, but...

MS. HAIG-BROWN: But this is a big, tough, granite mountain. I'd love to climb it some day. I kind of like climbing mountains, but apparently it's a really tough four- or five-day trip to get in there. You can helicopter in, but, I don't know, I'm just not ready to take a helicopter to the top of any mountain.

Anyway, the Campbell River itself actually runs through the chain of lakes starting with Buttle Lake and then Campbell Lake, and the main river is then only about three miles long. It's a big, wide, fast river. A friend of mine saw it for the first time quite a few weeks ago here, and he just couldn't get over it. He just said, "It's so big. It's so strong. It's just a beautiful river."

MR. SLOAN: In that river swim many types of salmon, right?

MS. HAIG-BROWN: Yes; all five species of salmon plus steelhead and trout.

MR. SLOAN: Your dad just loved fishing for them, didn't he? He even loved writing about it, too, it seemed. With some writers, it comes hard. I don't know if writing came hard to your dad.

MS. HAIG-BROWN: No, it didn't. He said over and over again that he was a writer who fished. He happened to write about fishing. The business of writing about fishing kind of caught on for him. He started out writing about nature. His first book was about an Atlantic salmon, but his second book was about a river on Vancouver Island—the Nimpkish River, which is the next major river north from the Campbell—where he spent his first three or four years in Canada. And his third book was about a cougar, a mountain lion. He came to writing about fishing a little later, but not too much later. In 1939, THE WESTERN ANGLER was published.

MR. SLOAN: And the Haig-Brown home today is a bed and breakfast?

MS. HAIG-BROWN: Yes, it's a B&B now, but mainly because my mother and father found themselves being crept onto by the town, as I think has happened to a lot of rural people. My parents weren't keeping as many cows and chickens anymore, and the town was looking to tax their land like subdivision land. So my parents hit on the idea of contacting the provincial government to see whether they wanted the property for parkland. And sure enough, they did. So it became what's called "greenbelt" property—riverfront land to be preserved to help keep the river healthy, as much as anything.

MR. SLOAN: Sure.

MS. HAIG-BROWN: Or to preserve the beautiful landscape. It doesn't matter what your motives are for preservation as long as you do it. Then, after my father died, his friends organized having the house itself declared a British Columbia heritage site. The Heritage Property Trust chooses to run it as an education center and a bed and breakfast. Income from the bed and breakfast pays for the basic costs of maintaining the property. It also means you can go there and sleep in my bed, if you want to.

MR. SLOAN: That's great. Now, how would one get there from, say, Los Angeles or San Francisco or Seattle?

MS. HAIG-BROWN: Well, once you get to Vancouver, British Columbia, you would then take a ferry to Vancouver Island. You'll want to go to Nanaimo rather than Victoria because Nanaimo is much closer to the Campbell River than Victoria. From Nanaimo, you'd drive up Highway 19 about two or three hours to the town of Campbell River. You'd want to drive through Campbell River, but instead of crossing over the Campbell River and going north, you'd take Route 28 westward, toward Gold River, which is on the west coast of Vancouver Island. The house is just under a half-mile up the road along the river.

MR. SLOAN: I remember reading RETURN TO THE RIVER in middle high school, and, as I told you one other time, they used to take my fishing books away from me. They used to tell me that if I could read those, I could read other things.

MS. HAIG-BROWN: That's truly creative teaching, I would say.

MR. SLOAN: Wasn't it, though? It was always a terrible blow, but it happened several times. But that book really turned me on to trout fishing—river fishing, especially.

MS. HAIG-BROWN: RETURN TO THE RIVER, as a matter of fact, is actually based on the Columbia River. Probably the choice to feature the Columbia was one of those pragmatic publishing decisions, based on the theory that a book about an American river was going to sell better than one about a Canadian river.

MR. SLOAN: Marketing raises its ugly head again.

MS. HAIG-BROWN: Because the fact is that the story...

MR. SLOAN: ...That the story doesn't make any difference.

MS. HAIG-BROWN: No, it doesn't, because salmon or any other creatures of the wild don't respect political boundaries. It's just that we get pragmatic sometimes.

MR. SLOAN: You know, it's a strange thing. We had an author on the show named Fen Montaigne *(See "Fen Montaigne on Fishing in Russia" on page 77)*, who wrote a book called REELING IN RUSSIA. In his book, he describes a seven-thousand-mile trip he took through Russia with a fly rod on his back. Yet today, he has been contacted to do a story for NATIONAL GEOGRAPHIC on the salmon in the Columbia River. It seems that when publishers think of salmon and rivers, they immediately think of the Columbia.

Tell me, do you have the same dam problems at the Campbell River that they have at the Columbia?

MS. HAIG-BROWN: Yes, to some extent. Mainly, the problem is the damming of the top lake in the chain, which is a long, narrow lake in the mountains, and the flooding of the shores. Just generally, the problem is that dams are a form of exploitation.

MR. SLOAN: Now, you do some work with the Nature Conservancy, don't you?

MS. HAIG-BROWN: I do volunteer work with the Nature Conservancy. I work in southern Alberta, on the edge of Waterton Lakes National Park, where I live. For your audience, Waterton Lakes National Park is a little bump just over the Canadian border on the northern edge of Glacier National Park in Montana. If you look on the map, there's this little bump of parkland extending into Alberta from Montana, and that's us. Of course, the two parks depend enormously on each other.

What we're trying to do at Waterton is keep the doorstep of the park from being developed by people building condominiums and generally wanting to camp on any nice spot that has mountains. Waterton is on a very narrow part of the Rockies—the eastern flank of the Continental Divide, in fact—so we're working to preserve habitat for grizzly and black bear movement. Of course, if you take care of the bears, which are the top predatory species, you take care of the whole environment, and everything else will be fine, too.

MR. SLOAN: Well, that's the interesting part, Valerie. If you buy into the slogan or anthem of "wild anything"—wild bear, wild trout, wild salmon—you have to buy into the concept of preserving the environment to support that species, with clean gravel, no logging, no clear-cutting, no despoliation of the Rockies.

MS. HAIG-BROWN: A man who worked for our British Columbia Division of Fish and Game once told me, "The one thing your father told me when I asked him, 'What should I do?' was 'Just protect the habitat, and the rest will take care of itself.'"

MR. SLOAN: True. Absolutely true.

Now, your dad did a little bit more than protect the habitat. He was a magistrate, wasn't he?

MS. HAIG-BROWN: Yes, he was.

MR. SLOAN: So he could fine the violators of the habitat if he wanted to.

MS. HAIG-BROWN: Well, there are some people who have pretty funny stories about my dad's career as a magistrate.

MR. SLOAN: How did he get into it?

MS. HAIG-BROWN: His version of the story is that he was the only guy in town who had a little education and no particular business connections. I mean, if they'd asked the local grocer to be the town magistrate, he would have found his customers up in front of him. So that might have been a conflict for him.

MR. SLOAN: Are you telling me that a little education and no business connections are the common denominators for becoming a judge?

MS. HAIG-BROWN: Well, remember, we're talking 1941 in a very small town. It was customary and common to appoint what are called "lay magistrates"—in other words, magistrates who don't have any legal training. My father actually defended that practice rather strongly and was quite offended when they laid off all the lay magistrates only the year before he died. He was on the bench for many, many years. In the small town where he presided, originally he held court on Saturday morning and Monday morning. He handled the week's traffic violations on Saturday mornings and the guys who had had a little bit too much to drink on Saturday night on Monday mornings. That was it. But it grew to almost a full-time job.

MR. SLOAN: Woe betide the fellow who violated a game law. I would hate to think what he got.

MS. HAIG-BROWN: You know what people said about him—and I think his children know this only too well? It wasn't the fine or the technical punishment he gave you but the lecture that was the worst part to endure. He was just so disappointed in people. He was not one who was prone to scolding and screaming. Instead, he would just say, "You could do so much better." I think that left a profound mark on people. I can hear him now.

MR. SLOAN: I've heard that lecture *(laughing)*. As a matter of fact, I have two children, and I think I've given it a few times.

We've talked about this next point a little bit before, but I do want to bring it up again. It seems strange to me, and maybe *strange* is the wrong word but I'll use it anyway, that your dad had four children—you being one of them—yet none of them was really as passionate about fishing as he was.

MS. HAIG-BROWN: I guess I've been asked that question many times, and I still don't know the answer, really. I think it was that he was a bit of a perfectionist. He wrote a book called A PRIMER ON FLY-FISHING, in which he starts out, "It can

145

all begin with a worm." Well, I can tell you that there were no worms in our house. There were dry flies. And they're really hard to keep floating when you're an impatient early-teen angler. But we loved going with him along the river. He didn't even fish all that much, and he certainly didn't take us every time he went fishing. He would have liked for us to catch onto it more, to coin a phrase, but he instilled in us an absolute *love* of rivers, there's no question about that. And I think now that that was probably more important than being terribly good at fishing.

He did teach us to cast. There was always a lot of casting going on on the lawn that swept down to the river—people trying out rods and landing a fly in an ashtray or a wine glass, or whatever. Apparently, I was really quite good at casting, and I do occasionally throw a line in the water. But it's always a little embarrassing because I always think that people think I ought to be better at it than I am. So it's intimidating, a little.

MR. SLOAN: Now, you wrote your own book about your mom and dad.

MS. HAIG-BROWN: Yes, I wrote a biography of both my mother and father, Ann and Roderick Haig-Brown, called DEEP CURRENTS. The book is kind of fun because I'm an editor, and I also do a certain amount of archival work. Sorting through the letters was interesting; my mother and father kept all the letters they ever wrote to each other. We were lucky because we lived in that house from the time I was born. I now understand how if you have a big enough house and you don't move all the time the way we do nowadays, the stuff just stays there.

MR. SLOAN: Would you comment on this? Here's a brief passage from Ted Leeson's introduction to THE SEASONS OF A FISHERMAN:

> What is true of writing is true of fishing. 'Neither sport nor art,' he [Haig-Brown] observes, 'should be unnecessarily cluttered and complicated.' It is this directness and clarity, simplicity without oversimplification, that makes Roderick Haig-Brown, as he says of Izaak Walton's friend and partner, Charles Cotton, a writer's writer and a fisherman's fisherman.

I think that kind of sums it up, don't you?

MS. HAIG-BROWN: I think it does; I think it really does. People think, "Oh, he must have had a wonderful array of tackle, and he must have tied a million flies," especially since fly tying has become such a big thing in the past twenty years. But he died twenty-four years ago. He was only interested in having a few flies, simple flies that did the job of imitating the natural hatch. He had rods, but he didn't go out and buy a whole huge collection of them.

MR. SLOAN: No, he didn't.

MS. HAIG-BROWN: In fact, some of the nicest rods he had were ones he inherited from his uncle Deci, in England, who taught him fly fishing. So he fished with him some, and of course the rods he inherited from him are the wonderful old bamboos that are so much back in fashion now. They're all there in the house in Campbell River—carefully guarded, of course—because people keep asking us if they can have just one of something for an auction. But we just say no, because if you started, where would you stop?

And the more important example of how he lived simply, of course, is in his writing. He used to say to me, and it's a pretty basic tenet of teaching good English writing, "Never use a three-syllable word when a one-syllable word will do." And I think that's a very simple way of describing the simplicity of his writing—which I think has a lot to do with what keeps it going on and on and on. His work is read because it's so readable.

MR. SLOAN: Did he revise a lot? Did he work and revise, work and revise? Or did his writing come as a total picture to him?

MS. HAIG-BROWN: No, he didn't revise a lot. Actually, his literary papers are all in Vancouver at the library of the University of British Columbia. If you look at those papers, what you'll notice is that he wrote in long hand with ink on the right-hand pages of big school notebooks. The facing left-hand pages of each notebook were to be kept for revisions. But most of the left-hand pages are completely blank. You can pick up the original manuscript for one of his books, which my mother would have gone on to type as the typescript for him, and find word for word the same thing that's in the book.

MR. SLOAN: Is that right? It came that way?

MS. HAIG-BROWN: Yes.

MR. SLOAN: God, isn't that wonderful.

MS. HAIG-BROWN: He spent a lot of time thinking and doing things like weeding the roses and cutting that gorgeous lawn. He spent time thinking and thinking, and then when it was sort of straight in his head, he'd go put it down on paper.

MR. SLOAN: Wonderful.

147

MS. HAIG-BROWN: When we were children, we were allowed to wander in and sit in his study, but you kind of knew that if he was leaning back in his chair with his feet on his desk, you'd probably better not interrupt him. If he had his pen actually on the page, well, you probably could interrupt him. I don't know what instinct told us that. It's only now that I realize what was going on. Of course, he had the flow of the thing in his head, and it was just a matter of getting it down once he'd got it figured out. So the revising was done in his head, if there was any to be done. Just by thinking was how my dad did it; a lot of thinking went on before he wrote.

MR. SLOAN: Well, as he says, fishing is the most complex of sports. Here's another quote:

> Good minds have always found it, because fishing is the richest and most complex of all sports but is not found in full measure without preparation. A man can learn for himself, even late in life, how to find it. But a boy, shown the right things early, will make them part of himself and build on them through a lifetime of experience.

Now, that's a wonderful quote.

MS. HAIG-BROWN: That's lovely. It's a wonderful quote, and I think in many ways he's describing himself. He was shown fishing as a boy, as he writes in A RIVER NEVER SLEEPS, by this Uncle Deci, whose actual name was Decimus because he was the tenth son of my father's grandfather. Another man, named Major Greenhill, was also very influential in my dad's sporting education, as it would have been called in England in those days. My dad's father had been killed in the First World War, or he would have gotten his education in fishing directly from his father, who certainly started it out and was a very keen fly fisherman and sportsman, again, as they call it in England.

MR. SLOAN: Is there any significance to the hyphen in Haig-Brown. What's the connotation?

MS. HAIG-BROWN: You can use it or not use it, but we North American Haig-Browns have taken to using it because it's the only way of keeping our last name together. Otherwise, we get called Brown, which is okay, too, but it keeps it simpler. If you're a Brown, you might as well have a Haig in front. His grandfather married Miss Haig, and his grandfather was Mr. Brown, and Miss Haig's father said, "You must double the name because we are the last of our branch of the Haigs." They were certainly *not* the last of the Haigs—there are plenty of them left in the world—but that's where it came from: my great grandfather Brown married Miss Haig.

MR. SLOAN: I got it. And the tradition lives on. In fact, there's a grandson, I've heard, who's a pretty good fly fisherman in his own right.

MS. HAIG-BROWN: I have a grandson, yes. It's my grandson you're speaking of. There's another grandson of my father's, a nephew of mine who's pretty keen on fly fishing and pretty good at it, too. But fishing's not a hugely all-consuming passion in the family. The all-consuming passion in our family is writing. My brother's a writer. I'm a writer. I have a sister who's an academic who writes, obviously, and another sister who's a teacher who's done some writing. We all write, and I have a daughter who's a published writer. It goes on. It's the writing. Books.

MR. SLOAN: Now, you told me there's a museum in Campbell River that has the tackle, and the University of British Columbia library has the literary papers.

MS. HAIG-BROWN: Yes, the literary papers are in the university library. The museum in Campbell River has some of the tackle on display, and some of it's at the house. The house isn't big enough to have all the tackle on display there. Also, the house is not a museum; it's a working B&B that's still a house. I mean, I can go there and feel like my mother or father are going to be in the next room, it's been kept so much the way it was when we lived there.

MR. SLOAN: I'd like to offer one more of my favorite quotes about fly fishing from your dad:

> Every fly fisherman has known the experience of catching fish after fish on a fly that has long since been tattered and torn beyond all recognition. Often, such a fly seems to take fish much better than the newly and tidily dressed specimen of the same pattern. I used to think the explanation was probably in the immediate conditions in the day and the way the fish were taken, but I have kept these battered flies sometimes and find that they still do well on another day, in another place, under quite different conditions. The explanation, I think, is that the dressing has become untidy in such a way that the fly works more flexibly and more naturally in the water.

Now, that is fabulous writing on a very simple subject. It really explains it. I mean, we've all had the experience he describes when we've been fly fishing:

you take this ratty old fly out to use, and it still does wonders.

MS. HAIG-BROWN: Right. Again, that quote represents his unique way of explaining something he's experienced. He's thinking and analyzing and thinking and analyzing. It probably represents something he'd been thinking about and analyzing for several years before he came to the realization of what it meant. Then he completed the process by putting it down so succinctly, in such neat words.

MR. SLOAN: Neat words. Your phrase "neat words" is absolutely on target. I don't know if that part of the creative process is something that can be taught, much less learned. I don't know if you can teach that.

MS. HAIG-BROWN: You're right, Steve: I don't think you *can* teach it. My father thought that the only way to learn to write was to do. And he started doing in his teens. His family had fits because he wanted to be a writer. His is almost a classic case of overachieving at it because his family had said, "Writing? Well, you can't make a living at that, so you'd better go out and get a real job." But he persisted. I mean, he did have jobs along the way in the beginning. He worked in logging camps in British Columbia, and he worked in London as, among other things, a film extra. This was when he was back in England for a couple of years being a writer. He just kept at it; he persisted. He tried to write short stories. He tried to write a couple of romances, although the romances usually seemed to be between a fisherman and some woman he met on the bank of the river. Not that those things sold particularly well—after all, that wasn't his genre—but you have to try.

MR. SLOAN: Exactly: in any case, you have to try. But you know something else? I have met some great fishermen who demonstrate similar persistence. I've met Ernie Schwiebert, for example. He has written some great works on trout. I've met John Rybovich, who built the Rybovich boats down in Palm Beach. He was a great friend of mine. What I have found is that good fishermen like this progress in a certain fashion: they catch fish, they become very good, they analyze their tackle, and then they move beyond fishing to an analysis and understanding of the larger issues surrounding the fish and their place in the world. These fisherman realize that killing anything cannot go on forever at the pace that man has set.

MS. HAIG-BROWN: Absolutely.

MR. SLOAN: These fishermen become, in effect, conservationists and protectors of the sport they love so much.

MS. HAIG-BROWN: Well, I think that applies to hunters, as well.

MR. SLOAN: Yes, I think it's happening with them, too.

MS. HAIG-BROWN: You have to know the setting and appreciate where your prey comes from. The more you appreciate that, the more you appreciate that that place your prey comes from has to be protected or there won't be any prey.

MR. SLOAN: Which, again, comes down to habitat.

MS. HAIG-BROWN: Exactly.

MR. SLOAN: There was another part of your dad's book that I'm planning to share with some colleagues of mine at a fisheries conference in Washington, D.C., next week: it's a description of natural predation, of how one fish feeds on another. Your dad describes how the coho come over the bar, and they're three or four inches long, silvery, and flashing in the sunlight. He describes how in the depths you see the steelhead, the larger fish, and suddenly—*bang*—one darts up and grabs one in. The net result is that very few of these coho make it up the river. But that's the natural order of things.

MS. HAIG-BROWN: Yes, that's the natural order of things. People complain about bears and how they go out and grab all the fish. Well, do you know what they've discovered on the coast of British Columbia not long ago? They've determined that, yes, the bears go out and grab the fish out of the river, eat just the bellies or whatever part they want, and then leave the carcasses up off the bank a long way. Well, they've discovered that there's an interdependence between the giant forest trees in the area and the dead salmon fertilizing them. Without the bears, you wouldn't get the salmon carcasses deposited up among the trees.

MR. SLOAN: Sure.

MS. HAIG-BROWN: The world is just so endlessly interdependent in ways we don't even know.

MR. SLOAN: We're all interconnected.

MS. HAIG-BROWN: But in the course of nature providing a bounty, or what looks like a bounty—an extra that we maybe think isn't needed, so we think we can catch them all, in the case of fish or game or any resource—not so. It's all needed. Yes, we can take a certain share, we human beings. But nature needs perhaps a larger share than some people have realized in the past. There's really no waste.

MR. SLOAN: I gave a speech recently up at the Catskill Fly Fishing Center and Museum *(See the Introduction on page 3),* and I mentioned your dad's name in it.

MS. HAIG-BROWN: Neat.

MR. SLOAN: We had an induction ceremony to the Hall of Fame. Joan Wulff was inducted, as were Vince Marinaro, Charlie Fox, and George Harvey.

MS. HAIG-BROWN: A deserving group of people, that's for sure.

MR. SLOAN: Absolutely. Institutions we mentioned like the Hall of Fame created by the Catskill Fly Fishing Center and Museum, the University of British Columbia library, and the museum in Campbell River all become tiny citadels that can be relied upon to preserve what was and, one would hope, what is. Are we scientifically ready for the next worldwide epidemic? Are we ready for the next pesticide that kills something we really don't want to harm? Unless there's eternal vigilance, we're not ready to meet these challenges, we're not ready at all. But these institutions help, they truly do help.

MS. HAIG-BROWN: Yes, because they remind people. I think that if there's any memorial my father has, it's the books. The books will go on telling people my father's message. I meet people, very young people, who are just getting started in their careers. They'll ask me, "Did he write any more books? I read one of his books. How many books did he write?" "Oh well," I say, "Go for it; there are lots more." And I meet people who are well established in their careers but considerably younger, even, than I am, saying, "He's the one who got me started. That's why I'm a biologist; that's why I care about the outdoors." He's an inspirer of people.

MR. SLOAN: That's a great legacy.

MS. HAIG-BROWN: In so many ways. Yes, it's a huge legacy.

MR. SLOAN: A *huge* legacy. You know, James Prosek came on this show *(See "James Prosek on Izaak Walton" on page 11).* He's a young man, only about twenty-four or twenty-five, but he's an accomplished artist. He graduated from Yale and went to England to trace the footsteps of Izaak Walton and chronicle his experience in his book, THE COMPLETE ANGLER: A CONNECTICUT YANKEE FOLLOWS IN THE FOOTSTEPS OF WALTON. In his book, Prosek offers an amazing statistic: Walton's COMPLEAT ANGLER is the third most popular book ever published. The Bible is number one, Shakespeare's works are two, and THE COMPLEAT ANGLER is three. Well, that says something.

MS. HAIG-BROWN: That definitely says something. Because certainly THE

COMPLEAT ANGLER is about a lot more than catching fish.

MR. SLOAN: Without a doubt.

Now, your dad must have had some interesting people wander through looking for him, probably without his even soliciting them. I imagine some people might have just shown up when they were in the area.

MS. HAIG-BROWN: Yes, a lot of people would just show up when they were in the area. I wouldn't say he solicited visits from anybody. He wanted to be writing and enjoying the river and that sort of thing. But it was the conservation work that mainly kept him from his desk in the end. He just felt so strongly that he had to be out there doing what was required and battling the battles. In the meantime, along came tons of interesting, famous, exciting friends, people we'd never met before.

MR. SLOAN: Who was his best fishing buddy? Did he have a best friend whom he fished with a lot?

MS. HAIG-BROWN: Oh, yes. That would be Van Egan, who still lives in Campbell River, two doors up the river from the house. Van was the person who, when my dad got really busy and stuck at his desk, would come along and say, "Come on, Roddy, let's go up the river for a bit." And Van Egan himself has written several books. Van had a lot to do with getting the place taken care of and the house taken care of. The river has coho spawning in it now because it has been somewhat restored and redeveloped in order to make it a better spawning stream. Van has done a lot of that work, as well.

MR. SLOAN: Your mentioning salmon spawning made me think of a paper I was given recently. It was written by the sixteen-year-old daughter of a friend of mine—she's just a high school student out here on Long Island—and deals with the magnetic resonance of anadromous fish species that go to sea. She thought about placing magnets on the upstream side of a dam so that young smelt and parr could find their way across these magnetic fields and down a chute where they wouldn't be chewed up by the turbines.

MS. HAIG-BROWN: Right.

MR. SLOAN: Now, I've got to tell you how much that impressed me, for a sixteen-year-old young lady to be thinking of that.

MS. HAIG-BROWN: That shows a lot of good, careful, solid thinking.

MR. SLOAN: Her work makes me optimistic that we can really solve problems like hydroelectric dams destroying fish migration patterns. I like to think that if we can get to the moon, by God, we can solve this problem.

MS. HAIG-BROWN: Well, I know what you mean exactly. I can't help thinking quite regularly, do we really have to go to the moon or Mars instead of fixing what's here? If we put as much ingenuity into correcting some of the wrongs on the surface of the Earth, we'd be a lot better off.

MR. SLOAN: Would you say that your dad was one of the first to really push for western fly fishing as we know it? I read some work by Zane Grey about fly fishing on the Rogue River for steelhead. But didn't your dad really pursue western fly fishing as well?

MS. HAIG-BROWN: Oh, I think so. When he first came west, he'd say, "Well, you know, I'm going to fish this river with a fly." Local people would say to him, "A fly? Oh, you can't catch those fish with a fly. You can't even fish that river with a fly. You have to hit them on the head with some hunk of lead or something."

But he ignored those people and went ahead and fished with flies a lot. When he first started, he couldn't find the flies he thought he needed. He used English flies, and he adapted and changed them until he developed a few flies that worked. They turned into the most messy, woolly, eaten-up, beaten-up things to catch fish that you'd ever seen. But he certainly went against the local knowledge in quite a few cases to take the fly to the river.

MR. SLOAN: Well, Valerie, this has been a fascinating opportunity to talk with the progeny of one of the greatest fishing writers who ever put words on a page. Valerie, I really want to thank you for coming on the show.

MS. HAIG-BROWN: Well, thank you very much for having me. I really appreciate it.

MR. SLOAN: Maybe this is not a series of one. I have an idea you and I will do this again.

MS. HAIG-BROWN: Oh, well that's good. I'd be happy to do it.

MR. SLOAN: Good, because I feel like we've just barely scratched the surface. Until then, I would entreat anyone to get a copy of Valerie's wonderful biography of her parents, DEEP CURRENTS, or a copy of THE SEASONS OF A FISHERMAN, a compilation of some of the best work of Roderick Haig-Brown, a name that will live forever.

JAMES CRONNIE
on Loch Lomond

AN INTERVIEW WITH JAMES CRONNIE ON FISHING SCOTLAND'S LOCHS, SUCCESSFUL STEWARDSHIP THAT IS RESTORING SCOTLAND'S SALMON FISHERIES, AND A UNIQUE NATIONAL FISHING TOURNAMENT TO PASS THE SPORTING TRADITION ALONG TO A NEW GENERATION OF ANGLERS.

In the United States, we have people who are river keepers. They maintain their rivers by keeping faith in the aspirations of the many who want the river clean, free from pollution, and useable for fishing, swimming, and boating. In some sense, Jim Cronnie can be thought of as a "lake keeper."

The lake Cronnie keeps is Loch Lomond, the largest freshwater loch in Scotland, located about forty-five miles north of Glasgow. Cronnie makes his office at the Loch Lomond Club, a hotel and golf course designed by Tom Weiskopf to harmonize with the natural habitat of the shoreline and mountains surrounding the loch. To say Loch Lomond is beautiful is a gross understatement. As one gazes out over the loch, one is often tempted to imagine that he or she will be the one to spot a monster emerging from its pristine depths, just like the legend of Loch Ness. Evenings on the loch are spent looking and casting to the ring in the rise. The loch's surface often reflects the Aurora Borealis. Loch Lomond is magical; there is always an air of mystery and expectation there. One is swept up into it.

Loch Lomond is Cronnie's home. Cronnie is a fisherman, conservationist, and dedicated organizer of educational and competitive events for the young anglers of his country. In this interview, Cronnie discusses the unique characteristics of Scotland's fisheries as well as some of the common challenges facing fisheries the world over.

MR. SLOAN: This is Steve Sloan on "The Fishing Zone," and I'd like to welcome our listeners this morning. We're broadcasting today from Loch Lomond, just north of Glasgow, Scotland. I'm joined today by a gentleman, Mr. James Cronnie, who is a fisherman extraordinaire. We're going to talk with Jim about fishing on Loch Lomond, fishing in Scotland, and fishing in this part of the world in general. I've heard that it's hot back stateside. Believe it or not, there's a heat wave here, too. It hit sixty-five today, and that's a heat wave in Scotland.

If you'd like to visit an absolutely spectacular place, this is the place to visit. Whether you like fishing or golf or both, Loch Lomond, or Lake Lomond, is gorgeous. More than twenty-one miles long, the loch has a fabulous shoreline, replete with castles. The loch was owned by the Calcun family, which was anglicized into the name *Calhoun.* If you remember your American history, you'll recall John C. Calhoun as the fiery South Carolinian senator who played a great part in the South's secession in the War between the States—or, as our southerners sometimes call it, "the last little disturbance we had down here below the Mason-Dixon Line." Loch Lomond today is owned by the same Calcun family that gave us John C. Calhoun, and it is absolutely spectacular.

So we're here today with Jim Cronnie, who is the gentleman in charge of fishing at the Loch Lomond Club and one of the most respected Scottish fishermen in the country. Jim, I'd like to give you an opportunity to say hello to our listeners in the United States of America.

MR. CRONNIE: Good morning all anglers in the U.S.A. It's a beautiful morning, as Steve says, here in Scotland but probably not what we would call the best fishing weather. But as we don't see days this clear very often over here, we're only too pleased to enjoy them when they do show.

MR. SLOAN: Jim's describing an absolutely still morning with no wind, about sixty-five degrees, with the sun out. We'd call it perfect weather in the U.S., but over here, Jim, I guess you've got to have a little wind blowing and a little wave action to get the fish moving.

MR. CRONNIE: Yes, I think it's just the same the world over. The old trout or salmon, he doesn't want to look up into the sky and see that big, bright light shining in his eyes. With a little bit of wind and a little bit of cloud cover, which I hope we'll see before your trip ends, we might manage to find a fish or two.

MR. SLOAN: Jim, Loch Lomond runs north-south. It's narrow and long and surrounded by beautiful mountains, and the southern end of it empties into the ocean. I wonder if you could describe the fishery itself for us. I know you have salmon, sea trout, brown trout, pike, and some other species here, but give us a little background about each one of them and what you might expect on Loch Lomond.

MR. CRONNIE: Yes, as you say, the lake—or *loch* as we call it here in Scotland— is actually twenty-one miles long and five miles wide. The loch is connected to the sea by a very short river, the River Leven, which is approximately four miles long. Migrating fish use the Leven to enter Loch Lomond and travel up through it to the various streams where they spawn at the back end of the year. Fish start entering the system, mostly sea trout and salmon from the Atlantic, in February and will travel through the Leven and into the loch right until November. Then, in late November, they will enter the small streams feeding the loch and spawn. Several islands lie at the bottom end of the loch, and it's around about these islands that we tend to find the sea trout in the evenings. Fishing for sea trout is probably my favorite type of fishing on the loch.

The loch is a multi-use loch, so it has quite a lot of amenities for pleasure boats, wind surfing, and various other water sports. Salmon these days, unless you get a really big wave [*i.e., choppy water from high winds—the Editors.*], tend to go fairly deep. So most of the people who catch salmon in the loch are trolling for them. There is a time, of course, at the back end of the year when they get very aggressive, and we may get one or two on a fly.

Also in the loch are northern pike, or the British version of the northern pike, which are some very large fish that lie amongst the islands and go in the weed beds. Some pike up to fifty or sixty pounds have been known to be in the lochs. The biggest caught in Loch Lomond was forty-two pounds. But skeletons of fish that weighed over fifty pounds have been found, and scientists tell us that these fish have been almost the "Loch Lomond monster."

There are also several other coarse fish species in Loch Lomond: perch, or *powan*, and a fish called a *ruffe*. But these are mostly fish that have been introduced in the last twenty years by bait anglers who have been fishing for the pike.

MR. SLOAN: Well, that's a lot of species. There's nothing more fascinating than the life cycle of the salmon, I think. It's spurred the imagination of some great writers, like Roderick Haig-Brown, who wrote RETURN TO THE RIVER, a book set out on the Campbell River in Vancouver, British Columbia *(See "Valerie Haig-Brown on Her Late Father, Roderick Haig-Brown" on page 139)*. But a lot of research has been done on salmon all over the world, and these fish have an unusual life cycle. They come into the same river where they were spawned, they've now determined, mostly by smell. Certain rivers—each river, as a matter of fact—have a distinctive odor, almost like a fingerprint when it comes to a salmon's sense of smell. They can find their way back to where they were spawned, and then it starts all over again.

And just as the behavior of salmon is identical throughout the world, the threats salmon face are similar. For instance, damming salmon rivers for hydroelectric power generation is a threat to salmon fisheries worldwide. Of course, Scotland is no different from the United States in the fact that hydroelectric power is important to industry and to people and their homes and farms. But, when you have hydroelectric power, you usually have a dam, and damming up the headwaters of some of these streams into lakes creates barriers between the salmon and the clean gravel they need to reach to spawn. If they don't get to clean gravel, their spawning process is ruined. Silt can enter the water through runoff from areas of the watershed devoted to logging or farming, or even damming itself. As the silt takes over the fishery, it kills the salmon off by ruining their spawning beds. Salmon move back and forth between the sea and their home waterway. A salmon that's been at sea one year and comes back is called a *grilse*. And Jim, grilse grow to about five pounds?

MR. CRONNIE: That's right; four to five pounds.

MR. SLOAN: So you've got one-year-old salmon that weigh four to five pounds, and then when they come back again, they might be even heavier. They grow very rapidly at sea. We know they eat prawns and shrimp and probably lots of other fin fish and minnows. They become very strong at sea, and when they come to the mouth of the river in which they were spawned, a change takes over. They stop eating extensively, and they move usually on the tides at dusk and at dawn. They start working their way back up the very same river in which they were spawned, which can pose lots of problems for them. Finally, they make their way up to clean gravel spawning beds, they spawn, and the cycle starts again. Now, to keep that cycle going, you need clean water, clean spawning beds, clean gravel, and pollution-free rivers. That's not such an easy combination to maintain in the modern age. I was just taken through Glasgow near here, Jim, and I was struck by the shipyards there. They built the *Queen Mary*, I understand, in the Glasgow shipyards, and during the Second World War they built a lot of other ships. So trying to get a pollution-free river for these salmon in such close proximity to heavy industry must not be easy. However, it's being worked on, I've heard.

Jim, why don't you tell us a little bit about the local fishery conservation associations here and the licensing efforts and the conservation plans that are underway?

MR. CRONNIE: Yes, Steve, you're very much correct in noting that the salmon have had a hard time over the past fifty years. The demands of civilization and mankind and this quest to go ever higher in industrial output and become ever more prosperous have put a lot of pressure on the natural things around us. I'm hopeful that nowadays there are several of us in the world who have recognized these factors, and we are trying to do quite a bit to reverse the process. The salmon, as you say, starts its cycle as soon as it hatches and smells its home water; it tries to complete that cycle a year later when it returns and tries to head upstream. The salmon does meet many obstacles on its way—the angler being probably the least of them.

You say you have a problem with the impacts of hydroelectric dams on salmon in your country. We have probably a much bigger problem with the impacts of deforestation on our salmon fisheries here in Scotland. In the late thirties and forties, nearly all of the hills and mountains in Scotland were heavily planted with coniferous trees, and we probably started harvesting them twenty years ago. That harvesting of those trees caused a great increase in the siltation of riverbeds in Scotland, especially the spawning areas, as you correctly said.

Various organizations in this area, such as the Loch Lomond Angling Improvement Association, have done a great deal of work over the past twenty years to alleviate the problems facing our fisheries here in Scotland. They have worked not only by helping to clean up the headwaters and the spawning beds but also in the building of hatcheries and nurseries to nurture young salmon. These hatcheries bring salmon to the fry stage and put them back into the loch and the river as free-feeding fry so that they have enough time to get the smell of the river into their nostrils and recognize their way home a year later.

Also in the last twenty years, a group called the West Galoway Fishery Trust was set up in the south of Scotland. The trust did a great deal of work with government bodies and various other river users. The trust employed a full-time marine biologist to produce a research paper, which pointed out all the faults with the current system and also gave us scientific information that could be used to change government thinking. And I'm very happy to say that because of the efforts of the West Galoway Fishery Trust, we've had a whole new change in the forestation procedures in Scotland, and legislation has been passed that allows foresters to fell trees and start the logging processes only in conjunction with the fisheries officer who controls the amount of waste being let back into the river.

And as you mentioned, Steve, you came up the River Clyde this morning. The Clyde is a prime example of how a river can respond to positive stewardship efforts. The River Clyde thirty or forty years ago was affectionately known as "the old smelly Clyde." Ten years ago, there was a complete change-around, probably having much to do with the fact that the shipbuilding industry disappeared around the Clyde. With shipbuilding gone, the Clyde cleaned up dramatically. We're very happy to say that there is now an annual run of salmon back into the Clyde, getting all the way into the headwaters. There are several areas on the Clyde where there are little management associations, such as the Clyde River Association itself. All these associations work very, very hard, and, as far as I know—and I haven't heard any differently yet—people who catch a salmon nowadays in the Clyde are so happy to see it that they return it to the river immediately. No fish get killed. The association and the anglers are trying to build the stocks of salmon back up again.

Of course, the Clyde in its upper regions is probably one of the best brown trout rivers in Scotland, even though it's also probably one of the lesser-known brown trout rivers in Scotland. This is a secret that, I think, most of the central belt anglers tend to try to keep to themselves. The brown trout fishery in the Clyde is one of those little jewels in the crown that is still there after many, many years of heavy fishing. The Clyde's a place where lots of anglers, fathers and sons, go out of the city and fish for many an hour and many a day. As Steve says, some days it works, and some days it doesn't.

MR. SLOAN: Well, Jim, we can bring these fish back. We can bring them back if there's a concerted effort between all interests, both commercial and recreational. I don't mean necessarily commercial *fishing* interests, although they'll certainly play a part in any solution, which I'll get to in a minute. By "commercial interests," I'm really talking about logging, hydroelectric power, farming, agricultural, and mining interests. If they could all get together and decide that they really *do* want salmon coming up their streams, they will have it.

Now, a salmon run in a river is indicative of a healthy environment in that river, which is indicative of good management, which is indicative that people care. So if you start at the bottom of the food chain with the fish and secure and protect *their* habitat, you know that up the food chain where we humans are located, you're going to have some good things happen to our environment. However, one of the negative effects of this pragmatic approach of viewing fish as a resource occurred, as I remember it, about fifteen or twenty years ago. Somebody was fishing for cod off Greenland, and they started catching salmon. Not only did they catch salmon from Greenland but they caught salmon basically from all the countries on the Atlantic—from Canada, from the United States, from Iceland, from Norway, from Russia. It seems that the cod fishermen had stumbled upon a salmon congregation spot, a place in the North Atlantic where these fish reassembled after they had gone out into the ocean to fatten up. From this congregation spot, they would then work their way back to their rivers of origin. But once the commercial fishing industry got wind of this spot off Greenland, the massacre of salmon on the high seas was enormous. Now, you've got to remember that in the Greenland economy a cash crop like salmon is terribly important. People made some serious money catching these fish on the high seas. Thankfully, that practice has been stopped now, by and large. I don't know personally of any other congregation spots, although there may be another one out there somewhere. But the point is that once that form of exploitative fishing stopped, we had a chance of helping salmon at the local level.

Jim, you were describing for us the process these salmon follow as they return from the sea and come back to the estuaries. You said they mill around a little bit so they can get some scent of freshwater and come back up the correct streams. You pointed out how they may go up the River Spey or the River Tweed or the River Clyde, but then they branch out into particular tributaries where they might have been spawned. So they've got to wait for that scent, too. Waiting seems to be an integral part of the migration process. Then suddenly people started planting drift nets and all kinds of traps in the estuaries to catch them, just as had been done at the congregation spot in the Atlantic off Greenland. In response to this threat to the salmon, you all got together. Why don't you describe for us what happened?

MR. CRONNIE: Sure, Steve. I'd say it was about twenty years ago or so, when I was secretary of a small fishing association with about four hundred members down in the southwest of Scotland. The government had changed the legislation at that time to say that the ratable values—the values that were used to calculate an annual tax on the rivers that the associations and the riparian owners all owned—were disbanded. I had an idea for a solution at the time. With a lot of help from a colleague of mine in the Scottish Anglers' National Association, we together contacted every single riparian owner in Galoway, which is in southwest Scotland, probably something like two hundred owners. We managed to persuade everyone to put the amount of money that they would have paid in ratable value taxes into a fund, and the proceeds from that fund were used to buy off the commercial stations in the estuaries of each of our rivers. I must admit that I was very glad and surprised at how smoothly it went and how well it was received by everybody who participated at the time. We raised £70,000, which was probably about $130,000 at that time, and with it managed to buy off all the main commercial nets on the lengths of the River Niff, the River Cree, the River Bladniche, and one or two others in that area. It was a very worthwhile and rewarding effort that we had in doing that.

MR. SLOAN: It's interesting, Jim. All over the world, people like you and me and the hundreds of thousands of people who tune in every Saturday to listen to this program all love fishing. I made a decision several years ago to steer this program away from becoming a sort of "how-to-do-it" broadcast and more toward a "what is happening?" discussion. I believe my listeners really want to know what's going on in fishery matters. I know that if you really love this sport, you shouldn't avoid becoming proactive in some of the efforts to preserve it and enhance the fisheries that provide its foundation. Your example of buying out those commercial interests is exactly the sort of proactive approach that makes for a win-win situation for everyone involved. The commercial fishermen who got bought out were probably happy because they realized their business practices might have been legislated out of existence over a period of time, in which case they'd be out of business and would not have received any money as compensation for their loss of livelihood. Instead, they got paid, and their payments were generated from individuals who contributed to the buyout fund. In turn, those individuals were able to rejuvenate the values of their properties through the invigorated salmon runs, and if any of them sold beats, provided housing, guided fishermen, or even put people up for the weekend to fish, the money they had contributed to the buyout fund was returned to them many times over. I mean, yes, it was a lot of money to raise in one shot. But over the years, I'll bet the return on the initial contributions to the buyout fund worked out to be a ten- to twenty-fold increase in the amount of money that had been raised. This type of win-win solution is going to go on in all parts of the world.

In New England right now, Jim, the federal government has instituted a buyout program because the cod, haddock, and hake fisheries have collapsed. The government is going to cod, haddock, and hake fishermen who have their own boats—boats that they were encouraged, by the way, to build with money borrowed from the U. S. government about ten or fifteen years ago—and telling them that they're going to buy these boats back to reduce the amount of fishing on the remaining stocks. So it's not just in Scotland that people are creating solutions to fisheries problems. All over the world these problems are endemic in the system, and these kinds of buyout programs will certainly help solve them.

Jim, I'd like to get back to a few questions I have about the fishing end of things now. What kind of tackle do you use, and would you describe a Spey rod for us? You fished on the River Spey recently, you told me, and did fairly well. Could you describe it and tell us about the difference in the tackle when you use that kind of equipment?

MR. CRONNIE: Well, Steve, the River Spey is probably one of the most famous salmon rivers in Scotland.

MR. SLOAN: Where is it?

MR. CRONNIE: It's probably a hundred and fifty miles north of here. It originates in the Grampion Mountains, runs through them, and flows to the east coast of Scotland. The Spey flows through Grantern and Spey out into the

North Sea, not the Atlantic. The Spey is a very clear, fast-flowing river, very much a fly-fishing river.

The Spey rods that have been developed in that area tend to be some fifteen to seventeen feet long. Basically, they are built to that length because the banks of the River Spey are very heavily wooded. Because there are a lot of trees along the Spey, you have to use what we call a "Spey cast," which is a version of a roll cast. You need a lot of length and power in your rod to get the line to roll over probably thirty-five yards across the river. With salmon fishing, the same technique seems to work the world over: you get across the stream, get the fly to come on the curve, and it's the curve and the dangle that we always hope will induce the strike to occur.

So the Spey rods, as I said, are fifteen to seventeen feet long, and you do a Spey cast in a miniature figure of eight. You literally lift your rod to your left shoulder, bring it across in front of your face, and whip it hard forward over your right shoulder. In the process, you make a figure of eight in your line, and then the line rolls off the surface of the river and right across. These Spey rods have been developed specifically for this river. But once they've learned to Spey cast correctly, I'm quite sure that most people would never do anything else because it requires much less effort than bringing the rod back above your shoulder and casting in the normal manner.

MR. SLOAN: So the two main advantages of the Spey cast seem pretty clear, Jim: it gives you the most distance, and it's less tiring. However, I know some people on the Delaware River in New Jersey, between New Jersey and Pennsylvania, who were fishing for shad, which come up on their annual run in early May. They use the Spey rod and use it very well because they can literally cover about 30 percent more water with casts across the river and down.

Jim, while we're still on the topic of fishing, I'd like you to describe for us how you started the International Junior Angler Fishing Match that's now held here between Scotland, England, Ireland, and Wales.

MR. CRONNIE: Steve, as you know, the youngsters in our sport, I think, are its future. There's no doubt about it: we have to help young people get introduced to fishing and help them learn to fish in the right way once they *are* introduced. We must give them proper advice and get them thinking in the proper manner when they go fishing. Approximately fourteen years ago, my friend Mr. Ernie Balgo and I had an idea that we should start a junior fly-fishing competition, a

Scottish youth championship. The fact that, of course, we had sons of fishing age ourselves at the time was a great factor in our decision. But our sons are now well grown up, and we are still at it, as I said.

In starting the championship, we thought that these youngsters should get a chance to not only fish in different waters but fish in competition against their best peers in the country. So we started the Scottish Youth Fly-Fishing Championship, and it's been running now, as I said, for fourteen years. We've got an annual entry of probably 150 youngsters from various clubs throughout the country, from as far north as the Shetland Islands to the very southwest corner of Scotland. We announce the championship to all the clubs and recruit contestants through the Scottish Anglers' National Association. We send out a letter to every club, asking it to nominate two or three of its best youths each year to fish in the Scottish Youth Championship. We then hold three heats and a final, usually at Loch Leven, which is probably the oldest trout fishery in Britain. Loch Leven is famous for its huge fly-fishing boats and its great trout fishing.

MR. SLOAN: Jim, is this competition for distance or accuracy? How is it scored?

MR. CRONNIE: Neither, Steve. It's actually a fishing competition that scores basically on the total weight of each contestant's catch at the end of the day. The boys go out and fish two in a boat, with a gillie. Each boat has an adult member in it just to make sure that the contestants don't get into any trouble or danger at all. They go out and they fish all day. We also allow them to kill and keep two fish, as they do in Scotland, and then we measure each fish. We award one point per centimeter of length. We then combine the total weight of the released fish and the total length points for the two keeper fish for each contestant to determine the winners. That's the way we do it.

At the end of the sessions, after the final, we have a Scottish Junior Champion and a runner-up. We have another ten places that go into forming the Scottish Youth Fly-Fishing Team, which then fishes an international match against England, Ireland, and Wales during the first week in August of each year. Each year, this international match is held in a different country by rotation. For example, we're down in Wales this year, fishing at a place called Lake Trawsfynydd. Don't ask me to spell it; after all, it's in Wales. But when I first went to fish that lake, about five years ago, it had a nuclear power station on it. The top six inches of the water was the temperature of warm tea, and then the water was freezing below. But nowadays, the water temperature is much more natural. Thank God that they've gotten rid of the power station.

These youngsters thoroughly enjoy this competition. We've been very lucky in the past few years to get sponsorship from institutions like the Bank of Scotland and various other sources, and we're able to keep the cost down to the youngsters.

MR. SLOAN: So you would have a total of forty kids: ten on each team, with one team from each of four countries? Then you have twenty boats, with two to a boat—a young fisherman and a gillie in each? How many days does the tournament last?

MR. CRONNIE: Usually, there are two practice days where the youngsters go out and try to find "the secret weapon" for the particular lake they're on, as we all have done in the past. Then they have the match day, which is usually on a Thursday. We would travel down on a Sunday, orient ourselves on Monday, fish Tuesday and Wednesday as practice days, have the match day on the Thursday, followed by an international dinner in the evening where the presentations and prizes are made to all these youngsters. We older fishermen like the dinner, too, because we can swap tales of the ones that got away. And no doubt the boys do that, as well.

MR. SLOAN: Jim, is the tackle they use all fly tackle? Is it all fly fishing?

MR. CRONNIE: Yes, it's entirely fly fishing and fly tackle.

MR. SLOAN: So the kids have to know how to cast and drift and haul back, and they've got to learn everything themselves. Now, do the clubs that the children belong to actually teach them these techniques at an entry level and continue to introduce new skills to them as they get better? Do the parents of the children that are competing and other interested people monitor this championship? Is that how it works?

MR. CRONNIE: Yes, Steve. I think it's very much the same the world over: the youngsters who get into fishing tend to come into it with their parents. The father takes his son fishing. But there are quite a few youngsters coming through now, especially from the inner cities, who have joined a club not necessarily through their parents but maybe through a friend or somebody else who goes fishing. There is quite a movement within the clubs in Scotland to encourage junior fishing by having competitions and various other events, such as fly-tying classes. To see some of these youngsters at fourteen years old, with their deft little fingers tying up flies that you and I could hardly even *see* nowadays—let alone tie—is quite a revelation and just great to see.

MR. SLOAN: Well, Jim, that sounds like a fabulous program. You know, when you talk about tying flies, it reminds me of a little anecdote about one of America's greatest fishermen that I'd like to share in closing. I once saw Lee Wulff, at the age of eighty-eight, about a year or two before he died in a plane crash—the crash of a plane he was piloting at age ninety-one—tie a number 22 fly *with his bare fingers*. Now, I actually *saw* him do that—saw it with my own eyes.

So, hey, keep fishing: it keeps you young. And this has been a delightful hour with Jim Cronnie at the Loch Lomond Club; it has made my day just to be in this beautiful setting. I just can't wait to go out on this lake. I know it's a calm day and the fish are not going to bite until evening, but so what? I'm going to give it a shot. And Jim, I want to thank you for sharing your time and insight with us this morning. Tight lines from Loch Lomond, north of Glasgow, Scotland.

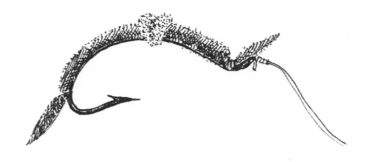

JACK SAMSON
on the San Juan River

An interview with Jack Samson on a unique and awe-inspiring fishery in New Mexico, the pursuit of permit in North America and Australia, and fond memories of subsistence waterfowling in China during World War II.

[Jack Samson is a close personal friend of Steve Sloan, and Sloan shares the following reflections on their friendship by way of introduction to the following interview—The Editors]

I *have known Jack Samson for a long time. We have had many exciting fishing adventures together. I think the strength and clarity of my memories of these times spent fishing with Jack are in some ways the most telling indicator of the strength of our friendship.*

For example, we fished the first Hemingway Tournament in Cuba in 1978. At the time, Jack was serving as editor of FIELD & STREAM, *and we were joined by his colleague, Ed Zern, the late humorist whose wit graced the final page of that magazine each month. We fished my boat, a thirty-six-foot Rybovich named THE NAN-SEA for my wife, Nancy. I remember us being shadowed by a Cuban gunboat when we asked to stay an extra day to fish. I recall that on the way home to Key West, we caught many dolphin fish on a fly as they hid under a gigantic log in the Gulf Stream.*

On a subsequent outing, I took Jack to Lizard Island, Australia, where he hooked, defeated, photographed, and then released a thousand-pound marlin, much to the amazement of the Aussies. The release of that fish started the Aussies rethinking the wisdom of killing such "granders" just for photo opportunities. I remember these and other fishing adventures with Jack clearly, but that "catch" remains a vivid memory even though it happened more than twenty years ago.

For a long time starting in the early 1980s, Jack had threatened, cajoled, and, finally, begged me to come down to the San Juan River to fly fish for the rainbows found below the Navajo Dam. Jack had practically pioneered the area through his writings and personal fishing trips. In fact, there is one run about a mile below the dam that is called "Jack's Hole" in his honor. For some reason, our schedules just did not coincide for eighteen years, but I eventually succumbed to a final plea and went with him. It turned out to be a fishing trip for the ages. In one afternoon, we caught and released 403 inches of rainbow trout—more than thirty-three feet of trout, *if my math is correct. When we finally quit at 6:00 that evening, even our guide said, "Wow, what a day!"*

Jack has written many books and articles. I am proud to have been included in many of them. He is a fishing buddy in the finest sense. Apparently, General Chennault found many of the same qualities that I have grown to admire in him because, when Jack was a young lieutenant in the regrouped Flying Tigers, he was asked by the general to take him duck hunting on the Chinese side of the Himalayas during the war.

The following interview with Jack took place at Rizuto's San Juan River Lodge, beside the San Juan River, near Farmington, New Mexico.

MR. SLOAN: I know where I put my rod and reel yesterday: in the San Juan River in New Mexico. And that's where I am this morning with a good buddy of mine, Jack Samson. Jack is a former editor of FIELD & STREAM magazine, FLY ROD & REEL, and SALT WATER SPORTSMAN, as well as the author of many books and hundreds of articles devoted to fishing and outdoor pursuits. In addition to being a renowned editor and writer, he is a fabulous fisherman. Yesterday, we had a day for the ages on the San Juan River, near Farmington, New Mexico. It was fantastic.

MR. SAMSON: It certainly was.

MR. SLOAN: Well, Jack, although you'd never know it, we're really not as far away from civilization as it might seem. What's the exact name of the town where the Navajo Dam is located and where the San Juan River originates?

MR. SAMSON: The exact town *is* Navajo Dam.

MR. SLOAN: We're talking about the San Juan River that comes out of the base of the Navajo Dam here in New Mexico. I've threatened to come down here for eighteen years to fish this river with you, and, boy, am I ever glad I did. Jack, I wonder if you could describe the San Juan River fishery here for us.

MR. SAMSON: Of course the river itself has always been here, but it ran through the desert in what they call the Four Corners area, which is where the four states of New Mexico, Arizona, Colorado, and Utah meet, way out in the High Desert country of the Southwest. The river has been here a long time, but it never had much in it, of course, except a few suckers and maybe a few trout. But in about 1963, the U.S. Army Corps of Engineers built a huge earth-filled dam across the river as a flood-control project. The dam created a twenty-five-mile-long impoundment called Navajo Lake. The dam itself is some three hundred feet high, which ensures that the water is pretty cold down at the bottom of the lake. When this water from the bottom of the lake comes out of the spillway at the base of the Navajo Dam and pours into the San Juan River, it's always cold. In fact, it's about forty-four degrees.

MR. SLOAN: Year round? It stays that cold in the summertime, too?

MR. SAMSON: Yes, even in the summertime. So the fishery is a cold, crystal-clear, big river. Around the latter part of the 1960s, people began to notice that there were some really big trout in the San Juan. From that time on, it's been a terrific tailwater trout fishery, holding huge rainbow trout and some smaller brown trout. It's a marvelous river, and its fish are big and strong and fast.

MR. SLOAN: Jack, we had quite a day yesterday. A lot of fishermen count the number of fish they catch, but not us. We counted the number of *inches* we caught and released. By the end of the day, we had released 406 inches of trout—more than thirty-three feet of fish. Not only did we catch a lot of trout, but I *saw* more big trout—and I'm talking trout between eighteen and twenty-four inches—in one day than I had in my lifetime. It was incredible. This is such a rich fishery, and, frankly, it's only an hour and twenty-minute flight south of Denver.

Jack, you live in Santa Fe, right? How long of a drive is it up here for you?

MR. SAMSON: It's about a three-and-a-half-hour drive.

MR. SLOAN: To put that in perspective for, say, a New York City angler like me, I can drive to Montauk Point in three and a half hours.

MR. SAMSON: The closest to what I'd call a big town is Farmington, New Mexico, and that's about thirty miles southwest of here.

MR. SLOAN: I've noticed that the river is very accessible; you can wade it in different spots. You can't wade all of it, but Tom, our guide from yesterday, took us out in one of those little float boats. At different spots, we just got out and waded. Tom would put us on a rock, and we would just wade and cast and wade and cast. It was incredible.

Now Jack, what about mid-day fishing, when the water warms up maybe half a degree or a full degree and the hatches start?

MR. SAMSON: Of course, the hatches on this river are kind of sporadic. You never really know whether you're going to get one or not. They can be brought on by slightly overcast weather or even by large clouds. The hatches don't last very long.

MR. SLOAN: Now, we're staying at Rizuto's, right?

MR. SAMSON: Yes, Chuck Rizuto's San Juan River Lodge. It's a nice lodge, neat and clean, and they have very good guides.

MR. SLOAN: They've got what, about six or seven boats that they charter?

MR. SAMSON: Right, six or seven of the MacKenzie-type float boats, like we used yesterday.

MR. SLOAN: How many years ago did you meet Chuck Rizuto, Jack?

MR. SAMSON: Oh, I'd say about fifteen years ago. I had retired from FIELD & STREAM and moved back to Santa Fe, where I had grown up. I had always wanted to learn how to fish this river, so I hired a professional guide. This was the time when they were just starting to guide on the river, back around 1983, and Chuck showed me how to fish the San Juan.

It's basically a nymph river. The fish are lying on the bottom of the river, or close to the bottom, and you've got to get your flies down to them. So you usually fish with a little bit of split-shot and a floating indicator, which is kind of like a bobber, above it. This rig helps keep the nymph moving at the same speed as the current so it appears as natural as possible to the trout.

MR. SLOAN: They make the indicators out of yarn here, I noticed. It's a red yarn, and you put it up your line from the split-shot. When that indicator twitches, don't wait—just strike. You flip your rig out, float it down, and, when the indicator twitches, just raise your rod tip. More often than not, there'll be a fish on, by God.

Now Jack, what's the title of your latest book?

MR. SAMSON: It's called PERMIT ON A FLY, by Stackpole Books.

MR. SLOAN: I'm sure you can get it at Amazon.com or ask for it in your local bookstore. Now, the permit has been quite an elusive fish for you. It has sort of been a lifetime quest for you to take a permit on a fly.

MR. SAMSON: Yes, a permit is a strange fish. You sort of get addicted to fishing for them after a while because they don't take flies well. Fishing for them becomes quite a challenge.

MR. SLOAN: This is mostly saltwater flat fishing, right?

MR. SAMSON: That's right; you fish for them on the bonefish flats. But permit on average are larger than bonefish, and they're strong and very fast, very smart, very wary, and very easily spooked. They're a fascinating fish, and I know guys who've fished all their lives on the flats and have never yet caught a permit.

MR. SLOAN: I've only caught one in all the fishing I've done. You're right: they're very difficult fish to catch. Now, you've uncovered a couple of new bonefish and permit flats, I understand. One of them is in Mexico, as I remember.

MR. SAMSON: Yes, off the Yucatan. The Yucatan Peninsula area is one of the more accessible areas to most Americans because you can fly down to Cancun, then drive south of Cancun for two or three hours to an area around Ascension Bay. There are a number of fishing lodges down there now. Years ago, there were only one or two, Boca Playa and Tasmaya, but now they've got about eight or nine. So it's not a hard place to reach, and you'll find lots of permit and bonefish and some small tarpon and snook.

MR. SLOAN: Jack, in addition to writing about permit, you also wrote the biography of Lee Wulff. You knew Lee, didn't you?

MR. SAMSON: Yes, I knew him pretty well. I met him while fishing in Iceland back in 1972, when I first became editor of FIELD & STREAM. He and his wife, Joan, were up on the Rimshaw River. I got to spend four or five days with him. He was a marvelous guy.

MR. SLOAN: He was about six-foot-four, wasn't he?

MR. SAMSON: I think everybody was so impressed by his writings that people thought he was much bigger than he was. He was about five-eleven.

MR. SLOAN: No kidding? Anyway, did he have any unique skills when it came to fishing, or is it just that he did it so much that he became really good at it?

MR. SAMSON: I think he was just consistent at it, and he was a stubborn guy. He wouldn't give up. The thing that always amazed me about Lee Wulff was that nobody really realized quite how unusual and courageous the man was. During World War II, he had been stationed up in Goose Bay, Labrador, to help entertain the troops stationed up there, take them out fishing, and show them survival techniques.

After the war was over, he decided to stay up there himself and go fishing for all the salmon that he had found. But he needed an airplane, so he went back down to the States and got a little Piper Cub and a set of floats to put on it. He flew it from Westchester County, New York, up to Nova Scotia and then back over that huge area of the sea to Labrador and Newfoundland. He used that Cub up there to fly in and explore all the rivers. In those days, there weren't any planes at all in that part of the world, except military aircraft. There were no airfields and no beacons or navigational aids at all back then. There were unusual currents and winds, too, and it was a million square miles of nothing. So he was really quite an unusual guy.

MR. SLOAN: His wife, Joan, is an unusual person, as well. I know her fairly well, and I know you do, too. Joan Wulff runs a fly-fishing school up in the Catskills. If you want to learn how to fly fish, get the rudiments or polish your technique up a little bit, I suggest you go up to Joan Wulff's school. Do you know where she's located, exactly?

MR. SAMSON: She's right on the Beaverkill River, but I don't know the town.

MR. SLOAN: She really knows how to teach people how to fly cast. It's funny, but yesterday, we were going down the river and we got into one spot where there were about a half dozen guys flailing away, and every one of them needed a fly-casting lesson. But they were catching fish, so don't get discouraged. Isn't that right, Jack? I mean, this is a sport that ought not intimidate us, right?

MR. SAMSON: That's right, Steve. Remember, it's supposed to be fun.

MR. SLOAN: With a little practice, we can really become quite accomplished at fly fishing. It's like golf, only it's a lot easier than golf.

Jack, you had this lifelong love for catching a permit on a fly. Suddenly you heard that there were some permit down in Australia someplace. Where was it?

MR. SAMSON: I had heard that they had permit in Australia, but nobody could ever pin it down. It was just sort of a recurring rumor I had been hearing. I asked Lefty Kreh about it one time—Lefty had been fishing down under for a couple of weeks—and he said, "No, no, no. We saw a bunch of tails on the flats, but they were all a fish called *trevally*, which is kind of like our jack crevalle." He told me he didn't see any permit there and he didn't think they had any. So I kind of forgot about it for a couple of years. Then, all of a sudden, I started hearing more rumors about them about a year ago. I got hold of a friend of mine over there named Steve Starling, who's one of the best outdoor writers in Australia. He said, "Yeah, we've got permit over here." It turns out that they don't call them permit in Australia; they call them *trevally*.

MR. SLOAN: So Lefty really *had* seen permit earlier? It was just that the Australians had a different name for them. Jack, what happened next?

MR. SAMSON: Well, a friend of mine named Mike McClellan, who lives out in Los Angeles and runs a booking operation for Australia and New Zealand called "The Best of New Zealand," confirmed that he, too, had heard the same rumor about permit in Australia. He put me on an Air New Zealand flight that flies from Los Angeles straight over to Sydney and Brisbane, Australia—a fourteen-hour direct flight. When I got over there, I looked up a man named Gavin Platz, who lives up around Townesville, on the northeast coast of Australia.

MR. SLOAN: Well, that's about twelve hundred miles north of Sydney, right?

MR. SAMSON: It's in Queensland. Gavin put me onto a guide named Steve Jeston, and, by golly, we went up there and fished an area right close to a large island called Hichinbrook Island. We saw lots of permit. We didn't catch any at all the first couple of days up there because it was rainy and kind of overcast. But we saw a lot of permit tails.

The next day, I went up to Cairns, Australia, which is about a two-and-a-half-hour drive further north, and fished with a guide named Peter Haynes. We saw a number of permit, and I hooked a small one on a fly, got him onto my feet, and he got off—the usual scenario, I learned. I was fishing with a guy named Cam Sigler, from Washington State. He hooked three small ones, and they all got off, but we saw a bunch of them. Then, of course, I saw some photographs that Peter Haynes had of some really nice-sized permit.

MR. SLOAN: Does the Australian permit look the same as the ones down in the Florida Keys?

MR. SAMSON: No, it's a little different. The dorsal fin, the tail fin, and the caudal and pectoral fins of the Australian permit are yellowish rather than black. But the Latin name for the Australian species is *Trachinotus black eye*, whereas our North American species is called *Trachinotus falcatus*. So it's really the same genus of fish, but it's new ground for us permit fishermen.

MR. SLOAN: Are the flats in Australia the same as those we find down in the Keys?

MR. SAMSON: Mostly. The Australian flats contain a series of small mangrove islands, and the flats go on for miles and miles and miles around them. That whole area from Townesville north, all the way up to the tip of what they call Cape George peninsula, is probably going to develop into a really good permit fishery.

MR. SLOAN: Well, Jack, if somebody says, "I'd like to go out and catch one of these permit on a fly," what kind of outfit would you suggest he use? What should he get?

MR. SAMSON: I would suggest maybe a nine-weight fly rod would be about the right size. You need a good reel, because permit are strong and they make long runs, with an excellent drag and probably at least 250 yards of backing on it—twenty-pound-test backing. You'll need a floating fly line. They primarily take crab flies.

MR. SLOAN: Right. That's what they're browsing; when they come into the flats, they're looking for crabs or critters on the bottom. You know, they've caught them in Key West off the wrecks, in deep water, by jigging and with deepwater sets. But when they get on the flats, they get very, very spooky. Does the same thing happen in Australia?

MR. SAMSON: Yes. I think they're spooky anyplace in the world.

MR. SLOAN: Jack, let's get back to the San Juan River for a little bit. There are pressures here, just like any other place. As the river goes downstream, it gets a little warmer and holds fairly large brown trout, I would suspect.

MR. SAMSON: Yes. A couple of years ago, the game department of the New Mexico Fish and Wildlife Service came up here and did an electro-shocking test on the river. I went along with them to watch. They shocked hundreds and hundreds of fish at each pool to see how big they were and how many of them there were, and, of course, they also tagged them for some further scientific study. They found that the farther down the river you went, the more and more brown trout you got. Incidentally, in terms of size, we turned up some football-sized rainbow trout on the upper parts of the river—fish that were somewhere around ten or twelve pounds. Big fish. Down toward the end of what's called "the quality water"—which is a special fishing water where you're allowed to keep one fish twenty inches long each day and you have to use barbless, single-hook flies—where the water gets a little warmer, we were turning over some great big brown trout. I'm talking about ten-, twelve-, and thirteen-pound browns—huge critters.

MR. SLOAN: Big fish indeed. By the way, Jack, this fishery is active all year round, right? You don't have to wait for any special season, do you?

MR. SAMSON: No, the best thing about San Juan River fishing is that it's good year-round. I think this river and the Colorado River, which runs somewhat to the southwest of here out of Lake Powell, are probably the only two rivers I know of in the Southwest that you can fish year-round. There's an average of about twelve inches of rainfall during the fall around here, so you have blue skies and sunshine most of the time. Even in December, January, February, and March, unless you happen to get a storm of some sort, you can get clear skies and sunshine, and it warms up to, say, fifty or sixty degrees in the afternoon. So you wear a light jacket.

MR. SLOAN: There must be an unconscionable amount of food in this river to support as many fish as I saw yesterday. It's got to be incredible.

177

MR. SAMSON: They estimated there were probably sixty- to seventy-thousand trout in about a four- or five-mile stretch of this river.

MR. SLOAN: That's about *ten thousand* trout per mile.

MR. SAMSON: That's right.

MR. SLOAN: And they're *big*.

MR. SAMSON: Yes, they certainly are.

MR. SLOAN: Now, Jack, I'd like to step down memory lane with you for a moment. You and I went to Cuba in 1978 with a fellow named Ed Zern, one of your staffers at FIELD & STREAM. What was Ed's official title?

MR. SAMSON: I guess you could call him the humor editor, for want of a better term. Ed was a very funny guy.

MR. SLOAN: You gave him the final page for his humor column, right?

MR. SAMSON: That's right.

MR. SLOAN: He had an interesting take on life. His page was marvelous, kind of cozy and warm and funny all at once. He was a good guy, he really was. He is not with us anymore, unfortunately, but we had a marvelous time together when we went to Cuba to fish in the Hemingway Tournament in 1978, the three of us. Do you think it would be possible that somebody might publish an anthology of Ed's work one day?

MR. SAMSON: I sure wish they would.

MR. SLOAN: I think the angling public would enjoy his work again, I really do. His material was almost timeless.

From Cuba, you and I went back to Australia some years later. I remember you called me up and said, "I want to catch a thousand-pound marlin and let him go." And, by God, you got one!

MR. SAMSON: I wouldn't want to have to do it again.

MR. SLOAN: It couldn't have been fun being strapped in that chair. But it was a very interesting fight, you must admit. That fish jumped a lot and was very active, and, if my memory serves me right, I don't think anybody ever had released a thousand-pound marlin in Australia before. I'm sure you were thinking about the terrible waste of all those magnificent fish before you went down there.

MR. SAMSON: Yes, it kind of struck me that it was an awful shame to kill fish like those. They're fifteen feet long and they weigh a thousand pounds or more. A lot of times, these big-game fishermen would bring them in, haul them up on a scale, and have a photograph taken of themselves with the dead fish. Then they would haul the fish out to sea and let the sharks eat it. It seems like kind of a waste of a natural resource.

MR. SLOAN: It is, and if you calculate that waste into all kinds of fishing, you can see immediately how the catch-and-release method we used yesterday over here on the San Juan River is really pro-conservation. Catch and release sustains the fishery for a long time and ensures that it will continue to be sustained into the future.

Now, where is your next fishing trip going to be?

MR. SAMSON: Well, I'm not really sure yet. I'd like to go back and do a little permit fishing down in that area of the Yucatan we mentioned earlier, and in Belize and Honduras, so I expect I'll be going back down there in October.

MR. SLOAN: You know, folks, we're out in the sun here all the time, and I noticed yesterday, Jack, that you use quite a bit of sunblock.

MR. SAMSON: Yes, I do—especially at this elevation. You're a mile closer to the sun out here in New Mexico than you are anywhere else. We're at an elevation of between five thousand and seven thousand feet, so you can get burned pretty easily.

MR. SLOAN: I would caution everybody about the sun, and also about the need to drink a lot of water because you just don't notice how quickly you can become dehydrated out here. Carry a little water with you if you're going to wade around the river here.

Jack, you told me a story once that I never forgot. You were stationed in China during the war, and you were part of the Flying Tigers, right?

MR. SAMSON: No, I was actually part of what *replaced* the Flying Tigers. The Flying Tigers were a civilian operation, a bunch of mercenary volunteer American fighter pilots who went over to Asia before Pearl Harbor and were fighting the Japanese under the command of General Claire Chennault. But when the Flying Tigers were disbanded in July of 1943, of course the war had started by then, and Pearl Harbor had been bombed. The Fourteenth Air Force was formed, and a lot of the Flying Tigers joined it. Then the rest of us

179

all were flown over from the States to join them. We called ourselves the Flying Tigers because we had an arm patch of a tiger.

MR. SLOAN: But exactly where were you stationed?

MR. SAMSON: Our main base was back in western China, at a city called Kunming. But most of our flights were toward the eastern part of China, in places like Guilin and Liuzhou, and we spent the war flying out to bomb cities along the Chinese coast that were occupied by the Japanese. We also were looking for Japanese shipping in the South China Sea.

MR. SLOAN: And the Himalayas were "the hump" over which they had to fly in all your supplies, right? Everything had to be flown in, I would assume.

MR. SAMSON: That's right. We were on the eastern side of the hump, and everything had to be flown in. They didn't have room on those supply flights for anything except bombs and ammunition, so we didn't get much food flown in. We had to kind of live off the land.

MR. SLOAN: Right. I remember your telling me how you gave a sergeant some money, and they flew back a shotgun and some shotgun shells for you.

MR. SAMSON: I guess I'm one of the few people who ever went through part of the war hunting ducks and geese.

MR. SLOAN: But this was for survival.

MR. SAMSON: Yeah, survival, but for fun, too, of course.

MR. SLOAN: Of course. And somehow, the general heard about it.

MR. SAMSON: That's right. General Chennault loved to hunt. He found out that somebody—and he didn't know who—was hunting ducks, so he sent a guy around to my barracks one evening to ask if I was the guy doing it. I told him I was. I thought I was going to get court-martialed. Instead of that, the general shows up with his driver the next morning at about dawn, picks me up, and we went duck hunting.

We had a great morning hunting. After that, this staff car would show up at my barracks about once a week, when it was still dark and early in the morning, and the old man and I would go hunt ducks. He was a wonderful guy. He was from Louisiana—a place called Waterproof, Louisiana—and grew up hunting and fishing. I got to know him that way. I was only a sixth lieutenant, and, of course, he was a one-star general, so there was quite a bit of difference in rank there. But we got to be pretty good friends. I went back after the war to work for him at a civilian airline, Civil Air Transport, for a couple of years.

MR. SLOAN: And was he also a fisherman, Jack?

MR. SAMSON: Not as much, no.

MR. SLOAN: Well, in any case, Jack, you and I have had a long, long friendship and a good one, and we've shared lots of fishing adventures together. As well as I can recollect, we've never had a bad fishing trip, including this one. And the good news is that we've still got a couple of days left.

What do you think we're going to do today on the San Juan River down here in Navajo Dam, New Mexico?

MR. SAMSON: Well, there are a couple of spots that my guide, Tom, was talking about last night that we didn't get to see yesterday. I think he's going to take us to where we can do a little wading.

MR. SLOAN: All right.

MR. SAMSON: And finally, there are a couple of large fish he knows about. He's an unusual guide. I mean, the first thing out of the chute yesterday, we were fishing this run, and he kind of walked up ahead, and he said to me, "Jack, you see this little run here where the river comes down? Well, there's a rock there, and just inside that rock, there's a little hole, and I see two pretty good fish in it." Now, that's what you call *guiding*. He's got good eyesight.

MR. SLOAN: Absolutely. And, by God, there were fish there. We took a nice fish out of one of those little holes. And then tomorrow, we'll go down the lower river, maybe?

MR. SAMSON: I think so. They have about four or five miles of what they call "the quality water," where, as I said before, you fish only with a single barbless hook on a fly. But from Rizuto's San Juan River Lodge down, there are about eleven more miles of river that are open to the public to fish in any way they want. I understand there are a lot more brown trout in that stretch.

MR. SLOAN: I can't wait to find out.

Jack, is there anything more you'd like to pass along to our audience about fishing in general or the environment and conservation? You've spent your lifetime involved in all these areas.

MR. SAMSON: As you know, Steve, I think that the most fun we get out of our sport is catch-and-release fishing. This river is a prime example of how catch and release can improve a fishery. There's a natural spawn here on the river, which is a good sign that it's a healthy, growing fishery. But to catch these fish and fight them, have a great time doing it, and then let them loose to grow larger is really about the most fun we can have.

MR. SLOAN: Well, that's a fact, Jack. These fish are too beautiful and economically important to catch only once.

JAMES MCBROOM

on THE RIVER BOOK

AN INTERVIEW WITH JAMES MCBROOM ON HIS STUDY OF
HYDROLOGY FOR THE FISHERMAN AND THE ENVIRONMENTALLY
CONSCIOUS.

ave you ever wondered why your favorite stretch of a river has changed from year to year? How are nature's forces contributing to these changes? How much has man contributed to water problems? James McBroom is a hydrologist; he studies rivers and streams. With a colleague, Laura Wildman, McBroom has written THE RIVER BOOK: THE NATURE AND MANAGEMENT OF STREAMS IN GLACIATED TERRANES, a fascinating study of the complex inter-relationships that make a river both a complete ecosystem in itself and a contributing part of larger regional and global ecosystems.

No serious angler can fish a trout stream today without some familiarity with hydrology. The very same river or stream flows that provide a home for the angler's quarry also carry its food. By providing shelter and food, the river represents a complete environment for the fish that inhabit it. You may never look at a trout stream or river in the same light after reading McBroom's RIVER BOOK or the following interview with McBroom and Wildman.

MR. SLOAN: My guests today are Jim McBroom and Laura Wildman, experts on water and rivers and what it takes to ensure that the former is clean when it's in the latter. Jim just completed THE RIVER BOOK, a wonderful introduction to the science of hydrology and our most precious commodity on Earth, water. THE RIVER BOOK shows how an appreciation and understanding of hydrology is the foundation for all that we, as fishermen, homeowners, or citizens, can do to ensure the vitality of our watersheds. Jim and Laura, who contributed to Jim's effort, will tell us what we each can do to make our streams and watersheds better.

Good morning, Jim. How are you?

MR. McBROOM: Good morning, Steve. I'm well.

MR. SLOAN: Great. Jim, you're a civil engineer by profession, right?

MR. McBROOM: That's correct. I'm a civil engineer, and over the past twenty years I've really developed an area of interest and experience in the field of water resources, which is a sub-section of civil engineering. Within that area, I practice in the fields of hydrology and hydraulics, so I do a lot of work dealing with rivers and water.

MR. SLOAN: Please give us a definition of hydrology.

MR. McBROOM: Hydrology is really the study of water and its various forms and uses. I study the water cycle, ranging from precipitation and rainfall and how much of it becomes runoff, including how much water flows in the streams and how much water soaks into the ground. I also study how much water is detained by wetland systems and water bodies such as reservoirs. Hydrologists look at water from a quantitative point of view: how much water exists in a given watershed and where it is and how it moves.

MR. SLOAN: Okay. Now you do some fishing now and then, don't you?

MR. McBROOM: Yes. Not as much as I'd like to have time to do, though.

MR. SLOAN: Well, nobody has enough time to fish. But when you do find time, where do you generally fish?

MR. McBROOM: Well, I've fished in small streams for brook trout and other native fish as well as fishing the Housatonic and the Connecticut River. I really just began fishing a few years ago, when my children got a little bit older and I was then able to take them out fishing with me. It's a family sport for us.

MR. SLOAN: Jim, you basically wrote THE RIVER BOOK for the State of Connecticut?

MR. MCBROOM: That's correct. The book project began about ten years ago. Laura and I were asked by the State Department of Environmental Protection, which is the conservation agency of the State of Connecticut, to put together an educational brochure, as they called it then, on floodplain management and how rivers interact with floodplains. As we began working on the project, we realized that there was an awful lot more to educating the public about rivers than just talking about the causes and effects of flooding. We began saying, "Well, let's add a little bit of information about the ecology of the river, and let's add a little bit about the geology and how the river channel forms." Soon, we had a lot of questions that we felt people would want to know the answers to. Why are some rivers wide and shallow while others are narrow and deep? Why do some rivers go in a straight line? Why do some rivers meander? Why do some rivers have high flow in the springtime? Why do some rivers dry up in the summertime? So, in addition to looking at the basic issue of flooding, we began to expand the scope of the work, and it just kept growing. We thought the subject hadn't been covered adequately locally and that we could inform the public about the value of river management if we could educate them on all the different facets of how a river operates. So the project gradually grew into what we now think of as the whole book.

MR. SLOAN: Your book does a great job of integrating the many sciences that constitute the study of rivers. First, you address hydrology, which we said is the study of precipitation and surface runoff and stream rates. You also look at ecology, which we've talked about a lot on this program, as the study of plants, animals, and their environment, with a particular emphasis on aquatic systems. Then you address hydraulics, which is the study of water velocity; water quality, which involves chemistry and biology; and then fluvial morphology, which is the study of the geologic origin of water, the alignment of slopes, and the movement and deposition of sediments.

In a general sense, Jim, do you feel we are we headed toward a greater awareness of these areas as they impact our streams, or have we still got a long way to go?

MR. McBROOM: Well, I think I can answer "yes" to both parts of your question. Yes, we do have a long way to go, but we also do have a greater awareness of the interrelationship between the different components of rivers and how they operate. I like to think that we can manage them from an educated point of view and thereby understand everything that impacts a river—from the effects of watershed hydrology to the importance of water quality, including contaminants that enter a river not just from traditional sources, such as the end of a pipe or a sewage treatment plant, that we think of as common point sources of water pollution.

We also recognize that our parameters of water quality in the river are affected by a variety of components—components like the runoff from our suburban shopping malls or the runoff from feeder streams or even the runoff from everybody's lawns that have been treated with fertilizers and herbicides. We need to build awareness of the fact that whatever we do in a given watershed begins to affect the river that drains it. One of the key messages in THE RIVER BOOK is that we can all play a role in river conservation when we recognize that what we do on our individual properties, what we do on the street, and what we do essentially *anywhere* in the watershed will ultimately affect the river. We tried to convey the notion of this linkage between what happens in the entire watershed, which is that area of land that drains water to a particular channel, and what the results are in the channel.

MR. SLOAN: Well, Jim, let's take that first example you mention, shopping centers and the paving of their parking lots. Every time we pave over our land, we take some portion of our ecosystem with it. I'm not against development because I develop myself. I'm in the real estate business some of the time, when I'm not saving fish.

But for the sake of an example, let's say a developer comes along and wants to build a shopping center and pave a twelve-acre parking lot for it. That's not really a big shopping center when you include the parking lot, which usually constitutes the total area of any shopping center at a ratio of about four or five to one. Anyway, the developer builds on and paves over this twelve acres, which was formerly naturally vegetated soil that would absorb a certain amount of rainfall. But now the developer paves this twelve acres with an asphalt covering that provides an impermeable conduit for the rain as it comes down and runs off somewhere. Then what happens?

MR. McBROOM: Well, with the reduction in the amount of water soaking into the ground, you do find more water reaching the river as runoff because it has now been prevented from infiltrating the soil. In a traditional type of development like the twelve-acre shopping center you just described, that runoff would cause a higher flow rate in the river during and immediately after a rainstorm, which causes erosion of the river channel. The increased flow makes the channel excessively large and can cause a lot of sediment to be disturbed. Now, there are ways of reducing these effects, and one of the philosophies behind the book is that for every action that occurs we have to try to have a reaction to it that will prevent or at least reduce adverse effects from occurring. We call this "mitigation."

MR. SLOAN: How do we do that?

MR. McBROOM: Well, if we have a shopping center with twelve acres of impervious cover, it may be that we can mitigate the effects of all that stormwater runoff by constructing a retention pond next to the shopping plaza to help hold the excess runoff and slowly release it back into the ground or slowly release it back into the river over a period of hours or days. This way, we wouldn't have a flash-flood type of condition with a lot of water reaching the river all of a sudden.

MR. SLOAN: Jim, we're being joined now by your colleague, Laura Wildman. Laura is a fisheries expert.

MS. WILDMAN: Hello Steve; Hi Jim.

MR. SLOAN: Welcome, Laura. Jim and I were just talking about the effects of development and paving of open land and the consequent effects on stormwater flows, Laura. Now Jim, you're suggesting building some type of retention pond for the water that would run off the asphalt that we covered the land with. The goal is to hold the water, basically, so that it can leach back into the groundwater system and stabilize itself.

MR. McBROOM: That's correct. Along with trying to control the amount of water, we also like to think of the retention pond as a way of trying to control water quality. The retention pond will also serve to catch any sediment that gets washed off of the parking lot or the road sand in the wintertime, if you're up north. It helps to catch any oil or grease that may have dripped off the cars and onto the parking lot. So we have a number of different components of the riverine environment that we're trying to protect by using that retention pond as a mitigation device.

MR. SLOAN: Well, we got a call about three Saturdays ago now from a fellow in Sacramento, California, which, in addition to being the State Capital of California is also in a great agricultural area and the center of a large farming community. This caller mentioned that *ten thousand* wells have been affected by agricultural runoff, primarily, but also by auto emissions and other contaminants in his area of California. The contaminants have found their way into the aquifer and now they are affecting the wells. That's very serious.

MR. McBROOM: It certainly is, Steve. That's why we always have to look for that balance between protecting the surface water and protecting the groundwater. One of the steps that is helpful for both the groundwater and the surface water is to try to reduce contaminants at their source by avoiding excessive discharges and by trying not to make discharges that could become potential contaminants of the groundwater. For example, we mentioned before that fertilizers from lawns are having a tremendous impact on our water bodies. We know that if we apply excessive fertilizers at the wrong time of the year, or if the fertilizers we apply are easily soluble, this can . . .

MR. SLOAN: What's the wrong time of the year for applying fertilizers?

MR. McBROOM: When you apply them outside the growing season. For example, some people apply fertilizer in the fall. Well, it really doesn't do much good in the fall because a lot of it runs off before it has a chance to stimulate the plant growth that you're looking for. If it runs off, it may simply stimulate plant growth in a pond or a river and turn the river green with an algae bloom, or it may soak into the groundwater and become a source of nutrient loading. So avoiding excessive use of fertilizers and following the manufacturer's instructions very carefully when we do use them are important parts of protecting the environment. These are steps we can all follow.

MR. SLOAN: Jim, would it be safe to say that all of us who own a home with a yard and a lawn are really part of a watershed? I wonder how it might be possible for each homeowner to come to regard his or her yard as a miniature watershed that contains paths for both surface water and groundwater to flow toward other channels of water or aquifers. I mean, whatever we do on our own little watershed will impact the rainwater that will fall on it and drain downhill or percolate underground and, eventually, affect a river, water quality, and, say, Laura's fish.

MR. McBROOM: That's correct and that's a good analogy. Laura's fish are very important not just for the sake of their role in the environment but because they also serve as a crucial indicator of the quality of the environment: they're almost like having a canary in the coal mine. The health and quality of our fisheries help tell us about the quality of the environment as a whole. So promoting the health of fish is not just good for fishing but also for swimming and other water recreation, for aesthetics, and for future generations.

MR. SLOAN: Laura, let's talk about the fish for a minute. If we're prudent in how we manage our little yard/watershed that we live on, what happens in the water? It clears up, gets better? What are the signs that things are getting better?

MS. WILDMAN: Well, when the water quality gets better, obviously fishing is going to improve. Some other measuring devices you can use to determine whether your river system is healthy is its clarity; you shouldn't see high turbidity in the water, at least not in a lot of the New England streams.

MR. SLOAN: What do you mean by the term "turbidity"?

MS. WILDMAN: Basically, turbidity is an expression of the level of suspended solids in the water. For example, one of the things we see after a rainstorm in a highly impacted watershed is a lot of sediment suspended in the water. Many species of fish have difficulty living in turbid water if it's not native to their area.

MR. SLOAN: Okay.

MS. WILDMAN: So, from a layperson's point of view, turbid water looks brown, so you can see that there's an impact just by looking at the water. But there are many other practices that we undertake that directly impact fisheries but aren't quite so obvious. For instance, Jim was talking about nutrient loading a few minutes ago. Nutrient loading can impact a river from something as simple as having your mulch or manure pile right next to the river and allowing mulch, leaves, grass, and manure to flow into the river. By allowing these materials to wash into the river, you're increasing its nutrient load. Sometimes nutrient loading isn't a problem for a fishery, but usually it is. When nutrient loading increases too high or too quickly, you're really impacting the fishery negatively. I also think THE RIVER BOOK makes it very clear that there are a lot of different types of rivers. Some people are confused when they see the suspended sediments in the river and they think, "Okay, there must be a problem here." That's not always the case. Some rivers really were meant to have suspended sediment in them. You see a lot of turbid rivers in the South, and the fish down there have adapted to those environments.

MR. SLOAN: For example, catfish and carp and other mud-loving fish?

MS. WILDMAN: Exactly.

MR. SLOAN: They rely on their sense of smell more than anything else.

Laura, what about that foam that we often see on rivers—the foam that suddenly turns brown and yellow and swirls around the back eddies. Is that indicative of any kind of problem?

MS. WILDMAN: When I first saw that foam on the river as a kid, I thought for sure someone must be putting hazardous waste in the river. But I found out later as an adult that that kind of foam is really a natural feature of a river. And not being an ecologist—I believe Jim knows a little bit about this, too—I believe that foam is formed from a protein build-up. But it's part of a natural process within the river, and it's not an indication that you have a problem.

MR. SLOAN: Okay. Jim, let's get back for a moment to that example Laura offered of somebody's mulch or manure pile contributing to the nutrient loading of an adjacent stream. Now, let's say this person lives beside this stream or river, and he's got his mulch to store or he's got some kind of fertilizer that he wants to put down. Are you recommending that he build some kind of a berm or some type of vegetative barrier? We shouldn't let our lawns go right down to the edge of a lake, river, or stream that we live beside, right? Is that one of the problems?

MR. McBROOM: That's correct. The scientific community has found that it's highly desirable to leave a vegetative buffer between human activities and the edge of any body of water. This buffer helps serve as a filter of upland runoff and contaminants *before* they reach the river- or stream-bank. Typically, a buffer might be anywhere from twenty-five to one hundred feet wide, and it can consist of multiple layers of vegetation. It's nice to have a high tree canopy that can help protect the river from excessive solar energy and shade the water. At the same time, it's desirable to have a layer of soft-stem vegetation, such as grasses, to filter the water that runs along the surface of the ground before getting into the river. So one of the ways to conserve riverine water resources is to provide this type of vegetative buffer—sometimes it's called a riparian buffer zone—to serve as a barrier from contaminants for the water in the river.

MR. SLOAN: Jim, let's talk a little about flooding, which all of us have seen either in the media or firsthand, if we were unfortunate enough to be living in a floodplain. We have seen flooding recently in places like Ohio and the Dakotas and other areas throughout the United States. Is this just nature's way of saying "hello" every now and then?

MR. McBROOM: Well, we have seen several types of flooding lately. Flooding is a natural phenomenon, and flooding existed before we ever came to this urban environment that we have in many of our communities. If you look at the geology of much of the landscape, it's been shaped by floods. For instance, broad, flat valleys that are full of sandy, sedimentary-type soil are the result of flooding. However, we've altered the situation, particularly in the smaller watersheds where the effects of small changes become noticeable much more quickly, by removing the tree canopy, filling in wetlands, reducing the size of the river channel, and increasing the amount of impervious cover that creates more runoff to begin with. All these practices intensify the flooding process. Particularly on smaller streams in urban areas, the human impact becomes much more noticeable.

On other rivers, we've altered the flood conditions by building dikes or levees that under normal conditions can force the river into a defined channel, which helps for navigation. But on the other hand, these channelization efforts don't allow the river to spread out as it would under natural conditions. In fact, the river may actually get deeper in the channel as a result of the dikes. So dikes and levees are kind of a double-edged sword: they're helpful in controlling small floods, but when they get overtopped in a larger flood, it becomes a disaster.

MR. SLOAN: Laura, one thing that fascinates me—and I don't know the answer to this question—is where do the fish go during a flood? What happens to them?

MS. WILDMAN: That's funny that you should ask that because I had someone ask me the same question recently. I want to make clear that I'm not a fisheries biologist; I'm a water resource engineer like Jim, but I do deal with the fisheries aspects of our projects.

Fish will take refuge in a variety of places during a flood. They will go out onto the flood plain, but they will also take refuge in undercut banks or behind rocks. Sometimes if the flows are fast enough, they will move to slower-moving areas, like up into tributaries or into the lower, slower parts of the river. Fish will often move when a storm comes in, unless they can find refuge behind something or in an area of lower velocities in the river, because, obviously, they can only tolerate certain velocities before their swimming speeds are outdone.

MR. SLOAN: That's interesting. I would assume that every time there's a flood, some of these fish may get into an area where they haven't been before. That's why suddenly some guy wakes up and says, "Holy smoke, what's this in my pond?" And there it is.

MS. WILDMAN: Yes, I'm sure fish have been introduced to different areas through flooding. In fact, flooding was probably part of the way that a variety of fish spread into different areas.

MR. SLOAN: Well, let's get back to urban America, where a lot of people live today. You see a lot of riverfront parks up in Hartford and around the Connecticut River where the edge of the river has been, for lack of a better term, *sculpted* in one way or another, either through rocks or maybe even through concrete or steel bulkheads. Is this helpful or harmful to a river? Should we be proponents of these parks, or should we say, "Let nature be wild and rough at the edges," and not have these modifications?

MR. McBROOM: Well, in general, it's detrimental to alter a riverbank to make it smooth and hard with something like concrete or steel. A lot of the fish, and not just the fish but animals that are lower in the food chain, depend upon the organic detritus from trees and overhanging branches to help serve as the base of the food chain. We find that a lot of the bacteria and fungi that live on leaves, and of course organic material along the bank, actually provide the base of the food chain. When you line the river channel with concrete or rocks or artificial materials, you reduce the amount of food sources for the fishery.

MR. SLOAN: Jim, we've got a lot of dams on our rivers—some of them based on the old industrial-type dam that was really designed to provide a power source and some of them like the ones out West that were built to create hydroelectric power and help water flow more efficiently to supply water for agricultural needs. What's the trend now? Are we trying to eliminate some of these dams, and how does that help clean up a river?

MR. McBROOM: Well, I think the trend today is toward a very careful review of any proposed new dam to see what its environmental impact will be before it's allowed to be built. In some areas of the country, dams are actually being removed in places where they're obsolete and no longer being used. For example, in some areas, we find dams that were built in the 1800s as a source of power for industry but are no longer being used by industries. Many of the industries that required their power may not even exist anymore. So these dams are serving only as a fish block; they prevent fish movement up- or downstream. They also spoil whitewater sports, and they trap sediment. Some of the dams are being breached, which means that you remove a portion of it to allow the water to flow through an opening. Other dams may be totally removed. In still other cases, like a project we're working on right now, we're building a channel around a dam that is being preserved for historical purposes. This channel will provide a bypass that fish can use, like an oversized fish ladder, so that we can then restore some of the migratory species into the river without their being blocked by the dam.

MS. WILDMAN: And that channel will provide a boat passage as well as a fish passage so recreational users will be able to get canoes and kayaks down the river as well.

MR. SLOAN: That's marvelous. I have fished a couple of tailwater fisheries. As you know, tailwater, by definition, is the river water that originates at the base of a dam as the water discharges through the spillway. When I think of tailwater fisheries, I think of rivers like the San Juan, out in New Mexico, which is for the first four and a half miles one of the most extraordinary stretches of trout-fishing water I've ever seen *(See "Jack Samson on the San Juan River" on page 169)*. I can't believe the size and population density of the fish in the San Juan; I think there are something like ten thousand fish per mile in that river—one big rainbow trout after another. What would you say the impact of that kind of fishery is versus the impact of the dam itself? Is it a positive that we have these good fisheries at the base of these dams? Or maybe the dam should be eliminated altogether. Or are there other factors that we need to weigh as part of the equation?

MS. WILDMAN: Well, I fish the San Juan myself, and I actually caught a beautiful rainbow trout right below the Navaho Dam. Fisheries just below very large dams with releases from the colder portion of the water, a low-flow release, basically, can really enhance fisheries downstream. You really see some great fish populations downstream from some of these larger dams like the Navaho. But not all dams have low-flow releases. Not all dams were designed to keep water behind them. A lot of flood-control dams don't even keep large bodies of water behind them. So dams have a mixed impact. While in some cases you will find a great fishery below a dam, as in the Navaho's low-flow, cold-water release into the San Juan, that's not always the case. Many dams are still blocking fish migration, so the species of fish in the river become a critical factor in the evaluation. If you were concerned about a salmon population, you'd really want to remove the dam because you'd want to be able to let the salmon go as far as possible upstream. That helps in the reproductive cycle. But if you're evaluating a rainbow trout population below a cold-water release on a dam, there's no question that the dam's providing a tremendous benefit to the fishery as well. In short, you have to look at the total effect on a given river and see whether or not the dam is benefiting the river as a whole. You have to play around with a lot of different issues for each particular river.

MR. McBROOM: In contrast to the benefits we just discussed with a dam like the Navaho, we find that some dams allow the water to become very warm and may cause a decline in the dissolved oxygen level. The area downstream from these dams may not be able to support fisheries well because of high water temperatures and low oxygen levels. So each situation is a little bit different and requires careful review individually.

MR. SLOAN: Let me ask you this now: when we go fishing in July and August, especially from the Northeast all the way down into the South and probably out in the Midwest and West, too, we start to see algae accumulating on our lakes and ponds. What's that from? Is that natural or are we humans contributing to its growth?

MR. McBROOM: Well, natural streams can have some algae, but we contribute a lot to that by allowing excessive amounts of nutrients, such as nitrogen and phosphorous, into our streams. Just as fertilizers are used to promote the growth of vegetation on land, they also promote the growth of aquatic vegetation, both floating algae and algae that's attached to rocks.

MR. SLOAN: We've all heard the word "choking" used to describe algae blooms. Are they literally choking these waters?

MR. McBROOM: Yes. Algae can choke the water physically by filling it with plant matter, and it can also choke the water chemically by depleting its supply of dissolved oxygen. By decaying on the bottom of the stream, these plants use oxygen from the water. When algae blooms reduce the amount of oxygen in the water, they can lead to fish kills.

MR. SLOAN: Laura, algae blooms would have to have an absolutely adverse impact on a fishery, wouldn't they?

MS. WILDMAN: Definitely.

MR. SLOAN: Now Jim, if we see a pond or a lake that's full of algae and is a mess, should we attribute it to a warm water condition, or could it be a warm atmospheric condition?

MR. McBROOM: Algae growth occurs primarily in warm weather conditions. Of course, in a pond, you have a lot of solar exposure, so a lot of the algae is using photosynthesis to grow. Because algae tends to grow in bright, sunny water, planting shade trees along the bank is a good way to counteract its growth.

MR. SLOAN: Now, what can you do if an algae bloom has already occurred and the surface of the pond is coated? Do you call in the pond-scum cleaner guy and have him rake it off and put it up on the land to dry out and decay?

MR. McBROOM: That's only a temporary solution. Some people manage their ponds by harvesting the weeds and removing them from the pond. But in general, they'll grow back after a while. A long-term solution is to try to remove the source of nutrients entering the pond, try to catch the sediment before it comes into the pond, and plant the banks around the edge of the pond to try to provide more shade. Try to exchange the water so it isn't sitting stagnant all day.

It's important to maintain the pond's watershed so that you have a continual flow of water coming through the pond. For example, if you have a lot of diversions or a lot of impervious cover in your watershed, the water rushes off down to the big rivers after a rainstorm, and it doesn't leave much water to flow into the pond day-in and day-out and maintain the kind of continual flow that a pond needs. This is a problem caused by a lot of the rivers we see in our urban areas; they have very high flow rates when it rains, but then they don't have much water in them during the summertime because the water has already left the watershed. We end up with low-flow problems in some of our streams during the summer.

MR. SLOAN: Jim, in your studies, don't we have something like a bio-cumulative effect at work here? For instance, if a river comes into a lake and then it goes out to another outlet through another river, the water leaving that first lake is going to carry with it all of the effluent that may have found its way into that first lake. If the lake is polluted because of, say, septic systems being too close to the water, then you would have even more pollution draining down through the outlet to the next lake. This cycle repeats itself with each succeeding lake downstream, with the river picking up more speed and more pollution from each lake and each tributary. By the time the river reaches the ocean, we've usually got a helluva problem that affects everything—fish, invertebrates, and the entire chain of life.

MR. McBROOM: Well, that's correct. The hydrological impacts that change the flow rate and the water quality impacts on the watershed are both cumulative, so they *do* tend to become worse and worse as one goes downstream. That's why we're trying to teach people how to manage their landscapes and their water bodies to prevent this type of deterioration from occurring. Then we try to mitigate any adverse effects that do occur so that we actually have net improvements in water quality.

MR. SLOAN: Jim, Laura, this has been fascinating. I want to thank you both for joining us today. THE RIVER BOOK has wonderful source material for anyone who cares about the environment and especially for fishermen who want to understand what they can do to improve their fisheries.

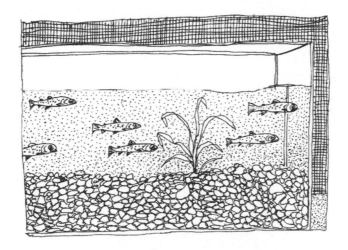

JOAN STOLIAR
on Trout in the Classroom

AN INTERVIEW WITH THE LATE JOAN STOLIAR ON HER WORK
WITH TROUT IN THE CLASSROOM, AN AWARD-WINNING
PROGRAM TO BRING FISHERIES EDUCATION TO YOUNG PEOPLE.

*J*oan Stoliar left these "mortal coils" on June 18, 2000. She bequeathed us a fishing legacy just as rich as that of Theodore Gordon, Edward Hewitt, Izaak Walton, and Charles Cotton. Stoliar was one of those rare fishing persons who looked beyond the technical proficiency in the presentation of a fly to a trout and was not interested in becoming an endless world traveler looking for new places to fish. She always had larger goals for her sport. She is survived by her beloved husband, Art.

A notable angler on any stream and a masterful fly tyer, Stoliar transformed her own consuming passion for fishing into helping other people who might otherwise never have been exposed to the sport find happiness, learning, and pleasure in it. Either of her two endeavors, Project Access or Trout in the Classroom, would have been sufficient achievements for any one person's lifetime. That Stoliar played such an instrumental role in the launch and success of both *is quiet testimony to her incredible vitality and energy. Project Access gains fishing access for the handicapped on trout streams, and Trout in the Classroom brings live trout eggs into inner city classrooms for students to watch the life cycle begin. Once the eggs hatch, the students nurture and return the fingerlings to a trout stream to release them into the wild. In the following interview with Sloan, Stoliar describes the pure joy of an inner city child in the process of completing this cycle.*

This extraordinary woman was also an award-winning book illustrator and graphic designer of book dust jackets and covers. Her most famous work in this field was probably the illustrations and cover art for Richard Bach's many books, including the best-selling JONATHAN LIVINGSTON SEAGULL. *She also created illustrations and designed covers for books by James Clavell, Johnny Carson, Truman Capote, and Wanda Landowska. Her illustration and graphic design credits in the fishing world are no less impressive:* DRESSING FLIES FOR FRESH AND SALT WATER, *by Poul Jorgensen;* THE BOOK OF LURES, *by Charles Fox;* FISHING THE MIDGE, *by Ed Koch;* THE WIND ON YOUR CHEEK, *by William J. Schaldach;* REMEMBRANCES OF RIVERS PAST, *by Ernest Schwiebert; and many others.*

Stoliar received numerous awards from the American Institute of Graphic Arts, the Printing Industries of America, and GRAPHIC ARTS *magazine. A champion of professional recognition and compensation for graphic artists, she served for ten years as design director of the Coalition of Publishers for Employment, and her design for Bach's* ILLUSIONS *was the first total book design to ever be copyrighted and generate royalties for its designer. New York City Mayor Ed Koch appointed her to his Commission for Distinguished Guests, where she served as a representative of the city in meetings with heads of state and other visiting dignitaries.*

You can learn more about her remarkable work by visiting the Project Access Web site at www.projectaccess.com *or the Trout in the Classroom site at* troutinaclassroom.com. *For an additional perspective on Project Access, please see the interview with Art Nierenberg, a Project Access co-founder with Stoliar, on page 65.*

"In a lifetime of achievements, I believe Trout in the Classroom will be [my] most enduring [legacy]," Stoliar once said. After reading the following interview with her, see if you agree.

MR. SLOAN: Today, we're going to talk about children, we're going to talk about fishing, and we're going to talk about a marvelous project that's bringing the two of them together. It's called Trout in the Classroom, and we will be talking this morning with its founder, Joan Stoliar. It's a wonderful, wonderful program, and we'll talk a bit about some of the ways we can all contribute to its growth and success.

Good morning, Joan.

MS. STOLIAR: Hi, Steve.

MR. SLOAN: Joan, as I just mentioned, you've created this wonderful program called Trout in the Classroom. Maybe you could start at the beginning by telling us how you came up with the idea for the organization.

MS. STOLIAR: Sure. You know, Steve, nothing in life is ever original with anybody. Never take full credit for anything; this is a marvelous piece of advice for organizations writing about what they do.

Trout in the Classroom got its start when I picked up a Trout Unlimited (TU) newsletter that mentioned an educational program, sponsored by a local chapter of TU in Deposit, New York, that involved hatching fish right in the elementary school classroom. Now, Deposit is part of our watershed, so I contacted the TU chapter and the teacher who had initiated the program. They directed me to California, where the State Board of Trout, Salmon, and Steelhead there had asked an elementary school teacher to devise a curriculum that would teach children about the ecosystem by using what they had on hand. Of course, they had much to be concerned about in California, in terms of their coastal water and their freshwater resources, so a curriculum that brought fisheries issues right to the students seemed to be perfect. It succeeded, and it's still the curriculum that the State of California uses.

So I sent for those curricula and proposed to Theodore Gordon Flyfishers, Inc. (TGF), a freshwater advocacy group, that this would be a very good vehicle for teaching not only New York City children about the environment but for connecting them with the upstate children who actually live in the watershed. TGF was very interested in sponsoring Trout in the Classroom, and the program became a beautiful vehicle for connecting these two groups of children.

MR. SLOAN: A child can live upstate and see a stream every day and walk by it— maybe even for his or her whole life—and not know how it works, what happens in it, or how it fits into the larger picture of his or her environment.

MS. STOLIAR: TGF has been involved in conservation matters for years. And working between the two communities, the upstate and downstate, has always had its challenges because of the tensions that exist between upstate and downstate New Yorkers over "their water." Many upstate residents resent the fact that "their water" finds itself downstate, in the Big Apple, where it becomes "someone else's water." We find that that tension doesn't exist as much anymore and for a couple of reasons. First, there's a new, young parent body, for instance, that responded to the program that was taking place in their children's classrooms. Secondly, the children both downstate and upstate were so excited about the program and brought home such enthusiasm for it that the adults in the community started responding. This is how you create an environmentally protective society: you start with the children.

MR. SLOAN: Absolutely. Well, let's start at the beginning and walk our audience through Trout in the Classroom. Let's say a teacher wants to teach his or her children about what happens in a stream or how trout live or where they get their eggs. Where does the teacher get the eggs to get started?

MS. STOLIAR: Well, ours come from the DeBruce hatchery in Livingston Manor, New York, about 120 miles northwest of New York City. In fact, that hatchery is part of the New York State Department of Environmental Conservation (NYSDEC) and supplies trout eggs to hatcheries in other parts of the state, as well.

MR. SLOAN: Now what do you need in the classroom to get this program started?

MS. STOLIAR: In the funded Trout in the Classroom program, the school receives $500 for the teacher to use to set up a chiller—some way of keeping the water cold—and a filtered aquarium. That $500 is a pretty reasonable number, I think.

MR. SLOAN: In other words, the $500 seeds the project and gets things going by covering the cost of the hardware. They start with an aquarium, a filter, and a chiller right in their classroom. What happens next, Joan?

MS. STOLIAR: Well, they can use a variety of configurations. The California curriculum suggests a configuration that involves running tubing into a little refrigerator to chill the water before it goes into the aquarium. Another system was built that placed the aquarium and its filter directly inside a Styrofoam box with a small air conditioner inside to keep the temperature low. Both systems worked. In fact, in Roscoe, New York, they had a hundred fish to put into the stream after starting with just two hundred eggs, and in Livingston Manor, they had fifty. Those are wonderful survival rates.

MR. SLOAN: Boy, that's terrific. You might not even get rates that good in a controlled hatchery.

MS. STOLIAR: And remember, Steve, that these were eight-year-olds who were running the show, the third grade classes in these two schools. You know what the promise is that TGF makes in administering the program? We provide the seed money, and then we leave good teachers alone to be good teachers. In turn, they use the trout hatchery in their classroom as a learning tool for almost anything they want to teach. They even involve the children in the math associated with their hatchery: for example, what's the percentage of fish that are still surviving? The teachers use it for art, too. You should see the wonderful art that has been generated through the program.

MR. SLOAN: I noticed that. You're right; it's fantastic.

MS. STOLIAR: The essay writing was outstanding, as well. In fact, the high school children and the intermediate school children wrote moving essays about their fish and its survival after its release. I was getting e-mail letters from the children in the Brooklyn school, before they brought their fish up to release it in the Willowemoc [near Roscoe and Livingston Manor], in which they were writing, "Tell us, what kind of a home is this fish going to go to?" I wrote them back to reassure them that the Willowemoc was a world-famous, perfect trout habitat.

MR. SLOAN: Absolutely. I can't imagine a better environment for a trout than the Willowemoc.

MS. STOLIAR: But the children were thrilled to hear that.

MR. SLOAN: That's a point well taken; they did need to feel reassured, I'm certain. After the kids have finished raising these trout, then the trout really are ready to go into the environment, right?

MS. STOLIAR: Yes, they are ready to be taken to the stream by the children. Of course, the teachers and I sometimes worry about how the children will feel about releasing the fish after six months of nurturing and loving. You know, you love what you grow, which is part of this program. You find out about responsibility, about how difficult and important it is to be responsible for another living creature. You learn how fragile the things that live in the water are, and you come to love them.

When it comes time to return them, how are you going to feel? Well, there was a great celebratory mood when we came to the stream and returned the fish, because as one kid, Floyd Frankie, explained, "This is their natural habitat. They're going home. We're helping them to go to where they should live." It was very exciting.

MR. SLOAN: It *is* very exciting, Joan. You've sent me a couple of letters that I'd like to share with our audience. Here's what nine-year-old Colleen Casey wrote:

> I think that the Trout Goes to the School project is a good influence for all of us. It was really fun watching the fish grow from little tiny eggs to bigger fish. We had a big problem once. A lot of fish died because some didn't eat, some were pinheads, and some got sucked up in the filter. I think that we all had a lot of fun, and I know I learned a lot about the fish. We went through three bags of food. The first food was really powdery, the second food was just a little bigger, and the third food is like coffee grounds. I don't want to let the fish go when it's time for them to go. I don't want to let them go because it was fun to watch them grow up.

Now, isn't that a marvelous letter, Joan?

MS. STOLIAR: It's a lovely letter. It's just what I was talking about when I mentioned the enthusiasm and the attachment for the fish that develops in the students. I'd like to read you a short poem written by a thirteen-year-old. He's a student named Luiz Cruz in the Brooklyn school, I.S. 318. It's called "A Poem without Much Care."

> A poem without much care involves a trout,
> A trout that has intense love from its caretakers,
> but pushes some away.
> Still, it changes lives, hopes, and its surroundings.
> Angelouse has no legs, no arms, but a heart,
> A heart that gives love back to the human in his life.

> By Luis Cruz

He's thirteen and lives in Brooklyn, Steve.

MR. SLOAN: A thirteen-year-old wrote that?

MS. STOLIAR: Isn't it exquisite?

MR. SLOAN: Yes, it's fabulous.

Now, Joan, I'd like to get back to some of the operational details of Trout in the Classroom. You had mentioned earlier that you obtain the trout eggs for the program from the DeBruce hatchery, up in Livingston Manor.

MS. STOLIAR: That's right, the DeBruce hatchery supplies them, and NYSDEC, which runs DeBruce, is very, very supportive of Trout in the Classroom. You must have permits from NYSDEC to receive the eggs. TGF promises the schools that it will do all the paperwork to get the permits so the teachers and students can collect insects and study them in class. You also are required to have a NYSDEC permit to put the fish back in the stream. So we've worked very closely with NYSDEC on the permitting process for the program, and the DEP (Department of Environmental Protection) in New York City is also very, very supportive and wants to see Trout in the Classroom grow and succeed in the schools.

The whole idea of the program is to help children become so completely sensitive to the environment that, as one teacher, Gloria Smith, said in Roscoe, "My children will never again throw a piece of paper in a stream."

MR. SLOAN: Good.

MS. STOLIAR: This is our focus. We strive to inculcate that sensitivity toward the environment throughout Trout in the Classroom.

MR. SLOAN: Well, they could tell their parents, too. Then we'd be in really great shape.

MS. STOLIAR: Well, their parents do get involved.

MR. SLOAN: I'm curious, Joan. Could you do this program with bass or carp if you wanted to?

MS. STOLIAR: Of course. In fact, they even do it with salmon in California.

MR. SLOAN: That's incredible. So, it's not only trout, folks. If you live in a state that may not have a trout hatchery but does have a largemouth bass or other production hatchery near you, you can have the same classroom program set up for those species. It works essentially the same way with any species of fish, and the focus and goal is identical: to get kids interested in their ecosystem early.

Now, as you mentioned, these fish go back into the stream after the appropriate permits have been obtained, and you make sure they don't have any fungus or other disease problems, right?

MS. STOLIAR: Well, if they survive, they probably don't harbor any diseases.

MR. SLOAN: This is true. And, of course, there'd really be no way for them to contract any disease in their aquarium environment.

MS. STOLIAR: That's right. And even the natural attrition that occurs often provides an opportunity for learning. You can understand, Steve, the kind of conversations that have to go on in the classes regarding the amount of attrition that takes place. We use attrition as an opportunity to convey the sense that nature is profligate: it puts out lots of eggs, but and not all of them survive. From the very beginning, the children are removing dead eggs with little eyedroppers as part of their daily maintenance process. These eight-year-olds are selecting the largest fry and maintaining their life. It's very difficult for them sometimes.

MR. SLOAN: Well, it's also an interesting way of teaching children about death.

MS. STOLIAR: Absolutely.

MR. SLOAN: It's very sanitary this way. It's emotional, but not wrenching like it would be for somebody in the family. They learn that animals are born and also die.

MS. STOLIAR: Well, there's quite a vivid example of that. Would you like to hear what happened in the high school?

MR. SLOAN: Sure.

MS. STOLIAR: Someone accidentally dropped the oxygen experiment chemicals into the tank, killing all the fish immediately.

MR. SLOAN: A complete wipeout?

MS. STOLIAR: Yes, an absolute wipeout. The teacher was devastated because he's a farmer, and he's used to handling animals and successful transference. He was devastated. The children were actually much more able to handle it. As a matter of fact, when the Brooklyn children came up to the watershed and met with their high school counterparts to tour the watershed with them, the high school children told them about how, after their own fish kill, they began to study total disasters, pollution, toxic spills, and legislation to deal with them. The fish kill in their classroom led them to study all the things you also have to know when you're dealing with protecting the ecosystem. They could impart this to the twelve-year-olds who came up from Brooklyn. In fact, I met one young man that day, and he turned to me and introduced himself. He said, "I'm

Rich. I'm the kid who killed all the fish." At that moment, he was tying a fly. And next to him was a twelve-year-old, and Rich said, "As soon as I finish tying this, I'm going to be helping Luis with his fly." That attitude was exactly what we were looking for with the program. Clearly, his class had put the fish kill behind them. And we were delighted to see the connection between the downstate children and the upstate children flourishing.

MR. SLOAN: Joan, tell us, if somebody wants more information about Trout in the Classroom in New York State, or even out of state if you know of comparable programs, where can you direct them?

MS. STOLIAR: They should write to Theodore Gordon Fly Fishers, Inc., Trout in the Classroom Program, P. O. Box 2345, Grand Central Station, New York, NY 10163. We'll be glad to share our experiences with them, and we'll share any useful information we have with them.

MR. SLOAN: All right. Now, Joan, I'd like to get back to some of the wonderful letters from the students in the program. Here's one from a student named Nick Vallone, who lives up in Otisville, New York, right in your backyard. Nick writes, "Over the year, I have learned that it takes a lot of work to raise brown trout. They are not exactly brown. The stages are eggs, alevin, and fry." I'm sure *alevin* and *fry* are new words for these kids. Nick continues:

> When they are little, they have something called an egg sack. If the trout don't eat, they are called pinheads. When we pour fish food in for the trout, they fight for it. In one week, they grow at least one centimeter. This project is fun because you learn a lot, and I like to learn.

That is fabulous.

MS. STOLIAR: It certainly is, Steve; it's a wonderful letter. You should see those children when they're involved with the program. It's just such a turn-on.

I believe that with this whole program, what we're really doing is looking ten years down the road. When you see an eight-year-old, you think of him at eighteen, in college. When you see the sixteen-year-old, you think of him at twenty-six and working. You hope that in the future, if there's a problem at one end or the other end of, say, the watershed, the city, or upstate, somebody will pick up the phone and call someone they've known for years who was in the program. See, TGF plans to keep these children connected. The teachers want to use the program to establish pen pals and use e-mail to keep these kids in touch. The schools already have computers. We hope that eventually the students will be trading information on a Web site. I really believe these children should go on knowing each other.

MR. SLOAN: So, Joan, how many Trout in the Classroom programs do you have up and running now?

MS. STOLIAR: Well, we did four schools for starters. This is our first year, and we're finding out how to make it run well. We're learning a lot while the kids are learning. You learn what the best age group is, or even whether or not there *is* a best age group for the program. We don't know yet.

MR. SLOAN: What do you *think* it might be?

MS. STOLIAR: I'm not sure yet, Steve. We've had success at every level, so it's kind of hard to tell.

We had four groups underway initially. Each age group has its own strengths. I can say that there are three children in the high school program who are now going on to college and majoring in environmental science. That's tremendous, I think. In the Brooklyn school, two of the children who were in the program and came up to the Catskills to spend an environmental weekend, which TGF funded, are going on to the High School of Art and Design in New York City, where the program is going to run this year. Now, in the High School of Art and Design, there are special education teachers who are interested in the program. You see, Steve, the secret to the program's success is recognizing that you are working with two important groups: the first group is the children who want to learn, and the second group is the teachers who want to teach with it. An excited teacher and eager students make Trout in the Classroom happen.

MR. SLOAN: Of course.

MS. STOLIAR: So the teachers who will be running the program in the High School of Art and Design are a special education teacher and another teacher who specializes in science. They see the program as a vehicle for bringing the special ed student into the mainstream. It's also a perfect vehicle to share with mainstream students. Two of the students from Brooklyn are going to be in that high school and will have participated in the program already. They'll be coming in as freshmen, but imagine how much status they will gain personally by knowing how to raise trout already.

MR. SLOAN: That's for sure; they'll be looked to as the resident experts.

You know, it's interesting. I was involved in a project where we tried to buy a property and raise tropical fish on it because it had a very good underwater spring that could pump clean, salt-free water. This was down in the Keys in Florida.

MS. STOLIAR: Interesting!

MR. SLOAN: You may not know this, but 98 percent of the tropical fish that are harvested die. Tropical fish merchants use cyanide, they use concussion grenades, they use everything imaginable to catch fish for resale. In the process, they're wrecking the coral reefs in the Philippines and in Borneo and in the Red Sea to harvest tropical fish for our aquariums here in the United States.

Now compare this sort of environmental devastation with something like Trout in the Classroom, where you go to the local hatchery, which is already rearing fish anyway, you get some eggs to put in your classroom aquarium, you raise them up, and then you put them back into the environment. That is a dynamite program.

MS. STOLIAR: Well, it certainly creates a different kind of sensibility in a child as he or she grows. You've got to give the new parent body, this younger parent body, credit also for their response to their children's excitement.

You know, that reminds me of the chamber of commerce in the town of Rockland holding the traditional two-headed trout dinner.

MR. SLOAN: The "Beamoc." One head is in the Beaverkill and the other is in the Willowemoc.

MS. STOLIAR: Well, right.

MR. SLOAN: I haven't heard that name for a while.

MS. STOLIAR: That's right; it's the trout that can't decide whether to go on the Willowemoc or the Beaverkill.

But do you know what their dinner focused on? It focused on the children. It had an exhibit of the children and their work and had the children there reading their essays and showing their artwork. The speakers all focused on the children as the future. I remember one wonderful quote from that dinner. The children had been working with a professor from Columbia for a couple of years, planting trees and developing an understanding of the need for trees, their shade, and their detritus for the insects. A paper written by several of the children contained the following statement: "No trees, no insects. No insects, no trout. No trout, no fishermen. No fishermen, the businesses would close and the town has to move away." That was the closing line for the dinner.

MR. SLOAN: You know what? That same cycle is true in saltwater and in freshwater.

MS. STOLIAR: Of course.

MR. SLOAN: No cod, no town.

MS. STOLIAR: But the grownups understand this relationship, and they're responding by educating their children about it. I think this understanding will create a great turnaround in many communities.

MR. SLOAN: Well, I'd like to read to you a little bit, Joan, and we can comment on this together. It's a passage from a log that a Trout in the Classroom teacher prepared. She writes: "October: Average temperature, eleven degrees C., fifty-four degrees F." So right away, this tells me that the kids in this classroom are discussing this program in a dual-temperature mode, centigrade and Fahrenheit. It says, "The eggs were delivered and placed into a small hatchery plastic container, which was filled with three inches of water. A small container was submerged into a ten-gallon river tank with water circulating through a small refrigerator—i.e., the chiller." She continues, "November thirtieth: We removed fifteen to twenty dead eggs. The dead eggs appear hollow and whitish in color."

MS. STOLIAR: Amazing detail, isn't it?

MR. SLOAN: It's incredible. And it goes on and on with all sorts of information about the progress. Here, the log states, "The average length was seven and one-quarter millimeters." Tiny little things are reported, like, "All the eggs hatched." Then, on the nineteenth of November, they began feeding them food. "The egg sack is down," she wrote. They looked healthy on the twenty-first, and on the twenty-fourth they fed them two times. There was one black fish and one deformed fish. "In general, the fish are more active," the log says. In December, the temperature went down to eight degrees centigrade and forty-six degrees Fahrenheit. The chiller was working. The average length was fifteen millimeters. The number of dead fish was twenty-seven. And she says, "The fish are slimmer and longer; they're vigorous. Each fish has about ten to fifteen spots."

Then going on in the month, some of the fish are light in color. The water is cloudy. On the fifteenth, the fish have a golden color on their bodies. Most of them are swimming around, and they are lightly colored, she reports. It says then that they took off a Styrofoam cover and the taped panels, and they maintained the cold water. But then, on the twenty-second, they removed some of the insulation. Suddenly, the temperature became too cold. Many of the fish died because of the sudden drop in temperature.

Well, that's no different, Joan, than what happens in a stream.

MS. STOLIAR: Exactly.

MR. SLOAN: This log is marvelous. Then the kid drew a graph of the temperature and added a key in centigrade and Fahrenheit. So, it really is like bringing a trout stream into the classroom.

MS. STOLIAR: Well, it's certainly bringing all the subjects together. I think one of the focuses right now in education is to have integrated programs through which students can do their math, their English, and their science. As you can see, even poetry has come out of this program already.

They really learned firsthand about events and consequences. You know, when you have a problem—for instance, they had that sudden drop in temperature and an enormous loss in the fish population as a result—you get to see the practical effects. They ended up with one fish that was about three inches long, and they named it Angelouse.

MR. SLOAN: Angelouse? What a great name.

MS. STOLIAR: Yes, Angelouse. Angelouse was the fish they were writing me about, asking about what kind of a river it would be going into. Well, many of them took the trip up to the Catskills on the bus. Some of them had never been in the country before and were going to have a weekend to spend with fine teachers. They were taught how to tie flies, they got to fish and learned to cast, they learned how to catch fish on the fly they had tied, they went touring the watershed, and they met the other students who also had participated in the program.

But coming up in the bus, they had this one fish, Angelouse. They had Angelouse in an aquarium bag with air and water that was submerged in successive buckets filled with ice. They were monitoring the temperature for three hours up to the Catskills, and they had to keep moving the ice back and forth. That fish arrived in perfect health.

MR. SLOAN: Isn't that wonderful.

MS. STOLIAR: It was so exciting.

MR. SLOAN: And Angelouse was released into the Willowemoc?

MS. STOLIAR: Into the Willowemoc, that's right.

MR. SLOAN: Now, that fish put into that stream, then caught later on and released, and caught and released again and again, will provide sport for thousands of people.

MS. STOLIAR: And the knowledge the children have gained about the ecosystem and its fragility will never be lost.

MR. SLOAN: Absolutely. Well, our knowledge has certainly been broadened today, thanks to you and your program. Thanks, Joan, for enlightening us on Trout in the Classroom. Tight lines and a good drift.

MS. STOLIAR: Thanks for having me, Steve.

RAMÓN ARANGUREN
on Trouting in Argentina

AN INTERVIEW WITH RAMÓN ARANGUREN ON THE HISTORY OF
A UNIQUE TROUT FISHERY IN THE ANDES OF ARGENTINA.

*R*amón Aranguren is not only an extraordinary fishing guide but has an *encyclopedic historical knowledge of Argentine fishing. He explains how rivers were formed in Argentina and then how they were stocked with brown and rainbow trout. There were no native trout in Argentina in 1904; today, a river in western Argentina hosts all four species: brook trout, brown trout, rainbow trout, and landlocked salmon. Aranguren's retelling of the journey of the first trout eggs from the United States to Argentina is worthy of a book in and of itself.*

Aranguren, who guides anglers for Chimehuin Safaris, also explains why the estancia Arroyo Verde, which Meme and Mauricio Lariviere own and use to host anglers from all over the world, is one of the most impressive trout-fishing spots in the world. The exceptional clarity of the water in the region has led to the development of specialized flies and fishing techniques designed to meet the challenges posed by the unique fisheries of the region. In the following interview, Aranguren

211

discusses with Sloan how one of the world's finest trout fisheries came into existence—in just under a century.

MR. SLOAN: I'd like to welcome our listeners to Bariloche, Argentina, where I am currently standing with our guest, a fabulous fishing guide named Ramón Aranguren. Ramón and I just fished the Traful River, and we're going to tell you all about it. It was spectacular, absolutely spectacular. We're also going to tell you how you can get to Argentina and fish with Ramón on this fabulous river that is as clear and pristine as any water you have ever seen—including, probably, the water that came out of your tap today. It's a beautiful day here today. We've been travelling, my wife and I, in Argentina, and I just felt I had to get out to try some of the trout fishing that this country is so famous for. I must say I'm glad that I did. We'll also tell you all about this particular area in Argentina, why it's such a wonderful spot for fishing, and how it came to be that way. Ramón has some marvelous stories that he'll share with you. I guess if we're going to talk about Argentina, Argentine fishing, and what's happening in this area, we need to establish our location. Ramón, exactly where are we in Argentina?

MR. ARANGUREN: We are located more or less two and a half hours by plane from Buenos Aires, about eleven hundred miles to the southwest of that city. Buenos Aires is the capital of Argentina, and we are located in the foothills of the Andes here in Bariloche.

MR. SLOAN: The foothills of the Andes, indeed. Everywhere you look, you see these incredible mountains with sharp peaks on them and then equally impressive lakes and rivers below. It's a non-stop flight from Buenos Aires, Ramón?

MR. ARANGUREN: Yes, it's a non-stop from Buenos Aires to here, and you can also get non-stop flights from Miami to Buenos Aires. You would have, I would say, a seven-hour direct flight from Miami to Buenos Aires. Then you would have your connection time, plus two and a half hours to the fishing area here.

MR. SLOAN: It's really not that much travel time to bring you to an entirely different world. We'll talk about the details of how to get here a little later on. We are on the eastern flank of the Andes Mountains. What is the exact name of the lake here, Ramón?

MR. ARANGUREN: We are at Lake Nahuel Huapi in Bariloche.

MR. SLOAN: Ramón, I'm familiar with how many of the rivers are formed in North America, with glaciers or springs or other geologic processes. How are the rivers formed here on the eastern flank of the Andes?

MR. ARANGUREN: The process is probably different from what you've seen on your continent. Here, most of our rivers—I would say 95 percent of those from northern Patagonia all the way to Tierra del Fuego—are born in lakes. During a heavy glacier era, the glaciers carved the basins of the lakes. Then, when the ice melted, those basins filled up with freshwater. The natural gradient is from the west to the east—that is, from the Andes to the Atlantic Ocean. So all our rivers are born in lakes, and they are very, very clear—especially the Traful, where we have been fishing.

MR. SLOAN: So you have lakes that feed the rivers that flow into another lake, basically. Is that how it works?

MR. ARANGUREN: That's correct.

MR. SLOAN: And in between the two lakes are these rivers, and their waters are as clear as gin—I mean, absolutely sparkling clear—which makes for excellent trout fishing. Ramón, this great fishing didn't just happen accidentally. Trout were not in here in the beginning. Most trout fishing here is for brown trout, especially in the Traful River, but the Traful is the only river to have browns, rainbows, brook trout, and landlocked salmon. Ramón, can you tell us how trout fishing got started here?

MR. ARANGUREN: In the Southern Hemisphere, there are no native trout—not even rainbows or browns. We had to introduce them. The Argentine government introduced them in 1904. The first shipment of trout eggs arrived from the United States via Southampton, England. In fact, we have a funny story about that trip. In March 1904, there was a very unusual shipment because it included a lot of whitefish eggs.

MR. SLOAN: By whitefish, do you mean the species that we used to find out West and in the Great Lakes of North America? But someone had figured they could use them in Argentina?

MR. ARANGUREN: Exactly. Then lake trout, brook trout, and landlocked salmon were included in later shipments. We received eight big shipments from the United States via Southampton because of the refrigeration of the eggs. There

213

were no official connections for ships with refrigeration between the United States and Argentina. But we did have that service between England and Argentina at the time.

MR. SLOAN: So, in other words, the Argentineans were selling beef to England, and that got the refrigerated ships going. The eggs had to be shipped from New York to Southampton, England, and then loaded on a refrigerated ship for the trip to Buenos Aires. Now how long did that take?

MR. ARANGUREN: That was more or less forty days of travel from New York to Buenos Aires. Then you had another, I would say, five days on a train to Nahuel Pan Station, and then you had another twenty-one days by oxcart, at least.

MR. SLOAN: Oxcart?

MR. ARANGUREN: That's correct; the whitefish eggs traveled by oxcart from Nahuel Pan Station to the place where they would be hatched and then planted.

MR. SLOAN: So really, we're talking about two months, altogether, to get the eggs here. Now, once the eggs got deposited and hatched, they took hold?

MR. ARANGUREN: Well, the first shipment was very successful. Then we had some problems because poor weather conditions caused them to lose some or most of the later shipments of brown trout eggs. So the brown trout was not introduced in Argentina until 1930, when we imported eggs from Chile, which had received its eggs from England or the United States. So we don't really know the origin of our brown trout. It doesn't matter: the brown trout is here now.

MR. SLOAN: I'll say; they're definitely here and they're doing well. I caught two pretty good-sized ones fishing here and released them both. Ramón, what is a ranch called here again?

MR. ARANGUREN: *Estancia.*

MR. SLOAN: *Estancia.* The ranch we are staying at is ten miles long on the river and covers how many hectares?

MR. ARANGUREN: It's got seven thousand hectares, more or less fourteen thousand acres.

MR. SLOAN: Fourteen thousand acres of the most beautiful valley one has ever seen. You will have the choice of fishing several different rivers with Ramón, but the one I fished with him, the Traful, was just out of this world. The Traful borders the ranch we just mentioned, which is owned by Meme and Mauricio Lariviere. The Larivieres are of French origin but came here many years ago and bought this property. It's a real working ranch, with cattle and horses, and, of course, ten miles of access to the Traful. It takes thirty minutes to just get from the road to your cabin, and then they have what I would call the ranch house, a beautiful house with rooms for up to ten people at a time. Two more people can be accommodated in a cabin on a lake that sits atop a bluff, where the vistas are simply beyond belief. All of the facilities at the *estancia* are run as a traditional bed and breakfast, with Meme and Mauricio as your gracious hosts. They serve breakfast, lunch, and dinner to their guests, and you can relax in the afternoon and meet some very, very interesting people. Now Ramón, what's the best fishing time here? When's the season?

MR. ARANGUREN: Well, from the beginning until the end—that's the best fishing time.

MR. SLOAN: Well, exactly.

MR. ARANGUREN: The point is that I'm not trying to be funny. We can offer very good fishing from mid-November until mid-April because we have five or six different rivers in the area. That is always our goal: to give our guests the best service and the best fishing available whenever they are here. We are not limited to only one place; we can move up to 250 miles around. That area gives us a lot of opportunities for fishing different waters and different hatches, different levels of water, and different techniques.

MR. SLOAN: Ramón, we ought to remind our audience that if they come down to the Southern Hemisphere, the seasons are reversed. Our North American winter is your South American summer, so for those who love trout fishing, you've got to reverse the season associated with the months on your calendar. For instance, as you get into late December, January, and February in the States, you'll find very good fishing conditions here in Argentina—just like those in May, June, and July up north. Then, when you get into May and June here, it becomes winter and is very cold because you're up in the Andes Mountains. The fishing season closes for six months so that the spawning fish are protected.

Now, Ramón, we fished yesterday on the Traful. We were primarily looking for landlocked salmon because they're in that river. What's the biggest landlocked salmon caught down there?

MR. ARANGUREN: In that river, the biggest landlocked salmon caught, we guess, was around nineteen pounds.

MR. SLOAN: Wow.

MR. ARANGUREN: That was four years ago.

MR. SLOAN: Four years ago?

MR. ARANGUREN: And I swear that there are fish bigger than that now.

MR. SLOAN: You've seen them?

MR. ARANGUREN: Oh yes. The problem is that they kill you. They open the hooks; they break the line. You know the story.

MR. SLOAN: Right. They're very strong, that's for sure. They primarily go up and down from the lake into the stream, and they then go back up into the river.

MR. ARANGUREN: That's because in the headwaters of the Traful, there are small streams that come in that have very small gravel on their bottoms, and this is where they prefer to spawn.

MR. SLOAN: What was the biggest rainbow or brown caught on the Traful, Ramón?

MR. ARANGUREN: Well, the biggest rainbow that I can recall was almost twenty-six pounds, or twenty-five and a half pounds, actually.

MR. SLOAN: That's some river rainbow. Remember, that's a fish that was caught by casting with a fly, not trolling a lake with a downrigger. There's a big difference.

MR. ARANGUREN: Yes. That trout is mounted; it was caught more or less ten years ago. We have seen other rainbows that big. The problem is that those fish are very, very difficult to catch because they can see you. We know two or three almost by name, but, you know, you go more or less within fifteen or twenty feet of those fish, and they can see you. So it's very difficult to catch them.

MR. SLOAN: I got here a little early in the year, and the river was up a little bit—crystal clear, but up. High water means sinking lines and all that kind of tackle required to get your fly down. But I took two fish here, one twenty-three and a half inches and the other a twenty-inch brown, saw lots of others, and had a marvelous, marvelous time fishing for them. Ramón, the name of your company is Chimehuin Safaris, right?

MR. ARANGUREN: That's right. It's named for a river that you haven't visited yet, but you will. The Chimehuin is one of the mightiest rivers in Argentina, and it's the holder, actually, of the record in brown trout. The record brown trout caught there on a wet fly is twenty-four and three-quarter pounds. We are not talking about inches; we are talking about pounds. In the same place in the Chimehuin, by the same man using a dry fly, the record is seventeen and a half pounds.

MR. SLOAN: Now, I'd like to see a seventeen-and-a-half-pound brown trout come up to my dry fly. Yes, before I leave this earth, I'd like to see that. That would be terrific.

MR. ARANGUREN: The story about that catch is amazing because the man was fishing in the lake, trying some flies that he planned to use in Canada for Atlantic salmon. He was casting over small trout that were rising. Suddenly, something took his fly, and he saw a tail going into the water. That's all that he saw. He said, "That's not a small trout." So he began to walk to the lake, to the beach of the lake, for a landing spot. At every outlet of a lake you normally have a narrow place surrounded by rocks. So when the trout realized that somebody was moving her to the place that she didn't want to go, she decided to go into the river. That man ran into the middle of the water with his waders on. You know the story. He was following the fish in the river while he held his rod high, and finally he landed that fish, almost five hundred meters downstream, in a calm place after one hour.

MR. SLOAN: Ramón took me to two spots up on a bluff. We were probably about a hundred feet up in the air, wouldn't you say, Ramón?

MR. ARANGUREN: On the second day, yes; on the other day it would have been, I would say, sixty feet.

MR. SLOAN: We were sixty to a hundred feet up on the side of a cliff where the river flowing below us had created this huge pool. You could see the bottom through twenty feet of water, that's how clear it was. I looked down in this huge pool where the river came racing around a bend, creating a big back-eddy in the crystal-clear water. We could see the bottom, and I saw a few things move down there that would make your pulse jump. Two trout—*mucho grande*—and a very large landlocked salmon were in that pool. So the big fish are in there, and that's the point. The best season is yet to come. I got here a little early, and the river is still up a little bit. It starts dropping in the beginning of December. By the time you get to January, February, March, and April, it's in prime shape. For those of us who like dry-fly fishing, what's the best time to be here, Ramón?

MR. ARANGUREN: We can fish with a dry fly anytime, but the problem is that you need to fish in faster water. Basically, the best dry-fly fishing is in January, February, and April. The end of February and March, which is our summer, is a little better because the water heats up and the fish don't move or feed all day long. They move only early in the morning and late in the afternoon during the summer in water that is well oxygenated.

MR. SLOAN: The Traful is in northern Patagonia, in about the middle of Argentina. This country is longer than the United States is wide—about seven thousand miles long. So we're about in the middle of Argentina, with thirty-five hundred miles north of us and roughly the same distance to the south of us. We're on the eastern side of the Andes that's part of the Nahuel Huapi National Park, one of the oldest...

MR. ARANGUREN: ...Actually, it is *the* oldest national park in Argentina.

MR. SLOAN: It's really the third oldest park in the world, isn't it?

MR. ARANGUREN: Exactly. The first was Yellowstone, the second was Kruger Park in South Africa, and the third was Nahuel Huapi. In a time of one and a half years, those three national parks were created.

MR. SLOAN: Well, it's amazing to me to visit this fishery now and think how far it has come in just under a hundred years. To have started with a small shipment of trout eggs from New York to Southampton, England, and then from Southampton to Buenos Aires, and then finally to here is just incredible— especially when you look at the quality of the fishery that exists here now. But I digress: let's get back to the famous trout of the Traful. We were fishing yesterday with streamer flies. The ones that were successful were thin and sparsely tied.

MR. ARANGUREN: That's correct. The problem that you have with the clear water here is that the fly appears bigger to the fish in clear water than it does in less-clear water. We discovered this after much trial and error. Therefore, we don't use big wet flies or big streamer flies. Sometimes in the night or in low-light conditions, you may want to use big flies. But on normal sunny days, you use bright flies that are quite small.

MR. SLOAN: You call them "sparsely tied" flies, right?

MR. ARANGUREN: Sparsely tied, yes. The fly is named the "Stormy," or in Spanish, *la stomba,* which means, "small hurricane to move across the water, making a disturbance." That is what this fly does. It goes through the water and makes a disturbance because it resembles a small smelt or fish. It's only tied with four feathers of black, or grizzly hackle, then four or five strands of hackle. The body is only wire, copper wire, the color of web hackle and the same color as the tail. That's all there is to the Stormy fly.

MR. SLOAN: We fished sinking-tip fly lines because the water was up. I would assume that when the waters drop, you don't need the sinking-tip line. But we fished 250-grain sinking line with a shooting head that cast very well. There's some wind here, so you've often got to cast across and up and then mend line a little bit as the fly comes downstream. But they seem to hit that Stormy fly, and one of the reasons they do, as you were telling me, is that these trout are cannibalistic: they feed on their own species.

MR. ARANGUREN: Exactly. In these rivers, the trout become cannibalistic when they are roughly between fourteen and sixteen inches. They stop eating only insects and begin to feed mostly on small trout or minnows.

MR. SLOAN: Also on smelt or whatever is swimming in the river, including crayfish, right?

MR. ARANGUREN: Exactly.

MR. SLOAN: Are the smelt coming out of the lakes?

MR. ARANGUREN: Yes, they're coming out of the lake, and there are a lot of local fish and also small trout. Only in the Traful do you have the four species of trout. You can count the four species of trout.

MR. SLOAN: Which are?

MR. ARANGUREN: Brook trout, which is originally from the United States; rainbow trout, which also came from the States; landlocked salmon, from Sebago Lake in the United States; and brown trout, from England.

MR. SLOAN: The landlocked salmon are from Sebago Lake in Maine?

MR. ARANGUREN: Yes, and we really appreciate them. The landlocked salmon are the most difficult fish to catch. I have been guiding for fifteen years, and the thing that thrills me the most about the Traful River is the salmon. I want to fish there because of the salmon. There are no other reasons. I can catch probably bigger browns in the Chimehuin or bigger rainbows in the mouth of the Limay, probably. I don't know; I never have tried for specific trout species. But I really do love to try for salmon.

MR. SLOAN: I can attest to that, Ramón. We were scrambling up cliffs and looking in the water for them. I would say we saw dozens of brown trout and rainbows from those perches that we were at.

MR. ARANGUREN: Browns and rainbows are, I would say, 85 percent of the population of the Traful.

MR. SLOAN: And the salmon here are a light color in the water—very, very pale, right?

MR. ARANGUREN: Yes, very pale.

MR. SLOAN: They're hard to pick up, even if you're up high looking down for them.

MR. ARANGUREN: That's because now the water is so fast that you cannot concentrate on the stones and therefore spot the trout and salmon. When the water is at a normal level, you can concentrate on the stones. When you find a shape, you can find a fish. And once you find one salmon, you begin to find more. Normally they live in tribes. The landlocked salmon in Argentina live in tribes. I don't know about their habits in the United States. My experience here says that the salmon live in tribes, and those tribes that go to the lake travel together. They live in the same pool.

MR. SLOAN: Ramón, how far is the Traful River from Bariloche? Forty-five, fifty miles?

MR. ARANGUREN: Forty miles.

MR. SLOAN: It's forty miles to the ranch from Bariloche, and then ten miles from the road to the main house, Meme and Mauricio's house at *Arroyo Verde* that we talked about earlier. It is beautiful. Even if your wife or your girlfriend doesn't like to fish but you do, it doesn't matter if you come here. Believe me, my wife came, and, as you well know, she doesn't like to fish. She fell in love with this place. Ramón stopped the car coming in, whipped out his binoculars, and said,

"Look at this cliff." In the distance was this mountain, and the sun was going down behind it. I saw a spot up there in the sky, and he said, "That's a condor."

MR. ARANGUREN: Yes.

MR. SLOAN: And we watched the condors for about twenty minutes as they flew out from this cliff, and they were...

MR. ARANGUREN: ...Flying in, actually.

MR. SLOAN: Yes, actually flying in.

MR. ARANGUREN: They were nesting there.

MR. SLOAN: Nesting. And they were at least three or four miles away, didn't you say?

MR. ARANGUREN: Probably, yes.

MR. SLOAN: But we could see them against the sky. Then we saw the songbirds and quail, some deer and cattle, and there were even English hares running all over the place. If you like to ride, the riding here is fabulous—never mind the fact that you're on one of the greatest trout rivers in the world. And the place also attracts interesting people from all over the world; even President Eisenhower fished the waters here. Interesting people go to interesting places, and this is certainly one of them.

Ramón, thanks so much for sharing your wonderful part of the world with me.

MR. ARANGUREN: My pleasure.

❧

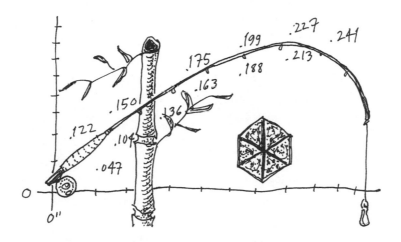

HOAGY CARMICHAEL, JR.,
on Being Everett Garrison's Boswell

AN INTERVIEW WITH HOAGY CARMICHAEL, JR., ON HIS APPRENTICESHIP WITH A MASTER OF BAMBOO FLY ROD BUILDING AND DOCUMENTATION OF THE ART

*H*oagy Carmichael, Jr., has the good fortune to be custodian of two of America's icons—the first being the works of his father, which included the evergreen immortals, "Stardust," "Up a Lazy River," "Georgia on My Mind," "Skylark," and, prophetically, "Gone Fishin'" and the second being keeper of the flame for Everett Garrison, the genius maker of bamboo fly rods.

Carmichael came to know Garrison well and reveals in this interview that Garrison was the first to approach construction of the bamboo fly rod from a civil engineer's point of view. Many of Garrison's calculations and formulas survive today in the fly rods we take for granted and so easily use.

Carmichael tells me that "Stardust" is played every ten seconds somewhere in the world, preserving his father's legacy. But fly fishermen of the world rejoice for how the younger Carmichael has preserved Everett Garrison's special niche in history. Trout fishermen everywhere salute him for his efforts.

MR. SLOAN: Hoagy Carmichael, Jr., is our guest today. Hoagy, how are you this morning?

MR. CARMICHAEL: I'm doing fine, Steve.

MR. SLOAN: Hoagy has made a lifetime study not only of his father's music, America's music, but of bamboo fishing rods and how they deliver our flies to trout. Hoagy, you met a fellow named Garrison. When was that?

MR. CARMICHAEL: His name was Everett Garrison, and he was from Yonkers, New York. I met him in 1968 when I was working at WGBH in Boston and was introduced to him through a friend of mine. Garrison and I fished the Catskills, actually, in a wonderful little club that you probably know called the Tuscarora Club. He had one of his bamboo fishing rods in his hand that looked a lot different from the little bamboo fishing rod I was using. His were all exquisitely handmade. He told me he hand-planed six strips of bamboo into six tapered pieces, all by hand. I swear to you, Steve, I didn't believe him. So I called him up and asked whether I could come to his home and actually see him do this. He sort of said no. That challenged me and got me curious about the process of making bamboo fly rods.

MR. SLOAN: Being refused is always a challenge.

MR. CARMICHAEL: He had never had anyone look over his shoulder before and act as an apprentice in training. I explained to him that I just wanted to see the process unfold. He relented, and I began to visit him regularly.

MR. SLOAN: I find that most artists do not immediately accept strangers into their creative process. You have to earn their respect bit by bit.

MR. CARMICHAEL: That's as it should be.

MR. SLOAN: Absolutely.

MR. CARMICHAEL: Garrison didn't have the time or the inclination to teach. When I met him, he was in his seventies, had a full-time job in New York, and made fishing rods at night for pleasure and extra income. When he died at eighty-one, he was still making fishing rods by hand.

MR. SLOAN: Interesting. Hoagy, you wrote a book on Garrison called A MASTER'S GUIDE TO BUILDING A BAMBOO FLY ROD. It was published by Meadow Run Press, a publishing house owned by our mutual friend, Bill

Trego. It's a handsome book in a beautiful jacket, just beautifully done. Garrison was a civil engineer and maintained a full-time job at this profession, right?

MR. CARMICHAEL: Yes. His engineering background really separated him from any other of the great classic bamboo rod makers. He understood chemical adhesion, why things bend, why they rebounded, and how they vibrated. He understood the moment of inertia, as in the stress curves in bridges that we only hear about when they fail. There was nothing empirical about this man. Occasionally he'd try some new glue mixtures and would experiment until he got what he thought was the right mixture. But Garrison figured everything out mathematically first. That was his nature.

MR. SLOAN: You write that it all started when a friend of his asked him to repair the shafts on some golf clubs. All he said was, "Well, I can do that." He made the shafts out of bamboo with some glued-together pieces.

MR. CARMICHAEL: That's right. In fact, he did it rather unsuccessfully, but he did try it. He loved fishing a little creek up in the Catskills in New York called Rondout, which you undoubtedly know. He fished that creek from time to time. As it turned out, a strange turn of events befell Garrison. He lived in Yonkers, just down the street from a man named Dr. George Parker Holden, who was recognized as an expert rod builder and fisherman who worked right out of his own home. Dr. Trotter, who was Garrison's doctor and good friend, was also a very good friend of Holden, and he introduced them. Holden had written a classic book called THE IDYLL OF THE SPLIT-BAMBOO. It turned out that all Garrison had to do was walk six blocks and he was on the doorstep of the bamboo-rod-making authority of the day.

MR. SLOAN: It's interesting, Hoagy: America always was and still is the home of cottage industries. I can think of several. Fly rods are certainly one. Fin-Nor reels, which started their production in a garage, are another. Certainly, a lot of fly tying started at a workbench in the back of somebody's shed or garage. Over time and with popular use, these homemade rods and reels and ties all became icons, true American icons.

MR. CARMICHAEL: Yes, some did. As you may know, Steve, I have this fairly extensive business in used fishing tackle, some of which is antique. I am always buying, selling, and appraising. I've probably taken apart about 800 mom-and-pop fly rods and all sorts of other tackle. The handcrafted work that this country has produced in fishing tackle is amazing. The number of hours that Americans have spent trying to figure out better ways to produce goods is just staggering and fabulous.

MR. SLOAN: The scope of fishing reel patents in the United States patent office is mind-boggling, too.

MR. CARMICHAEL: Yes, Americans are very inventive. The number of hours they have spent inventing fishing tackle alone is staggering.

MR. SLOAN: When Garrison first started building fly rods and met Alex Taylor, who owned a sporting goods store in New York, he made some rods for him to sell. They sold for forty-five dollars, and he had eighty hours of work in each rod. That works out to roughly fifty cents an hour, which wasn't even close to a living wage in those days.

MR. CARMICHAEL: Well, Mrs. Garrison told me that from 1932 through 1934, she never saw her husband during daylight hours. He was up early and gone and then back after dark.

MR. SLOAN: Hoagy, Garrison himself was not a well man, was he? He suffered from some neurological problems and depression. Maybe working all these equations out in his head helped him work through his bouts of depression.

MR. CARMICHAEL: When he lost his job at New York Central Railroad, he had to work. He had two children. He sort of figured out he might generate some income from having studied Dr. Holden's methods of making fly rods. What amazes me was that he was able to do all the necessary tapering and fitting calculations with only his little ivory slide rule. He gave that slide rule to me, by the way, and it is one of my most prized possessions.

Steve, you know fishing rods are tapered; they're larger at the butt end and, of course, much thinner out at their tip. That taper—that triangulation, that narrowing—is very important to the action of the rod. Garrison calculated the exact places where a rod should be a little thicker and a little thinner for just the right action. This precise tapering is especially important for bamboo rods. It is vital to how a fishing rod feels. Rod makers have different ideas about tapering. Jim Payne, the great Jim Payne—perhaps the greatest rod maker who ever lived—knew nothing about engineering, nothing at all. He and his father before him just figured these

226

things out by going out behind their shop and throwing a line and saying, "Oh, this one works and that one doesn't."

MR. SLOAN: Right: good old trial and error. But Garrison had it all worked out on paper, right?

MR. CARMICHAEL: Oh, God, he sure did. He was very proud of that fact, and I think if he were to come back on this earth for an hour—and God, I wish he could—he would say his calculations and formulas are what he is most proud of and wants to be most remembered for.

MR. SLOAN: I find it interesting that you, Hoagy, are fascinated by Garrison's calculations, especially because your background and lineage are so heavily steeped in music, which is frozen mathematics, really. The sound waves for the note "E" can only vibrate so many times per second to be a true E on a tuning fork. Garrison may not come back in any form we know, but it's clear to me that he had a disciple, and I'm talking to him this morning.

So, you did the original research on Garrison?

MR. CARMICHAEL: It's interesting, Steve, that when I wrote my book in 1977, there was no written information on how to make a bamboo fishing rod, other than one book that had been written forty years earlier. Nobody was really interested in the topic. Now, there are six or eight hundred bamboo fly rod aficionados. There's even a magazine dedicated to bamboo rod making published in Finland and Sweden. My book about Garrison's work has spawned this wonderful little new generation of fly rod makers. It's been very satisfying.

MR. SLOAN: Not only that, Hoagy, but I see in your book that Garrison himself only made 650 rods in his whole lifetime.

MR. CARMICHAEL: That's right.

MR. SLOAN: Considering the number of fly fishermen who enjoyed the sport from the 1930s through the 1970s, that's not a great body of work. However, those rods all were well made. Tell us how they were made with his special calculations. They were really quite revolutionary in their own time, weren't they?

MR. CARMICHAEL: Remember, Garrison made most of his own tools because he couldn't buy the necessary tools. He did all the bamboo work, the planing and all the gluing. He wound the silk on his own rods. He made all his own reels. He even made his own cases—metal cases with a top, bottom, and screw-off caps. He made his own cloth bags. Many times, he even made his own ferrules. This was a real cottage industry, and there was only one guy in the cottage. Payne and Leonard, the era's other great rod makers, had people working for them who were under their direction. Garrison was uniquely alone.

MR. SLOAN: Are any of his rods or anything else he made in the Smithsonian?

MR. CARMICHAEL: No, not to my knowledge.

MR. SLOAN: Isn't that interesting? That's a mistake.

MR. CARMICHAEL: Of course, the Catskill Fly Fishing Center and Museum now has some beautiful rods of his on display.

MR. SLOAN: By the way, you know that Lee Wulff was a civil engineer, too. It's kind of interesting how both men had similar backgrounds and shared a love of fly fishing.

MR. CARMICHAEL: Lee Wulff went to Stanford University.

MR. SLOAN: Right, exactly.

MR. CARMICHAEL: Nobody's dummy.

MR. SLOAN: Exactly.

I'll tell you what I'd like to do, Hoagy: I'd like to walk through the various components of a Garrison bamboo fly rod and ask you to comment on how these different parts each contribute toward the rod as whole.

Number one was the product itself, the cane selection. Where did he get the bamboo?

MR. CARMICHAEL: There is only one species of bamboo out of 1,200 different species that can be used for rod making. It's called *Arundinaria amabilis*, and it grows successfully only in China in a very small twenty-square-mile area. It's harvested in China, shipped over here, and dried and cured. You buy it in twelve- or eight-foot lengths, but the most sought-after size is usually twelve feet long and two-and-a-half inches in diameter. It is stronger than fiberglass of the same size—very strong.

You buy the bamboo blanks by the bundle, usually twenty in a bundle. There are good ones and there are very bad ones. You can tell by the weight, what we call the heft, and you can tell by looking at the ends and seeing how strong the fibers are. But Steve, these strains of bamboo that Garrison used are very strong. I mean, this bamboo is one-third the strength of steel per unit of area. In other words, if you hang four feet of it out over a ledge and you put a weight on it, it will support one-third of the amount of weight that steel of the same dimensions would support. Yet it weighs just one-fortieth as much.

MR. SLOAN: Is this bamboo considered a shrub or a tree?

MR. CARMICHAEL: It's a species of grass, actually. It grows fast and takes only two and a half years or so to mature. It'll grow forty feet.

MR. SLOAN: So now we've got a twelve-foot bundle of bamboo in a garage workshop. How do you split it?

MR. CARMICHAEL: Garrison used a sort of hatchet, a tool shaped kind of like a meat cleaver, to split the bamboo sections. You make a lot of mistakes until you learn how to split bamboo correctly. You have to follow the grain. The grain is there, so as long as you don't try to overpower the grain and you move the bamboo up through your splitter, it will split well. You must hold the splitter and move the section up through it, and then it will split itself.

MR. SLOAN: With the grain?

MR. CARMICHAEL: Yes. It's an acquired skill because bamboo has these nodes, or joints, about every fifteen or eighteen inches. Getting through those nodes and working with them is a problem.

MR. SLOAN: Those nodes are like little ridges and bumps, right?

MR. CARMICHAEL: That's right; they're dams. They're little fortification dams. They are God's gift to the rod maker, even though they have very little tensional strength and you have to be very careful how you handle them throughout the entire rod-building process.

MR. SLOAN: When you split the length of bamboo, what do you try to get out of it? A piece maybe an eighth of an inch or a quarter of an inch wide?

MR. CARMICHAEL: Well, let's just say you're doing a tip section. You'll need six pieces to make a hexagon. You'll get six pieces of bamboo approximately an eighth of an inch wide. The nodes should be staggered so that

229

you don't have them going around in a sort of single circle around the bamboo. You'll want to spread the nodes to keep that tensional weakness associated with each one as far away from any other as you can. Garrison, being the engineer, understood that he had to stagger the nodes for integral strength. He was using the same staggering, so to speak, that a six-cylinder engine firing on cylinders one, three, five, six, two, and four—that's the firing order, by the way, of a six-cylinder engine—uses to ensure its integral strength. Anyway, after ensuring that the nodes were properly spaced, Garrison then trimmed the bamboo section to length and had the pieces ready to be planed with his hand plane.

MR. SLOAN: Each piece?

MR. CARMICHAEL: Each piece. They would go into a metal jig—what we call a form—that was adjusted for just the right width all the way up and down. It was adjusted to make the bamboo thinner at the bottom and thicker at the top, where the ferrule goes. And then he would plane. Gosh, Steve, there's no way to explain how to do that, but I show the sequence in pictures in my book.

MR. SLOAN: Hoagy, now we've got the bamboo, we've got it split, and I would imagine it has been planed a lot. Now what is created from this process at this stage? Six triangles planed out of these strips form the basis of one section of a fly rod, correct?

MR. CARMICHAEL: Yes. You're trying to create six strips glued together in a tapered fashion. You've got to keep the apex of each triangle of each strip in the dead center of the rod section. It's an interesting concept: the strength of this bamboo is on its very outer edge, the outermost section of the bamboo column, in the big round stalk that you bought. So you never plane that outside edge; instead, you only plane the other two sides. You work a little on one side, then a little on the other, back and forth, forth and back. You essentially pare down the triangle. If you see it in your mind as a triangle that's a quarter of an inch thick, and if you keep slicing off the sides, then the diameter of the triangle drops. You don't have to plane the third side to accomplish that. So you plane with these long strokes in these long steel forms. You try to plane four feet at one time, or whatever the length of the strip is.

It's very time consuming, Steve. You have to hold everything just right. Everything's got to be in line. The sun and the moon and the stars have to be working in just the right way. I'm not kidding you: planing is the toughest part of it. It's very difficult. I'll bet Garrison threw away more pieces than he ever finished the way he wanted.

MR. SLOAN: Then what? When you get these pieces fitted together, you bevel and then wrap them, right?

MR. CARMICHAEL: You have to wrap them and then heat-treat them. The heat treatment is to try to wring as much moisture out of them as possible. Then you go back to the finishing planer, and you plane some more. At this point, everything has got to be perfect. You just plane them to the point where they're perfect. Each of the six strips is planed exactly the same into the taper you want. And then you slather them with glue and put them into a binding machine and bind them together, applying heat as you go along. You let them dry, and then you've got what we call a section—a glued section.

By the way, people have tried to make fishing rods, and have quite successfully, out of between four and eight bamboo pieces. However, once he did the math, Garrison decided that six pieces made for the best fit. The problem with using more than six strips is that once you get a lot of pieces, you end up with as much glue as you do bamboo.

MR. SLOAN: Sure. Absolutely.

MR. CARMICHAEL: So what you're trying to do is to get a completely circular cross section from the triangular pieces. Of course, there are going to be some edges on it, but that's fine. Five pieces, of course, do not make a circle because there would then be a stronger side and a weaker side. This is why Garrison chose six pieces.

MR. SLOAN: All the while he was doing this, he was making these fantastic mathematical equations to prove where he was—and how he could do it—in the engineering sense. He was continually working it out on a mathematical basis.

MR. CARMICHAEL: Yes, and experimenting with changing tapers and figuring out, say, why this tip to him felt just a little soft once you had thirty or forty feet of line in the air. He was always calculating how he could transfer the energy from his hand, through the butt section, through the metal ferrule, out to the tip of the rod. He was always seeking a difference of just four, five, or six percent so that he could take a little bit of the loop out of the back cast. Conceptually, he always knew what he wanted to achieve.

MR. SLOAN: What was this "differential screw" that he invented while he was making his rods?

MR. CARMICHAEL: Yes, he invented a tool called a differential screw. Every turn of that screw would change the diameter of the width of the planing forms by about *four one-thousandths* of an inch—the tolerances were that closely defined.

He figured out all the ways to work within those close tolerances. He was wonderful, you know. He was just a wonderful, classy, Ed-Hewitt-type man.

MR. SLOAN: Well, he was a genius. I'd call him a genius to be able to do that. To take the concept from his mind, to the raw product, to the bench, and then from the bench, to the finishing steps, and, once he's all done, have everything work well and better than anything had worked before: that's really the proof of his genius.

MR. CARMICHAEL: A Garrison rod is a great-feeling fishing rod—there's no question about it. Nobody has ever disputed that. They have a sort of a moderate action. You don't feel the butt, and you don't feel the tip. The power all passes through very smoothly and evenly once you start that forward stroke. He liked that about his fishing rods.

MR. SLOAN: Hoagy, you describe in your book that he had brought a couple of these rods down to the Anglers Club of New York, and John Alden Knight was there. Wasn't John Alden Knight the fellow who invented the solunar tables, too?

MR. CARMICHAEL: He is the same man. They called him the inventor of "the lunatic table."

MR. SLOAN: Right. Also in attendance was Otto von Kienbusch, who started and donated a marvelous angling art collection and library for Princeton University.

MR. CARMICHAEL: That's right.

MR. SLOAN: At lunch, they were talking about a rod with parabolic action. I think Charlie Ritz was involved with that, too, wasn't he?

MR. CARMICHAEL: Garrison had made ten eight-foot rods because he had been invited to go to the Anglers Club of New York down at 101 Broad Street. He brought them down to show them to this group and to talk about rod making. He ended up with only one rod as he drove home. He sold nine that night. He was thrilled. Kienbusch bought them; Alden Knight bought them. John Alden Knight was fishing with his rod and accidentally broke the tip off it. He sent it to Garrison for repair, and Garrison returned it and added a new top guide. But it changed the action.

Knight said, "I like that new action. Make one for me that has that same action." What Knight liked was that the rod had a little thinner butt and did not taper as fast up to the tip, and the tip was even a little bit bigger. So with a thinner butt and a little thicker tip, you had a taper that was slower in terms of its graduation down to a thinner tip. It worked more into your hand when you cast or false cast with it. The rod's action was called the John Alden Knight parabolic action.

Incidentally, another rod maker of note, Paul Young, used rods with that action for a long time. Some people like them; some people don't. It tends to launch the fly line a little bit more than the semi-parabolic or the more medium-moderate-action rod.

But those were the days, Steve, when history was being made. I mean, all those wonderful people were involved, like George Edward Mackenzie Skues, Edward Hewitt, and George LaBranche, and, a little later on, Charlie Fox, Vince Marinaro, and George Harvey. All these men were pioneering fly-fishing techniques and tackle. The first years of the twentieth century were a heady time for fly fishing.

MR. SLOAN: Not only did Garrison go out and invent a superior bamboo fly rod but along the way he invented a device called a blade holder. He studied and fiddled around with glues to make sure that the rods would stay together. Then he improved the ferrules and the corks and the grips and the guides. All of these improvements were done in his pursuit of style, his great style of methodical perfection.

MR. CARMICHAEL: The impregnation process, which Orvis and many other rod makers have used over the years, was Garrison's idea, too. Garrison developed both an open- and a closed-cell process. One was a vacuum process, and he didn't like it. He said he could feel the weight of the rosins—the impregnating rosins—in the bamboo. He really invented the impregnation process that used less glue and made the rods stronger but lighter.

MR. SLOAN: Hoagy, so not only did he engineer the cane into a rod but he also engineered ferrules, corks, grips, and guides? And he designed the reel blanks, the butt caps, even the aluminum cases, right? Then, for real perfection, he even repaired the ones anglers broke.

MR. CARMICHAEL: Oh, sure.

MR. SLOAN: What a guy. Boy, oh boy.

MR. CARMICHAEL: In fact, when he made a rod for you, he never threw away the excess bamboo. He tagged it with your name, and if for some reason you broke a tip section, he would go back to the excess he had tagged and be able to make the repair using the bamboo that came out of the exact culm that he had used in making the rod itself for you. This ensured that there would be no differences in the amount of what we call *modulus*, or elasticity, or the sort of bending capabilities of the raw material itself. Ain't nobody ever done that before.

MR. SLOAN: For sure, nobody's done that before or since.

MR. CARMICHAEL: That's a careful man.

MR. SLOAN: Yes, indeed. Hoagy, what did he mean by, and how would you describe, the "transfer of energy" when you're fly fishing? Let's assume you've got a rod like one of his in your hands for the first time. What are you trying to prove when you talk about transfer of energy?

MR. CARMICHAEL: It's a fascinating subject to me. If you stand on a lawn with a rod and a line, and you make your false cast backwards, and then your right hand goes forward quickly as you would with a cast, you're moving energy from a starting point...to where? From the middle of your head, down your cortex, into your arm to your hand, and forward from there. Well, that energy has to go somewhere, has to dissipate somewhere. So what does it do? It goes right up through that fishing rod and out to the tip. The line is connected to the tip. By connected, I mean it is balanced when you get the back cast on that little tip guide. So you drive that line forward.

Now, you've seen people—we've all seen people—who put too much energy into casting a fly line, and it puts great big waves in the line. If you drive the rod forward in a moderate way and there's not enough bamboo or material in the rod, you can't really transfer the line from forty feet behind you to forty feet straight in front of you effectively. If the rod is not in balance correctly when you drive it forward, the line just won't go anywhere at all. There's no bending to create the forward energy.

MR. SLOAN: So, Garrison calculated how to transfer that energy by creating what he called a parabolic action, correct? What is a parabolic action, Hoagy?

MR. CARMICHAEL: It's an action that you can feel, for instance, when you waggle the rod. You see people waggling rods in fishing shops all the time. When you do it, you can feel the bending part of the rod, the part where the bending starts, more down in the cork grip than you can with a more semi-parabolic, which would have its bending part in front of the cork grip, or a fast-action rod, which would be flexible more out toward the tip section. It is really the relationship of where the rod starts to bend. I suspect that you, Steve, use a more fast action rod. Right?

MR. SLOAN: Yes, I do. You and I talked about this and how Garrison had the engineering calculations done in his head to create the parabolic action.

By the way, if you have a garage that hasn't been touched, maybe you will find a gem of a Garrison rod when you go into it for a cleaning. Did Garrison put his name on these rods?

MR. CARMICHAEL: Oh, yes.

MR. SLOAN: Take a look in that cloth bag that the moths have worked on a little bit because there were only 650 of his made.

MR. CARMICHAEL: While you are there, be on the lookout for other antique tackle. Garrison, Payne, Leonard, Gillum, or reels by vom Hofe, Hardy, or Fin-Nor, all that sort of stuff could be very valuable. There are places today like the Catskill Fly Fishing Center and Museum, and the American Museum of Fly Fishing in Manchester, Vermont, that are repositories for some of this great classic tackle. Steve, you don't know it, but I've just given the Catskill museum a Garrison. They'll have it in the next three or four months or so. If you look in my book, there's a picture of one of the great characters, that old-timer Vern Heinie, who lived on the banks of the Beaverkill. Well, I have his Garrison, and that one is going into the Catskill museum, where it belongs

MR. SLOAN: Absolutely where it belongs. Of course, with today's graphite, plastics, boron, and the other material, they've basically copied what Garrison did with bamboo but put it into another form to use as fly rods. In this way, they don't have to spend eighty hours trying to make a beautiful fly rod.

MR. CARMICHAEL: Well, that's for sure. But it's a different material, Steve. It's a very successful material. These graphite or carbon fiber rods will throw a fishing line a mile. But they feel different. It's like the difference between driving a nice Honda Civic and a Mercedes or a Saab. There's a feel to natural bamboo that you cannot duplicate. You just cannot duplicate it at all.

MR. SLOAN: This is true.

MR. CARMICHAEL: Some people like to have nice cars, suits, cigars, and equipment. Other people don't care. That's fine. But, obviously, you could buy a nice fishing rod made in Japan or in this country for three or four hundred dollars. You can buy a nice Garrison for eight or ten thousand.

It's still very hard for me to deal with graphite. When I waggle it back and forth, I just don't get the same feeling as I do with bamboo.

MR. SLOAN: Hoagy, we've done it: it's time for us to waggle on out of here. Thanks a million for coming on "The Fishing Zone" with me and providing us with such interesting information on Garrison and his rod making.

MR. CARMICHAEL: I've enjoyed it, Steve. Thanks for having me.

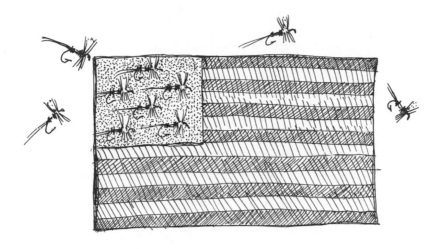

Joan Salvato Wulff,
the First Lady of Fly Fishing

An Interview with Joan Salvato Wulff on her life, philosophy of fishing, and the six-stage metamorphosis of serious fly fishers.

I always felt that no book about fly fishing would be totally complete without an interview with Joan Salvato Wulff. Joan reveals in this interview her life's philosophy and what it takes physically to be a champion fly caster. Joan, of course, has taken the sport to other dimensions. She was the first to break down the mechanics of fly casting into simple elements so that even the beginner could understand the dynamics of casting. People I meet at parties, dinners, and on a bridge overlooking my favorite trout hole where they have inadvertently spooked the trout tell me that they would like to learn how to fly fish. I have but one stock answer after these many years: spend a weekend at Joan's Wulff School of Fly Fishing in Lew Beach, near Livingston Manor, New York. The next best thing to do to satisfy this urge is to buy one of her videos or books on the subject. Joan has seen the best and was married to one of the greatest, Lee Wulff, a legend; however, it is no small measure of her own extraordinary prowess as a person, sportsman, and teacher that she stands alone as the first lady of fly fishing.

MR. SLOAN: Today we have a treat for you all, and I mean a real treat. We have Joan Salvato Wulff joining us. I just named her "the first lady of fly fishing."

Joan, how are you this morning?

MS. WULFF: Good morning, Steve.

MR. SLOAN: You're down in the Keys this morning?

MS. WULFF: Yes, I'm in Islamorada, one of my favorite places in the world.

MR. SLOAN: Joan, it all started where, in Paterson, New Jersey?

MS. WULFF: Yes. My dad had an outdoor store. He was a member of the Paterson Casting Club, and they met at a pond right near our house in one of the suburbs. The parents brought the kids, so there were lots of kids casting. The club was very active. I had to convince my dad that girls could do this, too. I convinced him to teach me and started at age ten to learn to fly and plug cast.

MR. SLOAN: You certainly took it to a few extra dimensions, I would say.

MS. WULFF: It was a long, slow process. I started out at a time when people were taught to keep a book under their arm while casting because it was supposed to be all in the wrist. I was ten years old, and I had to reach targets from twenty to fifty feet away. If they were thirty-five feet away, I couldn't do it. So I broke with tradition, let the book fall, lifted my arm, and was able to reach those farther targets. Everyone would come to me and say, "Now get your elbow back down. It's all in the wrist, you know."

That was really how I got started loving fly casting.

MR. SLOAN: What was *Skish*? The Skish tournaments?

MS. WULFF: Skish came along later. There were both accuracy and distance events. I was so young, I concentrated on the accuracy events. We had 30-inch-diameter targets. We had different events, like dry fly casting, where you did lots of false casting, and wet fly casting, where you just picked up the line and then shot additional line to reach targets. Then in 1950, some of the organizers came along and put it all together under the name of Skish tournaments.

MR. SLOAN: Now, there was an active circuit in those days, wasn't there? I mean, you could pretty well go into tournaments in different places in the country, right?

MS. WULFF: Yes, and I did. There were state tournaments, regional tournaments, and national tournaments. After winning some state and regional titles, I went to my first national tournament in 1943 in Chicago. From 1943 to 1960, I went to a different national tournament every year. I traveled the country that way. It really was kind of a great education.

MR. SLOAN: Not only did you go, but you won a lot of them. You also set the distance record. What was that cast? A hundred and sixty-some-odd feet?

MS. WULFF: The cast you're talking about was one hundred sixty-one feet. It was in 1960.

But let me just go back a little bit. When I was seventeen, a very wonderful caster took me under his wing. His name was William Taylor. He made bamboo rods, and he taught me how to cast pretty much in the style I'm doing now. He was a distance caster, and I used to gillie for him—which means he would cast his line, and I would pull the line back in and lay it out on the platform so he could do it again. The lines were made of silk back then. They had shooting heads that were probably fifty to fifty-four feet long. The tournament rules required that they weigh no more than an ounce and a half. In the beginning, the fly line head was backed by just braided line. In 1946, monofilament was introduced by the Golden Gate Casting Club in California, which was the first to use it as a backing.

So Mr. Taylor would do his distance practicing, and I would gillie for him. I really loved what he was doing, and so I just begged him to let me try it. His rod, of course, was too heavy for me. So he made a rod for me that was lighter, and I could get the best out of it. That's what really kept me interested in casting. I would get tired of practicing for accuracy, but with distance I had to use my whole body. I had to do everything perfectly. I couldn't even false cast because the tackle was so heavy. I had to pick up the line—a fifty-four-foot line—shoot line on the back cast, and then shoot it forward in one cast. That was how the one-hundred-sixty-one-foot cast was done.

MR. SLOAN: I can't even imagine it. That's beyond my ken, I must say. One hundred sixty-one feet, even today, is unbelievable.

MS. WULFF: The other thing was that, in 1951, there was a restricted event called "the Fishermen's Distance Event," and it required a nine-weight outfit for everyone. I could handle that cast as well as a man because, again, and we haven't talked about it yet, the whole problem here is that women have roughly 55 percent of the strength of men, pound for pound. So, I could never cast anything as heavy as a man could, such as the twelve- and thirteen-weight outfits they used, but I *could* handle a nine-weight outfit. In 1951, I won the national Fishermen's Distance Event against all-male competition. So that kind of gave me something to be happy about and to motivate me to continue.

MR. SLOAN: I read somewhere that you love dancing. Do you think that having your body in shape for dancing helped you with the fly-casting tournament events?

MS. WULFF: You bet I do. In the days when you had the book under your arm, people stood rigidly when they cast. And, again, because I am a woman and I had done some dancing but was weaker, I had to use my body. By using my body, I mean I had to shift my weight to cast effectively. Dancing and casting both have moves within moves, and so I really believe that dancing helped me, yes.

MR. SLOAN: That's fabulous. You've taken the skill and perfection of fly casting to really an amazing dimension. Today, you have a fly fishing school up in the Catskills, in Lew Beach, New York, right?

MS. WULFF: That's right, Steve. We have about a hundred acres about three miles up the Beaverkill from Lew Beach, near Livingston Manor. The telephone number is (845) 439-5020, or you can find us on the Internet at www.royalwulff.com.

MR. SLOAN: If anyone wants to take a weekend to learn how to cast and get started in this sport, I can think of no better place than your school up in the Catskills. It's world famous.

You have written many books on fly casting and fly fishing, as well. In 1987, JOAN WULFF'S FLY CASTING TECHNIQUES introduced many fly casters to the mechanics of casting, and in 1991 you published JOAN WULFF'S FLY FISHING: EXPERT ADVICE FROM A WOMAN'S PERSPECTIVE.

On that last topic, Joan, I have to tell you that J.T., my broadcast engineer, says he was bowled over by the length of that one-hundred-sixty-one-foot cast. I just told him you don't weigh more than 110 pounds. It blew him away.

MS. WULFF: I'll tell you, Steve, I'm much more impressed with it now than I was then. Back then, I was competing with men, and the man who won the tournament that day cast one hundred eighty-one feet. So that's where I was in those days: trying to reach those greater distances.

MR. SLOAN: You turned your attention from distance casting toward accuracy, publishing a book in 1997 from The Lyons Press called JOAN WULFF'S FLY CASTING ACCURACY. I guess once you learn how to throw a fly, then you've got to be able to put it where fish can strike it.

MS. WULFF: That's right, Steve. I've had a wonderful life. I always say I'm an ordinary woman who's had an extraordinary life through the magic of sport fishing.

MR. SLOAN: This is true. I'm just going to touch on that extraordinary life briefly. You'd also met an extraordinary man in your life—a man, unfortunately, who is no longer with us. Lee Wulff was an extraordinary guy.

MS. WULFF: Yes, he certainly was. I worked for the Garcia Corporation from 1959 through 1975. And in 1966, my boss called up one day and said, "How would you like to go fishing for giant bluefin tuna in Newfoundland with Lee Wulff?" My immediate thought was, "Lee Wulff? He's kind of a fishing hermit." Newfoundland, fog, giant bluefin tuna. I get seasick, but in spite of my misgivings, I heard my little voice saying, "Sure. When?" So I went to Newfoundland. I caught a 572-pound tuna, there was no fog, and Lee and I started our romance on that trip.

MR. SLOAN: To coin a pun, you hooked up.

MS. WULFF: We all hooked up.

MR. SLOAN: By the way, I remember the film that he made from that trip, which was marvelous.

MS. WULFF: There was more to that film. Fate had a hand in it. It was for the "American Sportsman" series, and Lee wanted to show that tuna fishing was a team sport. He wanted a woman to be the angler. He was even looking for a woman who had never caught a fish at all. They had Kay Starr, the singer, who was famous for her hit song, "Wheel of Fortune," remember? She was going to be the angler. She was very small and had never fished, but she became ill and couldn't go. And that was the reason that I ended up there.

MR. SLOAN: That *is* fate—absolute fate. You also made the transition from tuna fishing to the author of angling books and the producer of a very good videotape called THE DYNAMICS OF FLY CASTING, which was produced by Miracle Productions.

MS. WULFF: You're talking about a big stretch of time in there, a stretch where I was learning what I knew about fly casting. I had begun to cast naturally, and then I did a little teaching. But usually when you start teaching, you say, "Watch me," and then you say, "Do it like this." That technique puts the burden on the student to figure out what it is you're doing and what they are doing. So when we had the school and I gave little casting lectures, I started to focus on specific points and say, "Move your hand from point A to point B." So Lee and Nick Lyons said, "You've got to write a book." I had misgivings because I thought you don't write books until you really know everything you need to know. But Lee and Nick encouraged me and got me to put my teaching methods in writing.

I started writing, but I didn't know where I was going. It was a wonderful voyage of discovery because I uncovered what I knew just by having to put it all down on paper. It was the perfect way to reveal what I knew.

I found out that there were two parts to a cast. I actually pioneered a set of mechanics. People wrote books about casting and told you what the result was but not how to do it. They said, "Go fast, go slow, aim here, aim there," but I figured out that the process of casting was really just an acceleration to a stop! So the first part of the casting process is the slow start of the acceleration. That's when you're getting the line and rod under tension, and I called that "a loading move." Casting is all about bending the rod, and loading is the bending of the rod from the tip downward. Then, when you've got the rod about ninety degrees from where you want the fly to go, you push forward and change your hand position. I call that the "power snap." That power snap is the end of the acceleration.

So by having those two terms—and "follow-through" was the third part, by the way—I was able to write about casting. It was like a mathematical formula. It's still valid. I'm going to revise that book because I've learned more and want to add some things, and would probably write it differently now. But the basics are still good, and that's what my whole school system is based on.

MR. SLOAN: That is a marvelously cryptic description of fly casting.

242

You know what amazes me, Joan? People would never think of going out and picking up a golf club and starting to play golf immediately. Anyone taking golf seriously has to consider taking at least a couple of lessons to get the correct grip, the mode, the swing, the mental picture of the golf swing, the hit, the whole business. Yet, by the same token, so many people say, "Well, I'd like to go fly fishing," and they pick up a fly rod and think they can become instantly proficient without practice. It takes a little bit of teaching and a little bit of practice so that you can enjoy the sport. People get frustrated when the line falls at their feet or every cast hits the ground behind them or, worse yet, they get nipped in the back of the head by the fly.

MS. WULFF: Actually, Steve, it's like any other sport: it's both art and science. It's a lifetime commitment to learning. You're always learning new techniques with each cast, and you have to keep up to speed on how and when to apply them. Mostly, you have to learn to handle bad conditions, which might be high winds or being in a boat where the sides are high or low or whatever. You just can't cast one way when you fish. You have to be able to cast in all planes, from horizontal on the right to almost horizontal on the left. You have to be able to change your casting angles from vertically overhead, with your body standing straight and moving back and forth, to dropping a foot back and opening your body sideways. All those skills play into it. So casting is the one factor in your fishing that goes on forever and always needs to be improved.

MR. SLOAN: Absolutely. You have written these skills down as guidelines, call them touchstones, for generations of anglers yet to come. You have verbally and through your teaching methods broken down into their simplest parts the language and physical skills of fly casting.

MS. WULFF: Yes, the analyzing and the elements.

MR. SLOAN: We have come a long way from the silk lines that used to crackle and the running line that always knotted up. Just think of all the other things that plagued us right after World War II until technology took over and smoothed things out for us. It's a much different game today because the ingredients are different and better.

MS. WULFF: Yes, they are.

MR. SLOAN: You were part of the evolution toward lighter and lighter fly rods.

MS. WULFF: Well, I've lived through the history of fly rods, starting with bamboo. When I made that one-hundred-sixty-one-foot cast, the rod I used weighed six and three-quarter ounces.

MR. SLOAN: Wow.

MS. WULFF: I would have loved to have been able to do it again with graphite. Then we went to glass, and glass was pretty heavy, too—just about the same as bamboo. Then in the 1970s we got into graphite, and graphite was definitely lighter. Now I find—and again, I'm coming at this as a woman—that I always have to think about the weight of rods. I think that there are too many graphite rods that are heavy. I work with the R. L. Winston Rod Company to try to get out the word to women that they need to use lighter rods to do the same jobs that men use heavier rods for. You have to be able to master the tackle. I'm also trying to convince men to sell women rods that are lighter because a man in a tackle store generally says, "Oh, I love this rod. It's a nice light rod." But it usually may be an ounce too heavy for a woman.

MR. SLOAN: Absolutely.

MS. WULFF: That's kind of my mission in life: to try to get women and men to understand the limitations of our strength. We women have to use our strength very precisely, and I think that's what helped make me a better caster than I might have been otherwise. It just wouldn't work unless I did it right.

MR. SLOAN: I would say the R. L. Winston Rod Company is very lucky to have you on board as their adviser and consultant because you see casting from a very different perspective.

Joan, you endorsed a boat from Grand Slam Boat Company. What kind of a boat is made by Grand Slam?

MS. WULFF: Well, it's a wonderful 17-foot flats boat. A good part of fly fishing is to fish for any fish that will come near the surface to take a fly. That's why I love fishing in the Keys. The Grand Slam is a new boat company. They're headquartered in St. Petersburg, so I'm going to be enjoying fishing here in the Keys for the next couple of months out of a wonderful boat.

MR. SLOAN: Well, that boat is going to see some beautiful casts when you get up in the bow, I'll tell you that.

Generally speaking, there's been an explosion and a kind of a metamorphosis among people who fish for trout and salmon. They went out west trying to catch bigger trout. Then they went north and west into Canada for salmon. Many even went as far as Russia. Now, they've been going down to the Keys for a couple of decades to fish for bonefish, permit, redfish, and snook. It's just marvelous down there.

MS. WULFF: Don't forget tarpon.

MR. SLOAN: Tarpon, too; you're right. Fishing the flats in the Keys gives you a chance to use a little heavier tackle. Not much heavier, if you do it right. But you get a much stronger fish on the line, without any question. I assume you enjoy that as much as trout fishing?

MS. WULFF: I do, Steve. I love it—absolutely love it.

I'd like to get back to the tackle for a second. Tackle is set up so that you ask for outfits by number, and the numbers can be as low and light as number one and as high and heavy as number twelve. Perhaps thirteens are coming up, or even fourteens. That means that these rods can handle heavier lines. Of course, these rods weigh more, so when you're fishing for trout you might use anything up to a number six outfit, maybe even an eight. And when you go bonefishing and tarpon fishing, you get into those higher numbers. A seven-weight rod will do fine for bonefish, and an eight weight will work for snook and also for bonefish in windy weather. Then you go on up to tens and twelves for tarpon. Now, men use twelves. They're very heavy rods; they're very stiff. I use a ten weight because I can manage and master a ten weight. So there again is that man/woman strength thing.

MR. SLOAN: Women should really try the Keys and flats fishing. It gives them a chance to be with their guy and actually do some fishing. Flats fishing takes you away from the *mal de mar* of the ocean and the smell of diesel fumes.

My wife hates the ocean. She can't stand it, really. It just bothers her, and she gets seasick. It's a miserable day for her, and I feel miserable because I know she is uncomfortable. I might be having a great time, but I know there's somebody on board who's not doing that well. But she does like flats fishing because it's calm, generally speaking, and it's visual. You're in three or four feet of water most of the time.

MS. WULFF: That's right. And you're looking for fish.

MR. SLOAN: It's marvelous for women.

MS. WULFF: Yes, it is. But I do want to take exception to something you just said.

You said that flats fishing is great if a woman wants "to be with her guy." It's a different world now, friend. When I started, women went along as appendages. When we started the school in 1979, perhaps ten percent of our students were women. And now it's fifty/fifty or even more women than men. Women have come into their own in the world generally, as you know, and so they decide what they're going to do. They pay their own way; they travel. I'm so glad I've lived long enough to see all of this happen. And flats fishing is one of the things they love.

MR. SLOAN: This is true. I'll stand corrected—or sit corrected—but in any case, you're right. Women can do this. By the way, I make a point of seeking women as guests on this show to get their point of view out because it has been such a long time coming. Secondly, as you know, I was the one who wanted the separate IGFA fly rod records for women—for just the reasons you stated. A woman cannot handle a twelve-weight rod and maybe is at a little disadvantage on a world record fish because she can only use a ten- or a nine-weight. So that new category was approved after much debate, but Billy Pate and I and lots of others had been pushing for it. Now women can set a world record by themselves in their own category.

MS. WULFF: Yes, they can. I was a little bit undecided about all that because I had come up through the tournament ranks where there were events for women for accuracy. But in distance, I just figured I was competing against whoever was the best. But I know that women need encouragement and a helping hand just by providing them their own category, one in which they don't have to compete with men. That's made a real difference in bringing women into that competitive world that you're talking about.

MR. SLOAN: Joan, on another subject—what gave you the idea of the Triangle Taper fly line? How did that evolve?

MS. WULFF: Actually, that was Lee's design, and Lee was a man who was a free thinker, a pioneer. He sewed the first fly fisherman's vest, and he was the first to used deer hair on dry flies. He did many, many other pioneering things. So his idea for Triangle Taper, I think, came from the original horse hair lines. Fly lines started out being made of horse hair; they would braid them, starting with one and adding more and more to create a gradual taper. I believe that they may have been as long as one hundred feet in the old days. These were the lines used on rods that were fifteen or sixteen feet long.

MR. SLOAN: The old greenheart rods.

MS. WULFF: Yes. Two-handed rods. And so, of course, it meant that as soon as you have a single, continuous taper, that means that once you stop that rod and the loop forms, a heavy part of the line is kicking over a lighter part. That was what Lee picked up on without anybody talking to him about it. So that's where the Triangle Taper idea came from. It's a continuous taper for the first forty feet, in certain sizes. We've got Triangle Tapers for many uses. If it's a saltwater Triangle Taper, it's only thirty feet for the weighted section. If it's for salmon or something like that, you want forty feet so you don't have to retrieve as much. You pick that up and can cast the whole line.

It's been a very successful line design once people understood that it was not triangularly shaped. People didn't know what the word "taper" meant. As soon as they heard triangle line, they thought that's what it was—a triangular cross section. Today, after fifteen or more years, people finally seem to understand that it's the taper.

MR. SLOAN: I use it and I love it. There is a marked difference if you're a student of the game. It's dramatically better for me, anyway. I was just wondering what the evolution was. Lee's civil engineering background came into play a lot, and that was certainly one of his best products.

MS. WULFF: Exactly. He was an artist and an engineer.

MR. SLOAN: Joan, what do you see in your crystal ball for the future of tackle, so to speak? Are we going to have lighter rods, smoother lines? What's coming up that may be on the drawing boards? Anything?

MS. WULFF: Gosh, Steve, I've always been someone who used whatever was available. But I keep hoping that we'll have lighter rods for heavier lines, if we can do that. I think that all rods have become much better than they were ten years ago. It's hard to find a bad rod nowadays.

MR. SLOAN: That's a fact.

MS. WULFF: Except that it can be too heavy—I would say that. But most rods nowadays, at various levels of price, are good. I work with Winston, so I know that their rods have the best finishing components, and that's part of what makes prices go up in the fishing-tackle business.

MR. SLOAN: Fly rods today are basically indestructible, except for encounters with car doors and windows.

MS. WULFF: That's always been true. However, we all have some of those unfortunate encounters in our history.

MR. SLOAN: Now, you're a senior adviser to the Federation of Fly Fishers. You're a director of the Atlantic Salmon Federation. And an institution you and I both love, the Catskill Fly Fishing Center and Museum, counts you as a board member. You're also a trustee now of the International Game Fish Association, and we're very proud to have you in that role. All of these roles mean that you're giving something back to the sport, and I suspect that's been in your mind a long time.

MS. WULFF: Yes, Steve. Actually, you go through stages. In the beginning, all you want to do is catch fish by the numbers. How many did you catch? How many did I catch? The second stage is the biggest fish. That's so you can start bragging and showing pictures. The third stage is the most difficult fish. Now you want to catch the wily brown trout instead of the easy-to-catch brook trout. Then the angler wonders that this may not go on forever unless you put something back into it. So conservation is kind of the fourth stage that we go through. That's where these national organizations, the Federation of Fly Fishers and Trout Unlimited, come in. Joining them marks a point when you recognize the serious part of what fishing is all about. Yes, you can be in different stages with different fish. You might still be looking for the biggest tarpon or the biggest brown trout, while you go on.

MR. SLOAN: This sounds like the Montessori method of fishing.

MS. WULFF: So stage five is kind of where I am, which is just being there. Wherever I am, I'm happy to be there because game fish can only live in clean and beautiful places. So if someone asks me, "What's your favorite fish?" I say, "Whatever I'm fishing for." My favorite place is wherever I am. That's just how it is. And there is one more stage, which is that you want to replace yourself and become involved with a youngster, to get him or her away from the computers and out in the natural world so that this wonderful sport can go on with the right people fighting to keep the waters clean and the fish wild.

MR. SLOAN: You know, it's interesting. I went up to visit James Prosek, who's written some books, as you know.

MS. WULFF: A wonderful artist.

MR. SLOAN: We were talking about new books, and I said, "Jim, you should write a book called *Fishing for Single Parents*. Single parents are primarily women, maybe eighty to eighty-five percent of them. What can the mother do if the kid is out there on the ball field playing soccer or baseball other than sit on the sideline and catch her breath every time her kid either handles the ball or miscues? But here, with fishing, she can participate with him or her. She can actually do it. To me, it's an answer to the question of how to create quality time with children in their formative years. It really is an answer for bonding. It doesn't have to be male bonding all the time, either.

MS. WULFF: Right. I have this in my life with a grandson who is nine years old. When he was five and a half, I taught him to roll cast, and he became a very good roll caster. When he was seven, I gave him fly-tying lessons with one of my school instructors. So he has caught fish on his own fly. This year he is tying Royal Wulffs. He can cast; he can shoot line. And when he strikes a fish, he strikes it beautifully and smoothly. There's no craziness about it. It's just...I'm just thrilled with him.

MR. SLOAN: You should be. That's quite an endorsement. That's fabulous. Well, listen, here's another endorsement: Joan, what a wonderful beginning for your grandson. I can tell you're smiling when you tell the story.

MS. WULFF: I'm smiling listening to you say it.

MR. SLOAN: These are the six steps basically, and it's amazing how all of us go through the same process to get there—it really is.

MS. WULFF: Well, there may be other stages I don't know about yet. It's a lifetime sport.

MR. SLOAN: That doesn't make any difference. These are good enough. It has been a privilege having you on the program, Joan. You really are the first lady of fly fishing.

Thanks a million for coming on.

MS. WULFF: Thank you, Steve.

LEFTY KREH
on Casting Etiquette and much more

AN INTERVIEW WIH LEFTY KREH, PERHAPS THE MOST FAMOUS
FLY FISHERMAN IN THE WORLD, ON A VARIETY OF IMPORTANT
TOPICS—FROM BEAD-EYE NYMPHS TO ROLL CASTS TO BEING
COURTEOUS TO YOUR FELLOW ANGLERS

*T*here are some people who achieve greatness and expertise and are known by
one name only. A few examples are: Sandy for Sandy Koufax, Splinter for
Ted Williams, and Babe for Babe Ruth. Mention the name "Lefty" in fishing cir-
cles and there is only one conclusion: It is Lefty Kreh. Lefty has given of himself, his
humor, his expertise, and knowledge to millions of anglers all over the world. The
sport and the anglers he reached are much the richer from his tireless sharing.

MR. SLOAN: Hi, everybody. It is "I Fish and I Vote" time. Don't forget it,
four very important words. Cast your ballots as deftly as you cast your flies.

Today we have a treat, Lefty Kreh. That's all you have to say, Lefty
Kreh, and that really says it all for fly fishing.

Lefty, first things first. Are you really left-handed?

MR. KREH: Yes, I am, Steve, as far back as I can remember!

MR. SLOAN: Do you remember the first trout you ever caught on a fly?

MR. KREH: It was a brook trout up at Hunting Creek, near Camp David in Fairmont, Maryland.

MR. SLOAN: Is that where you are from originally?

MR. KREH: Yes. From Frederick, Maryland, right near there.

MR. SLOAN: Isn't Gunpowder Falls in that area too?

MR. KREH: Gunpowder Falls is near where I live now, about fifty miles from Frederick.

MR. SLOAN: Did you start fishing like most kids do, with a worm and bobber for trout, and then move on to lures and, eventually, flies?

MR. KREH: No. Joe Brooks actually got me into fishing, and I started off fly fishing. Trout were available in all the little streams around my home, so I actually caught my first trout on a fly.

MR. SLOAN: Lefty, you know, Joe was a very good friend of mine.

MR. KREH: He was a mentor of mine.

MR. SLOAN: A fabulous guy.

MR. KREH: Yes, no question.

MR. SLOAN: So you learned from one of fly fishing's true masters. But how did you get to where you are? You're not only a great fly fisherman, you're a great teacher. How many sportmen's shows do you think you've gone to over the years?

MR. KREH: I have no idea.... Too many to count.

MR. SLOAN: In the hundreds?

MR. KREH: Looking back—yes, in the hundreds.

MR. SLOAN: And you basically teach fly fishing and the ethic of the sport when you give your seminars?

MR. KREH: I usually give casting demonstrations, and sometimes seminars on trout, saltwater fishing, or freshwater bass. But I've found that what people really seem to enjoy is being able to talk to me one on one, asking about what they're specifically interested in. Most of the show owners leave my times unscheduled, and that way I can converse with people as I like, sign books, and so on.

MR. SLOAN: Is there any common denominator that runs through questions from the general public?

MR. KREH: Well, the most common denominator I get on the telephone shows I do is, where can I go with my wife where I can catch fish and she can have a good time? There are very few places where you can do both. One of them is Freeport, Bahamas, if the caller is interested in saltwater fishing. In the Bahamas there is North Riding Point Lodge, but there're also some other hotels that have guides. A guide can take you fishing on the Grand Bahama Bank, which has some of the best bonefishing left in this part of the world. A non-fishing spouse can shop downtown. They have a big casino, and in the evening you can go have a wonderful dinner and see a show and be entertained. So there's something there for both the wife who doesn't fish and for the husband who does.

MR. SLOAN: Trout fishing, of course, is another story. My wife likes bone-fishing, but that's it. If I take her trout fishing, the fly's in the tree, it's around her neck, and in about twenty minutes she's frustrated and she says who needs it? Then she sits there and reads a book, hoping I will come out of the stream at some reasonable hour.

MR. KREH: One way that you can take your wife trout fishing, where she can catch a lot of fish, with very little experience or skill and have a good time, is in a drift boat out West.

MR. SLOAN: True.

MR. KREH: There you only have to pick the rod up and drop the fly down, and the guide can manipulate the boat. The person doesn't have to cast more than fifteen or twenty feet. Because the boat is drifting with the current, drag isn't as much of a problem. I've seen a lot of women get into trout fishing with a fly that way, because they did have success at the beginning and then they got interested and learned how to cast better and to make drag-free drifts.

MR. SLOAN: You're absolutely right. Let me ask you something. If you had to pick an overall trout outfit, what would you pick?

MR. KREH: You'd have to pick two. First, what frightens most trout is the impact of the line on the water. So the lighter the line, the better. For most dry-fly situations I prefer a No. 3 weight line, which only weighs a hundred grains. That line is great for dry flies, small flies, that sort of thing. But if you're going to toss some heavy Woolly Buggers and Sculpins and heavy weighted nymphs, a 5- or a 6-weight rod really is a better tool. If you had to have one, I'd choose a 5, and then use a 4-weight line for dry flies, and a 5- or 6-weight line for heavy flies. Really, you ought to have a 3 and a 5, or a 3 and a 6.

MR. SLOAN: Lefty, you remember that commercial, I think it was a beer commercial, where this guy was casting a fly line and it was falling on the surface in slow motion. Then you saw this big splash as it landed. I was looking at that and I said, that's enough to spook every trout in the neighborhood.

MR. KREH: I remember that! And one of the very first things I tell my students when teaching casting, once the person understands the mechanics, is to aim almost all your casts at eye level or above. What happens there, Steve, is you expend the energy as the line turns over, and then it falls softly to the water. That's one of the biggest problems. One of the other big problems in dry-fly fishing is drying flies. Fishermen make a cast, and the fly drifts over the fish and it doesn't take it. They pick the fly up and false cast to get the water out to make the fly float better. Well, if you false cast that fly over the top of that fish, you flush minuscule raindrops out of the fly line down on the surface, which are very evident to the fish. What you really need to do is to pick up the fly carefully, false cast to the side, then come back and make the last presentation dead ahead.

MR. SLOAN: I absolutely agree. Dead right. I think the average angler thinks false casting is either beautiful or poetic. But it's devastating on the fish, because not only are there raindrops, but the line can spook the bedevil out of trout just with its shadow, especially in low water conditions.

MR. KREH: One of the main criteria for judging if a guy is a good caster is how few false casts he makes.

MR. SLOAN: I agree. Now let me ask you something else. Describe that eye level thing again. What do you mean by eye level?

MR. KREH: Well, I tell people to imagine that the water is at eye level. When you cast, you're throwing the line as if the water is even with your eye rather than throwing it down at the water. There're only two times that I know that you throw down at the water—unless it's trying to get underneath something—and that's when you have a wind in your face or a wind to your side. Almost every other cast, you would be better to aim. Whether it's a weighted lead-core line or floater, you'd be better to either aim at eye level, or if you're making a long-distance cast, especially with heavier line and a fly, even tilted upward above the eye level just a little bit.

MR. SLOAN: What's a tight loop, Lefty?

MR. KREH: We don't fly cast a line, although we write and say that. We unroll a line. If you unroll the line in a tight loop, where the top of the loop and the bottom of the loop are close together, then most of the energy is going toward a target. When you unroll a large loop, what you're really doing, Steve, is you're unrolling the energy of the cast around a curve, or dissipating part of it up and part of it down. So the larger the loop, the more energy is required to get to the target. There's a very easy way to get that tight loop, by the way.

MR. SLOAN: How's that?

MR. KREH: When you're casting, if you will think that you are trying to throw the line at the end (tip) of the rod, you're actually trying to make the line strike the end of the rod. Now if you do it real early in the cast, it *will* strike it. But your rod is always traveling in a very slight arc. So if we're talking about a vertical cast, for example, once the rod passes vertical, if you try to make the line hit the end of the rod, physically, mentally try to make it hit, you direct all the energy right at it. But because the rod is travelling in a very small arc, it will duck beyond that before the line gets there. Most people will tighten their loops right away.

MR. SLOAN: Gotcha. That's interesting. I never heard it explained that way before. I do it automatically, but I never knew why. That is a wonderful explanation to it. Let me ask you something. If you were, say, going into the one-fly tournament, or you had a choice, you were stranded on an island in the middle of Yellowstone or something, give me four flies that you would take with you and nothing else.

MR. KREH: Well, I would certainly take one dry fly, and that would depend on the season, of course. If it was in the fall, I would certainly use hoppers because hoppers have a lot of protein, and trout will travel quite a distance to get them. So if you don't drift a hopper perfectly over the fish, it does not matter much. A trout will take it. If it had to be one dry fly that you could use all the time, on hard-fished waters, I might use something like a Madame X or something similar, that looks like no dry fly at all.

MR. SLOAN: A generic dry fly?

MR. KREH: Yes. It has rubber legs and looks something like a crazy spider. But it looks like a lot of meat, and it looks buggy. So if there are no hatches, or sometimes right in the middle of a hatch, the fish will stop taking a tiny little fly, like a Blue-Winged Olive, and go to that bigger piece of grocery. So I'd use that. Then I think the best nymph that's been developed in the last few years was a Copper John Nymph.

MR. SLOAN: Name another fly you wouldn't be without.

MR. KREH: A guy in Pennsylvania designed what was called the Woolly Worm. I forget his name. Everet, I think it was. But anyway, the guys out West began putting a marabou tail on a Woolly Worm, and found out that it added action, length, and more appeal. Of course, the Woolly Worm has now been bastardized into the Woolly Bugger. There are so many different variations of Woolly Buggers now that you can hardly recognize it as a Woolly Bugger in some places. A lot of people just drift Woolly Buggers, dead drift them. But you can twitch them to make them look like emerging stoneflies. You can make them look like minnows. You can make them look like leeches. They just have an irresistible, buggy look about them.

MR. SLOAN: Do you ascribe to the little tinsel they put on it, the flash, so to speak, on a Woolly Bugger?

MR. KREH: A lot of times I use Woolly Buggers with tinsel or chenille in the body. But the one that I have had the best luck with, Steve, is a Woolly Bugger with a marabou tail. I take eight or ten strands of peacock herl and put it in the spinning loop in the back with a little piece of wire to strengthen it, twist it all together, and wind it up. A peacock body has just an incredible insect look about it. Then I'll wind the grizzly feather over that body. If I had to have one Woolly Bugger, a peacock Woolly Bugger would be the one I would take.

MR. SLOAN: It's funny how that one type of material makes the fly breathe, or flash.

MR. KREH: It's got all kinds of colors in it.

MR. SLOAN: Right. Well, we have four flies. Lefty's survival kit. Go get yourself these four flies. You'll never be without a fish. Tell me about when you're casting... I've read Harvey's books and I've read Joe Humphreys's books. As a matter of fact, Humphreys did an interview with us on their leader system that goes from 0.21 to 0.17, or down to .09. *(See "Joseph Humphreys on Nymph Fishing" on page 127.)* Then they add some tippet which is basically 5X. They don't fish heavier than 5X, or lighter than 5X. Do you believe in that knotted system?

MR. KREH: I've fished with Joe and George many times, and I think that their leader system is a fine system. However, I have for some years now used commercial leaders for trout. I make all other leaders, but when you start making so many inches of this and so many of that and so many of this, it gets very complicated trying to make that thing come out correctly. And tapered leaders of any kind—salt water, trout or anything—have to unroll to the target. To do this, by the way, the butt section of any tapered leader ought to be half the total length of the leader.

MR. SLOAN: Half the length of the leader?

MR. KREH: Half the length. And you don't want a stiff butt section, either, but flexible material. Your fly line unrolls to the target. Your leader must also unroll to the target or the fly won't get there. To do this, you must have flexible weight in the back end of your leader. By the way, the only trout leaders that I know about on the market today that have the 50/50 ratio are the ones made by Scientific Anglers, called the Mastery Series.

Steve, you can take a 16-foot leader and 7 or 8 feet of fly line, and because that 16-foot leader has an 8-foot limp but thicker butt section, it'll turn over with absolutely no effort.

I would recommend that anybody who wants to fish dry flies buy that particular leader. I don't recommend products, as a rule, but that leader, that Scientific Anglers Mastery leader is the best turnover leader I've ever seen.

MR. SLOAN: That's key. You make a wonderful cast and all of a sudden the fly flops down right on the leader, and it's no good. It's a problem. I would assume this 50/50 leader will lay out a nymph or even a small streamer just right as well?

MR. KREH: When you have heavier flies on, you need the advantage of that heavy butt effect to keep that energy transmitting through the leader after it leaves the fly line. So if you have little short butt sections that get shorter and shorter and shorter, what happens is that you've diminished the amount of energy that can be carried through the leader to the line. The same thing holds true on bonefish. If I use a 14-foot bonefish leader, I use at least 7 feet of 50-pound [test]. When I build leaders other than for trout, I use good, top-grade monofilament spinning line.

MR. SLOAN: You know what bothered me about that whole knotted system. Up in Henryville, Pennsylvania where I fish for trout, we use very small flies. We're always using 18s or 22s, matching the hatch. I use ants, I like to fish with ants. If they can see a little 22, or 24 jassid fly, by God, they can see a knot. So I like to fish knotless leaders, even at 12 to 15 feet.

MR. KREH: There is another advantage to knotless leaders. If you fish where there's growth or watercress, and a lot of the trout streams do have that type of underwater vegetation, those knots in your leader can gather up a bunch of junk and can actually break your tippet and spook the fish as well.

MR. SLOAN: Absolutely. So, what connection do you use between the end of the fly line and the end of the leader? Do you use a loop-to-loop or do you make some other kind of connector?

MR. KREH: I use loop-to-loop for several reasons. One, I've been using them for over forty years. Never had one hang up in the guides. Two, loops seal off the end of the line where water can seep up and sink it. But the big advantage is if you're fishing on, say, the Letort in Pennsylvania, which requires 10-, 11-, 12-foot leaders, and then you leave there and go to the nearby mountains and fish a brook trout stream, you can't cast an 11-foot leader on a tiny brook trout stream. The loop system gives you flexibility, lets you switch leaders quickly.

What I do is simply unloop the big long leader, and then loop on a 6- or 7- or 8-foot leader for the conditions. Now, a lot of people will take a nail knot and they'll knot a piece of monofilament on the end of the fly line and put a loop in that. Why they don't just put a loop on the fly line, I've never been able to figure out.

MR. SLOAN: Me neither. Some of the fly lines are made with that long Chinese finger connector. I take that off and just make the smallest loop I can.

MR. KREH: The other thing, too, is that most monofilament or clear fly lines lay the mono over a core. And if you put a nail knot on there, like a lot of people do, and you stretch it, what happens is it shears the outer surface off the core and your whole leader will slip right off the fly line, whereas a loop in the line is not going to slip. I've never had a loop fail me on sailfish or any other species.

MR. SLOAN: You mentioned something about mono clear lines. I switched from the blue, yellow, and gray fly lines. I experimented with everything and finally went to the clear mono line, even though it sinks a little bit. I don't mind it, even dry-fly fishing. If it sinks, the fish can't see it. I usually fish low-water conditions, and the clear line really is superior about spooking the fish.

MR. KREH: The only problem is that it's slightly heavier than other lines and it comes down. But Monic now makes a floating clear line, as does Scientific Anglers. Cortland is working on floating clear line.

One of the problems with clear lines is accuracy. You can't see them in the air! People don't realize that they actually watch their line in flight. In fact, if you have noticed, there are very few experienced fly casters who wear long-bill hats.

MR. SLOAN: I do.

MR. KREH: But the reason is that if you wear a baseball hat, you actually can monitor the flight of the fly line almost from the beginning to the end, and you'll get more accuracy. But if you've ever fished in New Zealand, on the north end of the South Island, they insist on using very drab olive or gray lines. People's accuracy just goes to hell, because they can't see the line. Monofilament lines are the same, and they will affect your accuracy. However, what they're now calling "ghost tips" can help correct this problem. You use a floating line with a clear sinking tip. That way your line is not far underwater if you need to make a back cast, except for the tip section. So you can make a back cast easier and quieter.

Stu Apte is probably as good a tarpon fisherman that lives, and he just swears by that clear-tip-type fly line. Mitch Howell, who's won four or five of the Redbone bonefish tournaments—the best in the world compete in those—believes that the clear tip or clear line is one of the major reasons why he's won those tournaments. Clear lines do have a lot of advantages. I also think they're really critical in northern, clear lakes.

MR. SLOAN: I just switched everything to clear line four years ago. Lefty, help me out here. I noticed in my casting, I have a little drift to the right at the end of the cast. I compensate for it. You know, it's like windage, so to speak.

MR. KREH: You mean your line hooks to the right?

MR. SLOAN: It just kind of goes right. I know if I'm casting right, the line is going to fall from left to right instead of right to left. So I don't know, maybe it's in my technique or grip?

MR. KREH: When you come forward and your line comes to the right, line goes in the direction at tip-top speed. So if you turn your hand very slightly to the right as you stop, the leader will kick off to the right. If you turn it to the left, it kicks off to the left. But if your thumb stays right behind the handle from the target, when you stop the line will go perfectly straight.

MR. SLOAN: You were telling me during the break that you've got a little tip on the pickup. Sometimes a guy casts a clear line and he does not know how much line is out or has been retrieved.

MR. KREH: He doesn't know whether he has too much line in or not enough. If he has too much, of course, he's got to make a false cast. If he doesn't have enough, he can't roll out the line, which is underwater, up and out of the water to make a cast. What really helps is to go to some water nearby and make some casts, and find out at what distance can you roll your line out of the water conveniently to make it easy for yourself. Make a little mark with a marking pen on the fly line by your index finger. When you get home get some 8-, 10-, or 12-pound—I like 10 best of all—test monofilament. Make about a 7- or 8- turn nail knot on that mark and trim it nice and neatly.

Now you'll make your cast, and as you strip back you don't even have to think about it or look at it. Sometimes you'll hear it coming in the guide, but it doesn't affect your casting. But when that little bump comes over your finger, you know exactly where you should be for a smooth pickup. I can roll this up in the air, make a back cast, and shoot the line. Incidentally, monofilament, clear lines shoot better than other lines on the market.

MR. SLOAN: Lefty, what's the essence of a good roll caster? Because when you're in a tight spot and you can't make that back cast, the roll cast will catch you some fish.

MR. KREH: The biggest problem with roll casting is that people think that roll casts are made differently than regular casts, especially on the forward cast. You're making a back cast that is different because you're not permitted to throw the line behind you. All the instructors and the videos teach you to take the rod, hold it up near vertical, let the line drop behind you, and slash down. The line is going to go in the direction in which you speed up and stop the rod tip. What you really want to do is try to make a regular forward cast at eye level.

So you want to bring your line back, and let it stop just enough for the surface tension to grab it; the farther you can take your rod back and the lower your hand, the better the cast. What gets a lot of people in trouble in roll casting is they put their hand up by their ear or head. Now, the hand is going to descend as it's coming forward, which means that the line is going to come down at an angle, too. You should lower your hand when you start your roll cast forward; attempt to make a regular forward cast, stopping straight ahead, not down toward the water. When you make a roll cast, it should not look like what you looked at in the books and videos, a big round rolling line. That means you threw the line around in a big circle. Your forward casts and your roll casts should look alike.

MR. SLOAN: I've found over the years that when I make that big high loop, you know where my fly winds up, don't you? Right in a tree!

MR. KREH: Or in a pile right in front of you.

MR. SLOAN: Exactly. But get that hand low, and you can shoot it under the branch. It's very effective, especially in nymph fishing. Let me ask you something. An angler has got the rudiments down. What kind of exercises should he do and what should his practice methods be? I mean, you wouldn't pick up a golf club and say, all right, I'm ready to play. You'd go out and take lessons and practice.

MR. KREH: There are three tools that are good for practice. One is a rope. Take a rope about 50 feet long, put a nail in either end, stretch it out on a lawn and then drive the nails in the ground, so the rope remains taut. If you don't want to do that, you can just use a garden hose. You stand with the garden hose or rope in front of you with your rod tip about one foot on the other side. The line is laying on the ground.

Now, you make a back cast and throw it low to the ground, like you're going to throw it on the grass behind you. Then you throw it in front of you. Each time you make a back or forward cast, you stop. If the tip of the rod is on your side of the rope or the line, you are making a big loop in throwing the line down in a heap behind you and in front of you. If you can keep the rod tip on the far side of the rope when you stop each time, you will learn to throw tight loops immediately. A second thing that helps on loops is a Hula Hoop. You just go to Wal-Mart, which sells Hula Hoops for three or four bucks. You tape one to a pole and you start trying to throw your loop through that Hula Hoop. It's amazing. Even people with real tight loops quite often can't throw one out of ten through the Hula Hoop because they throw a tight loop but don't have any accuracy with it. This will define your accuracy. When you're really ready to polish your accuracy, particularly for dry flies or bonefish, take a mousetrap and cock it so it will go off if you hit it. Use a lightly weighted fly from twenty feet away. The average person will throw most of the first ten to twenty casts and not come within three feet of the trap.

Then what happens is that they begin to really focus on the trap. They won't hit the trap that often, Steve, but after a while all their casts are coming close. The reason is the same reason as when you shoot deer. If you hunt deer and shoot at the deer, you're not going to kill many deer. But if you focus on the shoulder or a specific spot on the deer, then you're likely to hit that spot. You hit what you really focus on. Many people do not look intently at the spot they went to hit, but they look at the fish or something in the general area. They're not really focused for accurate casting.

In fact, when you're fishing for cruising bonefish, many anglers look at the fish—and that's why they hit bonefish on the head instead of leading the fish. You want to actually focus tightly on a spot where you want the fly to land in front of the fish.

MR. SLOAN: It's called hand-to-eye coordination?

MR. KREH: Most people don't know that. People wonder why some of the better fly or plug fishermen can go along a mangrove shoreline and drive flies or plugs or lures into tiny places with great accuracy. They can do it because they are not looking at the shoreline. They are intently looking at that tiny little pocket that they want the fly to get into.

MR. SLOAN: Lefty, people ask me, are you a good fly caster? I say yeah, pretty good. If you stand about 50 feet from me and put a cigarette in your mouth, I'll take your eye out every time. Well, your tips are great even for the hot stove league in the winter. You could do that in a gym or you could do it out on the lawn in the snow. You can do it anywhere.

MR. SLOAN: There's no distance involved there at all.

MR. SLOAN: Do you do any exercises for your hands, to keep them strong?

MR. KREH: No. I don't think you need a lot of strength for casts up to 90 feet. I think a lady who only weighs 110 pounds, but casts correctly, can cast as easily as a guy who weighs 210 and is a lumberjack. Beyond about 85 or 90 feet, what makes distance is doing things correctly, but also how fast you can speed up and stop the tip at the end of the cast. A much stronger person can actually develop more speed and have the muscle to stop the rod faster. So beyond about 85 or 90 feet, muscle comes into play. Before that, it doesn't.

So it really isn't how hard you do something, it's how short and fast you make the tip stop after you've moved the rod through an arc.

MR. SLOAN: Lefty, let me ask you this. You come on a stream that you basically haven't fished before. You come to a pool. What's the first thing you do before you really start casting?

MR. KREH: First, I don't get in the water if I don't have to. The reason is that water transmits sound four and a half times faster than air. So any sound you make in the water is going to be transmitted to the fish four and a half times faster than if you make the same sound on the ground. So stay out of the pool, and fish from below it. In other words, stay in the pool below it, which muffles sound. The two places where you're most likely to encounter a trout are the back end of the pool or at the head. Those are the two places you want to fish most carefully. Examine them carefully before doing anything. One of the things that will really help you is to carry a pair of small field glasses. With field glasses, you can scout a pool before you even get to it and often see fish that, as you move up, slide under a rock or under the bank. Secondly, field glasses will often let you see what's floating on the water. If there's a hatch or terrestrials floating on the surface film, you can actually identify them without taking a sample.

Once you approach the pool, stay as low as you can. On small streams I tell people that their hip boots ought to wear out at the knees before they ever wear out at the sole. That's another tip, by the way. If you fish in hip boots, the manufacturers sell you the boot with a strap hanging outside, on which your fly line hangs up.

MR. SLOAN: Every time.

MR. KREH: If you remove the strap from the buckle and turn the buckle upside down and reinsert the strap, the strap goes on the inside of the boot and eliminates the problem. Anyway, when I approach a trout pool, the first thing I do is try to figure out where the trout are before I even try casting. I don't get in the pool unless I have to, and then I start fishing at the bottom, being very careful not to splash the fly line and spook the fish at the bottom. If you spook them, Steve, as you know, a lot of times they run right straight up through the pool and all the others get the message. Danger!

MR. SLOAN: An early warning system.

What's your take on beaded nymphs?

MR. KREH: Well, first of all probably 90 percent of the food that trout eat are nymphs, and probably 80 or 90 percent of that is taken within 10 inches of the bottom. Most people don't realize that. They think that nymphs are taken all over the place. Except when they're emerging, most nymphs are either moving around on the bottom or are being swept along on the bottom. So the closer you can get your nymph to the bottom, the more trout you're going to catch.

Bead-headed nymphs came from Denmark, and I can't think of the name of the man who invented them years ago. The main purpose of bead nymphs is to get down to the bottom. For that reason, you should have bead nymphs of just different weights. Now, they don't have to be different sizes, just different weights. I don't like real big beads most of the time. I think fish may figure something out. What I recommend is that you have some light brass beads, and then you also have some tungsten, which will really take your fly down.

The big key here is, "Can I get this fly close to the bottom?" Use whatever bead nymph you need to get down in that very low strata of the bottom where most of the food is going on. Nymphs aren't big and the fish don't get a heck of a lot of food out of one, so they're not going to chase nymphs all over the place unless you've got a hatch of some kind or emergers are coming up. Most of the time they're going to prefer to take those nymphs as they come to them, so they don't have to go up in the water column to fight them. So you use beads to get the fly as close to the bottom as you can.

MR. SLOAN: Lefty, do you ascribe to strike indicators made of yarn or cork?

MR. KREH: The only people I know who don't like indicators are people who spent 20 or 30 years learning to fish without them and now are ticked off because somebody can put one on and go out there and catch fish like they did. Hell, yes, I use indicators. I think yarn makes the best indicators. One reason for it, in most cases, unless you're using unusually large yarn, is that it'll come in and out of the guides without hanging up, which I find to be an advantage. So yes, I believe in indicators. I use them all the time.

MR. SLOAN: All right. Hey, I learned the old way but I'm coming around.

MR. KREH: Let me say one thing about indicators. I believe that your indicator should be yarn, should be partly black and partly bright colored. The reason for that is when a bright-colored yarn goes into a shaded area, it shows up well. But a real bright one, like chartreuse or orange, is not as easy to see as black when there is glare on the water. So what I do, I take a half a strand of black and a half strand of bright yarn, like bright yellow or chartreuse, and twist the two together so that I have a multicolored indicator. This lets me see better under all conditions.

I didn't mean to interrupt you, but that is a good tip.

MR. SLOAN: That's a helluva tip. That's terrific. Let me ask you something else. How many books have you written on fly fishing?

MR. KREH: Twenty-two.

MR. SLOAN: Twenty-two books! You said Lyons Press published a lot of them, which you and I both know very well. They published one of mine. But PRESENTING THE FLY, you said, was a very good one.

MR. KREH: I think it's by far the best book I've written. It's a big book, it's a 40-dollar book. It had a lot of wonderful reviews, and I think it's good for the guy just getting started, and I think it's for the guy who's been at it a long time. It also covers steelhead, bonefish, tarpon, sailfish, and trout. In other words, it covers the whole spectrum.

MR. SLOAN: PRESENTING THE FLY...what's your latest book?

MR. KREH: I revised one called ADVANCED FLY-FISHING TECHNIQUES, which has been selling pretty well. The main reason I did all those books is because when I got married, I thought Bill was a guy's name.

MR. SLOAN: You discovered there were some numbers with him.

MR. KREH: Love is blind and marriage is an eye opener.

MR. SLOAN: You are famous for your one-liners.

MR. KREH: I've been married 56 years to my best friend and I'm very happy about it.

MR. SLOAN: Fabulous. What are the trends, Lefty, before we get into fishing etiquette? What are the trends today in trout fishing?

MR. KREH: The major trend today in trout fishing is that more and more rivers and more and more streams are not stocked with trout, so you don't have dumb fish that've been eating pellets. Trout get caught a lot of times, and they finally get smart. So what you have to do now is you have to go to smaller and smaller flies. Years ago, if you remember, Size 12 to 16 was the standard for flies. Except for rare cases, most standards now are for Size 16 to 24, usually 18 or smaller on hard-fished streams. We're not talking just dry-flies sizes. Nymphs, and ants too, will catch more fish than if you're fishing with larger flies.

There has also been a refinement in tackle. Today, leaders have to be a little longer so when you get the splash from the line it does not spook the fish. Shy gear is what I call it. We're using lighter lines, longer leaders, smaller flies. And all these things together will help you get more fish. If you're going to a new area, you're better off starting small than you are starting medium or large.

MR. SLOAN: True. You know what I do? I put a little ant on right away if I don't know the water.

MR. KREH: You know, Steve, everywhere I've ever fished for trout, there are ants. I use both sunken ants and floating ants, and I tell you, if I had to have four or five flies for all trout, one of them would have to be an ant.

MR. SLOAN: You're right, floating or sinking it makes no difference. They'll take it. Now, you're in a stream or you're coming up on a pool, you see a couple of guys fishing there. What's the etiquette today? Is it the same? Are we getting better? Or do people not give a hoot? What's up?

MR. KREH: I think most people who encroach upon your water or do things that are against good fishing etiquette don't realize that they shouldn't be doing this. I find that if you're very nice about it and you explain to them, "Look, you just waded to the lower end of this pool and sent shock waves all the way up this pool, and put every trout down so neither you nor I are going to catch anything. But had you let me fish through the pool first, or were you well away from me or not entered this pool at all, I could have had a good time and I wouldn't do that in the next pool to you."

Most of the time people accept that.

MR. SLOAN: Maybe for the first time. They may have never heard it before.

MR. KREH: I think most people are nice people, and I don't think they want to tick you off or ruin your day either. Now, of course, if you are on the offensive, then they will become defensive. But if you try to do it in a way that's not offensive at all, then I think people appreciate that. In fact, a lot of people thank me and say they didn't realize they were doing this or that or the other.

MR. SLOAN: Lefty, continuing with etiquette, let's say you get into a spot like Hendrickson's Pool on the Beaverkill, one big long run, and you see a guy come in there and he stays in that one spot for hours, casting and casting. To me it's a diminishing return after a while.

MR. KREH: Of course it is.

MR. SLOAN: Ideally, he should make maybe a dozen casts, then move down a foot or two.

MR. KREH: After he tries a couple flies and a couple different drifts, yes. What I do if I realize he's really screwing things up, I just walk up slowly and I explain that, "Look, you've offered to fish here, all these different

things and nothing works, they're probably not going to bite. You'd probably get more fish if you'd just move downstream and did the same thing,
just keeping moving along." Of course, I also point out that fishermen
think that every fish they see in the stream is starving to death, when actually he might have just filled up on nymphs. So it might be a good idea just
to move down and try something else.

MR. SLOAN: I agree. To me, if you cover all the water, you've got a helluva
lot better chance of catching something than if you stay in one spot.

MR. KREH: Oh, sure. You know what? The secret of fishing in the Smoky
Mountains, for example, which has 2,400 miles of trout streams, is to fish
fast. The reason is that those streams—and there are streams in other
places like this, that's why I mention it—the trout don't have much food.
So there will only be a few trout in every pool.

So if you go in like you would on a stream that has a lot of rich food, and
you work over a stream that doesn't have much food, you're wasting your
time because the few fish in the pool will probably either take your fly or
reject it after maybe five, eight, ten casts. Your best bet then is to move up
and hit the next pool and the next pool and the next pool. I learned that
the hard way, because those Smoky Mountain hillbillies were cleaning my
clock down there until I found out why they were fishing fast. You need to
move around.

MR. SLOAN: Lefty, do you carry a thermometer with you?

MR. KREH: Yes. Actually, I carry one that's fantastic and costs ten dollars.

MR. SLOAN: What kind is it?

MR. KREH: It's a tiny rectangle about two and a half inches square and
about a quarter inch thick. It runs on a triple-A battery. You buy them at
Radio Shack, and they give up to a tenth of a degree. Very small and
they've got a probe on a wire. You drop that thing in the water, instanta-
neously it says it's 52.7 degrees. It costs ten bucks and I use that all the
time. That's one of the secrets of fishing in the summer. In the summertime, you want to fish early in the morning if you possibly can. Later in the
evening is okay, but early morning is best. The reason is when the temperature gets too high in the stream, it's not going to kill the fish but it
shuts down their metabolism so they don't feed.

268

MR. SLOAN: Lefty, just talking to you has raised my metabolism. I want to go fishing with all your tips. Thanks for coming on the show. Tight lines and a good drift, always.

❦

AFTERWORD

During the late spring of this year, we marked the 500th consecutive live broadcast of "The Fishing Zone" radio program. Many of the interviews I conducted originated from our quaint, modest clubhouse out at Henryville, Pennsylvania, beside the waters of Brodhead Creek. At Henryville, there was always a special peace and calm that descended on me just before airtime. It was amid the smoke tendrils of the fire I lit at 5:30 A.M. getting ready for my guest's interview and the murmur of the stream so close, so inviting, that somehow the experience always intensified my thought process and brought me into focus for the show. In early spring and fall, it was the frost in the air and on the ground; in summer, the cool of the early morning always heightening my senses and energizing my thoughts. I could hear the soothing sounds of the tumbling water, which only added expectation and immediacy to those interviews at streamside. Somehow, the crackling of the wet logs and the haze of the wood smoke from the old fireplace gave those interviews a pace and peace I could never have achieved from a radio studio. Thank heaven for modern telephone and satellite technology.

Of course, many interesting guests appeared on the show over the years, and to all of them, I extend a hearty and sincere thank-you. You know who you are, and I treasure our experience together. However, there are two individuals whom I did *not* interview but who have nonetheless left a lifelong impression on me. The first of these is George Harvey. I met George several times and, through him, Dan Shields and Greg Hoover. George was a pioneer in codifying the various disciplines of fly fishing and weaving them, starting in 1935, into a college curriculum at Penn State University in State College, Pennsylvania. His teaching of techniques, his sharing of a lifetime of study, and his selfless imparting of knowledge to an entire generation of young anglers is a truly remarkable accomplishment for which we should all be thankful. He is without question the "dean" of the contemporary masters of the sport.

The second individual I did not get to interview, regrettably, is Harry Middleton. Harry's early and sudden death in his late thirties was a tremendous loss for the sport of fly fishing. I dedicated one show to a posthumous review of his second book, ON THE SPINE OF TIME, a beautifully written account of fly fishing for wild trout in the Great Smoky Mountains. I found something unique in the compelling, melancholy language of this book; reading it was like listening to Scott Joplin's music—original, plaintive, sad, and unquestionably American. ON THE SPINE OF TIME touched me deeply, and I still use it as a personal reference, a touchstone, for writing and interviews.

Harry will be remembered also, however, for his first book, THE EARTH IS ENOUGH, and his related book, THE STARLIGHT CREEK ANGLING SOCIETY. Harry was less concerned with the minutiae and details of fly-fishing techniques than he was with the sheer *magic* of the sport; he was consumed by the magic of wild trout, wild places, and living a life devoted to and inspired by the natural world. He reached out to stardust, to moonbeams and their shimmering glow on clear, wild waters that were full of promise and possibilities. Harry was endeared to old rag-tag flies concocted out of the worn and tattered upholstery of ancient, discarded sofas. Harry's books and prose are infectious, and with his untimely passing he has come to symbolize a new and unmistakably fresh point of view—a way for one to arrange life's mysteries through the sport of fly fishing with grace, dignity, reverence, and, at times, light-hearted irreverence.

Fly fishing for trout can reveal much of the human condition, and it drives and inspires devoted anglers and writers like George Harvey and Harry Middleton. Most of us are inhabitants of that vast middle ground of angling—passionate weekend participants, near-experts, enthusiastic beginners—and it is only through the richly diverse writings and efforts of others that we can truly see and appreciate the dimensions and importance of this sport we care so much about. If we are truly attentive, perhaps we will allow it to treat us to a certain glimpse of our place in the natural order of things.

I can only hope that in some small way I have brought some of the best contemporary angling writers and concepts to the forefront in this book, with the firm belief that as the years go by, the very best is yet to come.

Stephen Sloan
New York City, 2001